Explaining Prices in the Global Economy

NEW DIRECTIONS IN MODERN ECONOMICS
General Editor: Malcolm C. Sawyer,
Professor of Economics, University of Leeds, UK

New Directions in Modern Economics presents a challenge to orthodox economic thinking. It focuses on new ideas emanating from radical traditions including post-Keynesian, Kaleckian, neo-Ricardian and Marxian. The books in the series do not adhere rigidly to any single school of thought but attempt to present a positive alternative to the conventional wisdom.

A list of published titles in this series is printed at the end of this volume.

Explaining Prices in the Global Economy

A Post-Keynesian Model

Henk-Jan Brinkman

Department of Economic and Social Affairs of the United Nations Secretariat, USA

NEW DIRECTIONS IN MODERN ECONOMICS

Edward Elgar

Cheltenham, UK • Northampton, MA, USA

Published by
Edward Elgar Publishing Limited
Glensanda House
Montpellier Parade
Cheltenham
Glos GL50 1UA
UK

Edward Elgar Publishing, Inc.
136 West Street
Suite 202
Northampton
Massachusetts 01060
USA

A catalogue record for this book
is available from the British Library

Library of Congress Cataloguing in Publication Data

Brinkman, Henk-Jan, 1961–
    Explaining prices in the global economy : a post-Keynesian model /
Henk-Jan Brinkman
    (New directions in modern economics series)
    Includes bibliographical references and index
    1. Prices. 2. Keynesian economics. 3. International economic
relations. I. Title. II. Series.
HB221.B68   1999
338.5'2—dc 21   99–21830
                                                          CIP

ISBN 1 84064 044 8

Printed and bound in Great Britain by Biddles Ltd, Guildford and King's Lynn

Contents

PART II   EMPIRICAL EVIDENCE

Tables

Figures

Selected abbreviations

ERDI   Exchange Rate Deviation Index = ratio of exchange rate to purchasing power parity = ratio of PPP-converted GDP to exchange-rate converted GDP

I$ International dollar = dollars with same purchasing power over total US GDP as the US dollar, but purchasing power over GDP categories is determined by average international prices rather than US relative prices

ICP   United Nations International Comparison Programme

IP   International price = average price of a category = quantity-weighted average of the purchasing power-adjusted prices in all International Comparison Programme (ICP) countries; sometimes referred to as price index

PL   Price level = ratio of purchasing power parity to exchange rate = the price level of one category as a percentage of the price level in the numéraire country with the exchange rate being used for currency conversions = reciprocal of Exchange Rate Deviation Index; also called the relative or (real) national price level or price index

PPP   Purchasing power parity (PPP) = the number of national currency units required to buy goods equivalent to what can be bought with one unit of currency of the numéraire country, usually the United States

Preface

This book, which is based on my dissertation, constitutes a symbolic bridge between the two universities where I studied. At the University of Groningen in the Netherlands, I was introduced by Professor Angus Maddison to the concept of purchasing power parities (basically prices in different countries for the same bundle of goods). Subsequently, at The New School for Social Research in New York, I became interested in the post-Keynesian approach to price formation, which is quite distinct from the neoclassical price theory that I had encountered in Groningen. In this book I combine these dissimilar interests by explaining price differences across countries with theories I became acquainted with at The New School.

Soon after I finished my PhD qualifying exams at The New School, I started working for the United Nations, where I have focused on development issues. This specialty filtered into this book in various ways. Chapter 11, for example, was originally presented at a department seminar. I also benefitted tremendously from working a few floors above the United Nations Statistics Division, where I had easy access to an abundance of data. Nonetheless, the views expressed in this book are mine and do not necessarily reflect those of the United Nations.

A number of people have been invaluable in the writing of this book. I would like to thank my dissertation supervisor, Will Milberg, who encouraged me to focus my research, as well as other members of the dissertation committee, Lance Taylor and Edward Nell, who provided useful comments on earlier drafts. I also would like to acknowledge The New School for its financial support by way of the Prize Fellowship which I received from 1987 to 1990. Without that fellowship, I would not have come to the United States and my life would have taken a completely different course, but that is another story. Two other persons warrant mentioning: Carol Lutfy because she opened a new world to me, and Rose Unes because she transformed the typescript quickly and meticulously. Without her, this book would never have seen the light of day. Finally I extend my gratitude to many other friends, colleagues and The New School faculty for their comments, assistance, support and encouragement, despite the fact that I often wanted to react to their inquiries, as my son does to mine, by saying: "I don't want to talk about it." (Mick, dit is opgedragen aan jou!)

HENK-JAN BRINKMAN

To Mick

1. Introduction

Will prices of Big Mac hamburgers ever be the same across the world? Will the price of a pound of coffee? What about a haircut? Why does a certain Canon camera costs $352 in France and $237 in Germany, despite the fact that transportation costs are much less than $115 and that there have been no tariffs and little exchange rate uncertainty between these two countries for several years?

The traditional explanation argues that prices of goods that can be traded across borders (tradables) would be equalized through international competition if transportation costs, tariffs and other impediments to free trade did not exist. But competition cannot equalize prices of goods and services that cannot – or can only at great cost – cross borders. The prices of such goods and services (nontradables) will thus be different across countries. Because of the existence of nontradables, exchange rates, which are partly determined by the movement of goods (tradables) across borders, can differ substantially from the purchasing power of currencies. As a corollary, exchange rates would still deviate from purchasing power parities even if trade barriers, capital flows and expectations were assumed absent. So the traditional argument goes.

In fact, the first systematic studies of the purchasing power of currencies, confirming the experience of many travelers, found that prices were generally lower in developing countries. This was attributed to the low prices of many services (nontradables) and explained by labor productivity differences. Thus if wages are equalized across sectors within a country, if higher wages prevail in the country with higher productivity and if productivity differences across countries are smaller in nontradables than in tradables, then relative prices of nontradables will be lower in low productivity countries than in high productivity countries. This is an argument that Ricardo already formulated in the nineteenth century but was only formalized, independently, by Balassa and Samuelson in 1964.

A number of other explanations for price differences across countries have been proposed since then. Some rely on factor endowments, some on economies of scale and others on financial repression. Most of these explanations have in common that they depend heavily on neoclassical price theory and on a dichotomy between tradables and nontradables, often equated with a dichotomy between goods and services. They assume that goods are perfectly tradable across borders at zero cost and services are nontradable at any

1

cost. But this ignores the fact that all goods have nontradable components and that services have tradable components and are increasingly traded in international markets, partly as a result of the technical advances of the last decades. To take full account of the tradable component in nontradables and the nontradable component in tradables, input–output relations have to be considered.

Yet abandoning the dichotomy between tradables and nontradables is not only a matter of taxonomy. It also relates to the structure of markets. Perfect competition and the complete equalization of prices can only exist when transportation costs and tariffs are zero. It is therefore not surprising that both tradability and perfect competition are best – yet still imperfectly – approached by homogeneous, primary commodities whose nontradable component is still rather small and whose prices are set on international commodity exchanges.

No study addressing price levels across countries has made market structures its central focus. Market power has been mentioned by, for example, Officer (1989, p. 362), and OECD (1992b) concluded that cartels are to blame for the high price levels in Switzerland. But market power has never been fully incorporated in the models designed to explain price levels across countries.

Most previous explanations for price levels rely on neoclassical theory, which argues that prices are determined by demand and supply. Prices are set instantaneously by a fictitious Walrasian auctioneer and if demand is different from supply the auctioneer will change the price until demand is equal to supply. This theory inter alia ignores uncertainty, economies of scale, externalities and market power.

The starting point of this book is the notion that markets in capitalists economies are imperfect and segmented. In contrast to the neoclassical paradigm, producers, not auctioneers, set prices. Producers have discretionary power to set prices and the degree of market power, which depends on the number of producers and on product differentiation, differs from industry to industry and from country to country. Prices are not determined by demand and supply as in the neoclassical models. Firms prefer to maintain capacity partly unused so that they can increase output and keep prices constant when demand rises, partly because of uncertainty about the reaction of rivals and the reluctance to antagonize customers. Yet firms are likely to increase prices when costs increase, particularly when the rise in costs is large, industry-wide and permanent, or else they will face bankruptcy.

A post-Keynesian markup pricing model is particularly suitable to take account of market power and intermediate inputs, factors ignored in previous studies. Moreover, the model is not vulnerable to the capital critique, like some of the recent explanations for price level differences, and the effects of trade barriers and economies of scale will be more explicitly addressed. Instead of a tradable/nontradable dichotomy, a continuum will be adopted, based on input–output relations, transportation costs and other trade barriers. Transportation costs and trade barriers have received, surprisingly, little attention in the empirical literature on price levels. More transportation costs will be passed on to consumers when the producer has more market power. Higher prices for intermediate inputs will filter through into the prices of the final good. On the other hand, a tariff on final demand imports – especially when perceived as temporary – is viewed by a domestic firm similarly to a price increase by a rival domestic firm. In such a case, it is likely that the domestic firm will raise production instead of prices. Labor productivity differences are also important factors but they are complemented by factors such as market power and input–output relations. Thus a high price for a Big Mac might reflect the market power of McDonald's, based on image, product differentiation and the nontradability of crucial inputs such as labor and restaurant space, rather than an overvalued exchange rate or trade barriers. Incorporation of market power, intermediate inputs, economies of scale and trade barriers to explain prices across countries gives the model a richer theoretical and empirical content than previous models. All in all, this book offers a fresh look at an old problem and the new approach will be tested with new data sets.

The book is organized as follows. Chapter 2 will review the literature and examine four other explanations for price level variations across countries. This chapter will also discuss the validity of these theories and present a survey of the existing regressions results. The next five chapters will present the theoretical model. Chapter 3 gives the core of the post-Keynesian markup pricing model and the theoretical assumptions underlying it. The next chapter develops a method to measure productivity within an input–output framework. Although the preferred method has to be adapted because of lack of data, it dovetails nicely with the model outlined in Chapter 3. Chapter 5 examines the most important behavioral relations behind the pricing model: the determinants of the markup. Three factors will be discussed: the need to generate profits to finance investment, market structure and the power of labor unions. In its turn, the market structure is determined by the concentration of sales and product differentiation. Two other factors affect prices, but they will be the topic of separate chapters as they influence several components of the price equation and not just the markup. Chapter 6 covers economies of scale and Chapter 7 deals with transportation costs, international trade barriers and foreign market power. The next four chapters confront the theory with the facts. Chapter 8 describes the price levels data and the different tests that will be performed in the subsequent chapters. The model will be tested by regression analysis on three different data sets. Chapter 9 tests the model on sectoral price levels for Japan and the Republic of Korea, Chapter 10 on price levels for GDP for a cross-section of countries, and Chapter 11 for price levels for investment goods, also across countries. The book will conclude with a summary of the test results and the implications.

PART I

Theory

2. Structural explanations for price levels

Before we turn to the theories, we must first define clearly what we are trying to explain. To compare prices across countries, they have to be expressed in a common unit and refer to the same good or service. The price data used in this book are based on purchasing power parities. Purchasing power parities (PPPs) are defined as the number of national currency units required to buy goods equivalent to what can be bought with one unit of currency of the numéraire country, which is here the United States. PPPs are however not directly comparable across countries because their units are national currencies per dollar – rupees per dollar for example – or rather national currency per international dollar (I$). An international dollar is a dollar with the same purchasing power over total United States GDP as the US dollar. (See also List of Selected Abbreviations and Appendix 1.) To create units that are comparable across countries, PPPs are divided by the exchange rate. The result is called the price level. Thus the price level (PL) is defined as the ratio of the purchasing power parity (PPP) to the exchange rate (ER), that is PL = PPP/ER, or, say, (DM/$)/(DM/$). Purchasing power parities, and thus price levels, are calculated for total GDP but also for components of GDP, such as cereals, food, consumption or investment

To explain price levels, nearly all authors start by distinguishing between goods with relatively low, or even zero, transportation costs (tradables) and goods with relatively high or infinitely high transportation costs (nontradables). Moreover, tariffs are almost always assumed zero – Clague (1986b) and Feldman (1991) are exceptions. The distinction between tradables and nontradables is common in international trade theory, going back at least to Ricardo (see also Salter, 1959; Taussig, 1927; Viner, 1937). Ricardo argued that the prices of tradables are determined on world markets and that prices of nontradables are determined by domestic costs and demand (Ricardo [1821] 1948, chs 7 and 28). Prices of tradables would be equalized through competition, but prices of nontradables can differ between countries, although some have argued that prices of nontradables could also be equalized because of substitution in consumption between tradables and nontradables and substitution in factor use (Kravis *et al.,* 1978, pp. 219, 221). If, in addition, the share of tradables in GDP is equalized across countries, then the price level is completely dependent on the prices of nontradables (Kravis and Lipsey, 1988, p. 475). (Of course, it is not clear how competition can equalize

7

weights.) To yield the relatively low price levels found in developing countries, the prices of nontradables have to be lower than the prices of tradables. The precise relation between the price level and the price of nontradables is, however, dependent on the particular index used (Desser, 1994; Kravis *et al.*, 1983, pp. 214–15; Officer, 1989).

Nearly all authors consider nontradables to be equal to services (Balassa, 1964, p. 585; Bhagwati, 1984, p. 281; Clague, 1985, p. 999; 1986a, p. 321; Feldman, 1991, p. 1383; Officer, 1989, p. 368; Panagariya, 1988, p. 514; Quibria, 1990, p. 359). This is less than satisfactory because it ignores the fact that many services, such as banking, insurance and communications, are tradable and are in fact traded. Moreover, construction is often (for example, by Kravis *et al.*, 1982) viewed as a nontradable, but this is also a simplification. Finally, there are some goods, such as coarse grains and rootcrops, that can be considered nontradable. But let us ignore this problem for the moment and ask: how can the low prices for nontradables or services be explained? (We will address the issue in Chapters 4 and 7.)

2.1 FOUR DIFFERENT EXPLANATIONS

Four different explanations for the low price level in developing countries have emerged in the literature. The first theory is based on productivity differences between rich and poor countries in tradables. The second theory argues that different factor or resource endowments are the cause of low price levels in developing countries. Economies of scale play the central role in the third explanation and the existence of financial repression in the fourth. Demand factors have also gained some attention in the literature, but they cannot be considered independently from supply factors.

Productivity Differences

The most common explanation for the low price level in developing countries is based on the productivity gap between rich and poor countries and also originated from Ricardo. Ricardo ([1821] 1948, p. 87) wrote that "the prices of home commodities ... are, independently of other causes, higher in those countries where manufactures flourish." After Ricardo, it took about a century before Harrod clearly identified the problem in 1933 in the first edition of his *International Economics*, although it was also discussed by Taussig (1927, ch. 5). Harrod (1957, p. 62) stated that "it may be expected that the price level of C goods [domestic goods] will be higher in the more efficient countries" because the differences between national levels of efficiency is smaller for nontradables. He attributed these efficiency differences to differences in the level of natural resources, scientific knowledge or capital. Therefore, Harrod can also be thought of as being the originator of the factor endowments explanation (see below). He also indicated that "when C goods are taken into account the Theory of Purchasing Power Parity is no longer true."

This argument was formalized independently by Balassa (1964) and Samuelson (1964) and can be summarized as follows (see also David, 1972, p. 981; Kravis *et al.*, 1978, p. 219; 1983; Kravis and Lipsey, 1983, pp. 4–5; Marris, 1984, pp. 41–5; and Samuelson, 1974, pp. 604–5). If international trade equates prices of tradables, save for transportation costs and tariffs, if wages are equalized across sectors within a country, with higher wages prevailing in the country with higher productivity, and if productivity differences across countries are smaller in nontradables than in tradables, then relative prices of nontradables will be lower in low productivity countries than in high productivity countries. This argument is schematically presented in Table 2.1. The table shows that prices of tradables could be equal across countries because low wages are combined with low productivity in developing countries and high wages are combined with high productivity in developed countries. But prices of nontradables are higher in developed countries.

Table 2.1 Differential labor productivity

	Developed Countries		Developing Countries	
	Wages	Labor productivity	Wages	Labor productivity
Tradables	high	high	low	low
Nontradables	high	low	low	low

Factor Endowments

It was not until the 1980s that other explanations for the low price level in developing countries were put forward in a formal model. The explanation that received most attention was based on differences in endowments of factors of production or natural resources. This explanation was first put forward by Kravis and Lipsey (1983, pp. 12–13) as an alternative to the productivity differences model and was more fully developed first by Bhagwati (1984) and subsequently by Quibria (1990) and Falvey and Gemmell (1991). Bhagwati criticized the assumptions underlying the productivity differences model, in particular the model of Kravis *et al.* (1983), and provided a model that assumed that productivity differences do not exist. He further assumed that the poor and the rich country have identical production functions for the two goods and the one service in the model. In both countries, the service is produced with more labor-intensive methods than the good. However, the poor country is labor-abundant, leading to a lower wage–rental ratio. Factor proportions are too different for factor price equalization. The poor country will produce a nontraded service (S) and a traded good (Y) with more labor-intensive methods than the rich country. The rich country also produces Y, another traded good (X) and a nontraded service with more capital-intensive methods than the poor country. In the poor country, one unit of Y exchanges for more S than in the rich country because of the lower wage–rental ratio. Thus services are cheaper in poor countries.

Other authors (Clague and Tanzi, 1972; Isenman, 1980) have put forward arguments along the same lines of reasoning: X-goods (or services) are more intensive in the use of A (natural resources, human capital, and so on) in all countries and in an A-abundant country, the prices of A will be lower, and therefore X-goods will be cheaper. Clague (1985) built a specific-factor model that went along these lines but also accounted for other influences. Two specific factors (both natural resources) are used in the production of exports and import-competing goods, respectively, but not in the production of domestically consumed services and tourist services. He analyzed the effects of natural resources, efficiency, tourism, the terms of trade and country size. Other things equal (that is, GDP per capita), more natural resources will lead to a larger supply of tradables and therefore to lower prices of tradables. Then, it is somewhat obscure how this leads to a higher price level but he alluded to the following explanations. Costs of tradables are lower in the resource-rich country but prices are equalized across countries; hence the windfall profit is spent on nontradables, raising its prices. Alternatively, higher tradables production might lead to a higher demand for labor, bidding up its price. The higher wages will be equalized across sectors and hence cause an increase in the prices of nontradables. Clague (1988a, p. 531) suggested an intuitive explanation: "the abundantly endowed countries would have lower prices of tradables relative to the prices of nontradables ...; since the exchange rate is related to the prices of tradables while the PPP is affected by the prices of nontradables, the PPP/exchange-rate ratio is expected to be higher in the abundantly endowed countries."

Clague (1985) assumed that increases in efficiency are confined to tradables. Hence prices of services are solely determined by the wage rate and higher efficiency is associated with lower prices of tradables. International tourism increases the demand for nontradables, leading to higher prices. For the terms of trade, the results of the model were ambiguous. Country size does not affect the price level because Clague assumed constant returns to scale. The next explanation, however, drops this assumption.

Economies of Scale

The third explanation of the price level is suggested by Panagariya (1988). His argument is based on the assumptions of economies of scale in manufacturing and constant returns to scale in agriculture and services. Only services are not traded. He assumed that the factor endowments in the rich country are a multiple of those of the poor country. Apart from this, the countries are the same, including relative factor endowments. He further assumed average-cost pricing in manufacturing and fixed prices in agriculture and manufacturing. Prices of services are determined by demand and supply under the assumption that the income elasticity of demand for services is unity. The country with a larger amount of factor endowments will have a larger supply of services but also a larger demand. The demand and the supply curves both shift to the right when factor endowments increase. But under certain assumptions about the value of some parameters in the supply and demand equations, he concluded that the prices of services rise with the amount of factor endowments. In particular, the assumption on the value of the economies-of-scale parameter, restricted to lie between zero and one, is crucial.

Financial Repression

The fourth explanation for the price level is the existence of financial repression in developing countries (Feldman and Gang, 1987; 1990; Feldman, 1991). This explanation cannot be considered independently and the authors do indeed view their model as complementary to the productivity and factor endowments models, although they ran regressions with and without GDP per capita, which is usually considered a proxy for productivity or factor endowments differences.

The term "financial repression" is used to describe a "set of policies that aim to extract revenue from the financial system and to use the financial system to funnel resources into specific sectors of the economy ... via forced sales of government debt to the banking system ... [and] interest rate controls" (Feldman and Gang, 1990, p. 341). Their argument is based on the assumption that, owing to financial repression, there is a low real interest rate that causes a shortage of savings and raises the cost of credit, especially in rural areas. This means that the credit market is rationed at the demand side.

Feldman and Gang used the Harris–Todaro model of migration, which explains the movement of labor from rural to urban areas by wage differentials. They argued that, because of the higher interest rate in rural areas, consumption is curtailed and labor leaves for the cities where a minimum wage exists. In the cities the migrants enter the informal, low-pay service sector. As a result of the inflow, the wages will fall and so will the prices of services.

Demand Factors

Finally, demand factors have been taking a more prominent place in recent models as a determinant of price levels, but they cannot be considered independently from such supply factors as productivity, factor endowments and economies of scale. Balassa (1964), Samuelson (1964) and Bhagwati (1984) ignored demand factors, except for the effect of tourism. Clague (1989, pp. 376–7) argued that, if one had appropriate demand variables, they should be brought into the equation. He did not think, in contrast to Officer (1989), that the share of nontradables in GDP could play this role. Other scholars also introduced demand factors in their models (Clague, 1988b; De Gregorio and Wolf, 1994; Falvey and Gemmell; 1991, 1996; Panagariya, 1988; Quibria, 1990). Some scholars explored the effect of government expenditures on the price of nontradables because government expenditures are disproportionate on nontradables (Rogoff, 1996, p. 663).

Bergstrand (1991; 1992) explored the role of demand in more detail. He assumed that tastes are nonhomothetic, which implies that the income-expansion path through the indifference curves is not a straight line. Hence the income elasticity of demand is greater than one for luxuries and less than one for necessities. Then price levels are higher in countries with higher GDP per capita because nontradables are luxuries and tradables are necessities.

Zietz (1996) focused on the demand for nontradables as an important determinant of the price of nontradables relative to the price of tradables. He argued that the demand for nontradables increases when the share of elderly or school-aged in the population rises, the crime rate increases or when the number of households per capita grows. These factors increase the demand for such nontradables as education, health care, housing and law enforcement.

2.2   VALIDITY OF ASSUMPTIONS AND THEORY

Where are we now? There are four explanations for price levels: the productivity differences model, the factor endowments model, the economies-of-scale model and the financial repression model. But what are their relative merits? First we take a look at the theoretical foundations and assumptions.

Capital Critique

Sraffa (1960) and Garegnani (1970) have pointed out that the assumptions underlying a neoclassical production function are rather peculiar. They explained that there is a smooth ("jelly") monotonically increasing relation between the wage–rental ratio and the capital–labor ratio only if there is a uniform capital–labor ratio throughout the economy. This is the case in a one-commodity world as typified by a "corn economy" that only uses corn to grow corn. The smooth production function breaks down as soon as it is recognized that capital is a produced commodity and is not an endowment that falls from heaven. Any model that does not assume a uniform capital–labor ratio is vulnerable to the capital critique from the economists associated with Cambridge University in England.

The labor productivity model does not rely on any neoclassical assumption, as demonstrated by Pasinetti (1981, pp. 256–8) and is therefore not vulnerable to the capital critique. Balassa (1964, p. 585), Samuelson (1964, pp. 145, 151) and Kravis *et al.* (1983, pp. 211–15) explicitly restricted themselves to labor productivity. However, there are some formulations of the productivity model that do use capital and are subject to the capital critique (De Gregorio *et al.*, 1994; De Gregorio and Wolf, 1994; Falvey and Gemmell, 1996).

The factor endowments models of Bhagwati (1984), Clague (1985) and Quibria (1990) do not assume any productivity differential, but essential to their argument is a smooth production function and a monotonically increasing relation between the wage–rental ratio and factor intensities, which are not required in the productivity differences model. Although factor endowments models do not make any assumption regarding productivity differences across countries, they can often allow for them (Bhagwati, 1984, p. 283; Clague, 1985, p. 1000; Falvey and Gemmell, 1996; Quibria, 1990, pp. 364–5;).

The models of Panagariya (1988) and Falvey and Gemmell (1991; 1996) are also subject to the capital critique in the way they are presented. It seems, however, that Panagariya (1988) does not need to make the assumptions about capital to reach the same conclusions. From the assumptions of economies of scale in manufacturing and constant returns to scale in agriculture and services, it intuitively follows that manufacturing prices are relatively lower in the larger economy independent of the production function.

In sum, for theoretical reasons the factor endowments and economies-of-scale models are less satisfactory than the other two models. But what is the empirical validity of the assumptions?

Labor Productivity

The labor productivity model makes assumptions regarding wages and productivity differences. The model assumes that labor productivity differences across countries are smaller in nontradables than in tradables; that is, that labor productivity of tradables is higher in rich countries than in poor countries and that this gap is larger than the gap in labor productivity of nontradables between poor and rich countries. In other words, the ratio of labor productivity of tradables to labor productivity in nontradables increases with rising per capita GDP, or the reverse of this ratio declines with rising per capita GDP. Usually, nontradables are equated with services, and tradables with industry and agriculture. There are some studies in support of this assumption.

Kravis *et al.* (1983, p. 204) regressed the ratio of services productivity to commodity productivity on PPP-converted GDP per capita and found a statistically significant negative relation for 20 countries in 1975.[1] Many authors quoted the famous studies of Kuznets and Chenery and Syrquin in support of the assumptions. In Kuznets (1971, Table 31), the ratio of product per worker in the services to the industry sector declines with rising GDP per capita across countries in 1958.[2] However, Chenery and Syrquin (1975, Figure 9) showed with a schematic figure that across countries this ratio only falls after a per capita GNP of about $300. Below $300 the ratio increases slightly. Similar evidence for 42 developing countries can be found in Blades *et al.* (1974, Table 31). Data from a later publication by Chenery and Syrquin (Chenery *et al.*, 1986, ch. 4) can be used to regress the ratios for 1960 and 1980 of labor productivity of services to labor productivity in industry[3] on GNP per capita of 1976. The estimated coefficient of GNP per capita is positive but insignificant. The ratio of labor productivity of services to labor productivity in agriculture decreases when GNP per capita increases, but is again not statistically significant.

The assumption that productivity differences across countries are smaller in nontradables than in tradables can be translated into movements over time, instead of across countries. In that case, productivity in the service sector increases less than productivity in the commodity-producing sectors when per capita output increases. Balassa (1964, p. 593) already substantiated this argument. Data from Maddison (1980; 1987; 1991) also support this interpretation. Between 1950 and 1976, the growth rate of output per person in the services sector was the lowest of the three major sectors in 13 European countries and the United States. For Germany, Italy and the United Kingdom between 1870 and 1950, and for Japan between 1906 and 1950, the growth rate of labor productivity in services was not always the lowest of the three major sectors, but it was always lower than in industry (Maddison, 1980, pp. 53–5; 1987, p. 684; 1991, pp. 149–51). See also Kuznets (1971, Tables 45 and 46) for 13 OECD countries between 1860 and 1960. Elfring (1988, pp. 49–65) surveyed and calculated labor productivity growth rates for the post-World War II period in some OECD countries and concluded that all studies point to a slower growth rate for services compared with agriculture and industry or goods. Blades (1987, pp. 180–81) confirmed this conclusion for OECD countries if services are compared with goods, but not for all subcategories. The growth rate of labor productivity in manufacturing was, for example, lower than in transport and communications and finance, insurance, real estate and business services. In agriculture as well, the growth rate of labor productivity was lower than in market services, while in nonmarket services (government and private nonprofit services) the growth rate was lowest of all subcategories.

Gemmell and Wardley (1990) provided some evidence on Great Britain in the nineteenth century and Bhalla (1970, pp. 534–8) for two developing countries: Philippines and Taiwan. In these two countries, some subcategories of the service sector have among the highest growth rates in labor productivity. Blades *et al.* (1974, Tables 34 and 35) confirmed in most cases a relatively lower increase in labor productivity in the service sector for developing countries, although, again, some subcategories match or have higher labor productivity increases than the goods-producing sectors. Gemmell (1985, pp. 64–6) showed that, for Egypt, labor productivity for services was larger than for goods during the periods 1960–1965 and 1970–1975. During the period 1965–1970, this conclusion was reversed but he dismissed this result as specific and abnormal. Chenery *et al.* (1986, ch. 4) provided evidence for 34 developing countries. Between 1960 and 1980, the ratio of labor productivity in services to labor productivity in industry decreased in 10 countries and the ratio of labor productivity in services to labor productivity in agriculture decreased in 11 countries.

There are some problems with this evidence. First, as was made clear, aggregation masks the difference within the sectors. The service sector is a very heterogeneous sector. Some subsectors, such as transport and communications, can show high productivity growth, while others, such as personal services like haircutting, display usually low productivity growth (Baumol, 1985; see also section 4.2). The different empirical studies do not use the same definitions. Second, many authors have pointed out that the measured productivity is likely to be biased owing to methodological problems. Often output in the service sector (or subsectors) is underestimated because it is measured by using input indicators, such as labor, or gross output and assumes constant labor productivity. Consequently, productivity in the services-using sectors is overestimated (Denison, 1989). Third, in many cases labor productivity in the service sector rises faster than in agriculture, which is also a goods-producing sector (Lancieri, 1990, p. 36).

In conclusion, the evidence for assuming that the productivity differences across countries are smaller in services than in goods production is mixed. The support for the assumption is mostly found in time-series studies in the developed countries for the period after World War II and is strongest when certain subsectors of the service sector, such as personal services, are compared to manufacturing.

Wages

The assumption that wages are equal across sectors is made not only in the labor productivity model (Balassa, 1964, pp. 586–7; Samuelson, 1964, pp. 145–6) but also in some of the other models. The models of Bhagwati (1984) and Quibria (1990) are crucially dependent on the economy-wide wage–rental ratio but Panagariya (1988, p. 514) did not need to make any assumptions about wages or other factor prices because he assumed that relative factor endowments are the same across countries. Feldman and Gang (1987; 1990) explicitly assumed a difference in wages across sectors.

Only Balassa (1964, p. 587) quoted some evidence on the tendency for interindustry wage equalization. Other authors fail to provide any information on wage equalization or wage–rental ratios.

The assumption on wage equalization is clearly contradicted by the facts, which has entertained labor economists for a long time. Wages are not equalized across sectors, not even when controlled for a number of factors. Indeed, these interindustry wage differentials are rather stable over time and correlated across countries, in developed countries, in developing countries and among them (Abuhadba and Romaguera, 1993; Amadeo, 1994; Gatica *et al.*, 1995; Gittleman and Wolff, 1993; Wood, 1978, pp. 175–9).

Moreover, the productivity model (implicitly) assumes that higher productivity in tradables is translated into higher wages instead of higher profits (Rogoff, 1996, p. 658). This, however, is not automatic and depends in part on the success of labor unions in increasing their share of the pie.

Factor Endowments

Kravis *et al.* (1983) published some capital–labor ratios to support the productivity differences model. The same data are used in other studies as well to support the factor endowments model (Bhagwati, 1984; Kravis and Lipsey, 1983). The data in Kravis *et al.* (1983) were from another study, which estimated labor and capital requirements on the basis of a sample of input–output tables. Although they do not discuss the method in detail, it seems that the capital and labor requirements are not based on capital stocks estimates but solely on the input of goods from the capital goods-producing sectors.

These figures showed that the capital–labor ratio is lower for services than for commodities in all income groups (except one) and that the capital–labor ratio for services monotonically rises when GDP per capita increases. For commodities, however, the capital–labor ratio does not increase monotonically. In the second lowest income group this ratio is higher than in the third and the fourth. Bhagwati (1984, p. 285) concluded that this is in support of his explanation because the ratio of prices of services to commodities also does not increase in these income groups. Kravis *et al.* (1983, p. 207) also pointed out that the capital–labor ratio in the transportation sector (a service) is among the highest in any country, whether it is poor or rich, and that textiles (a commodity) is not always more capital-intensive than some services.

Financial Repression

The financial repression explanation, put forward by Feldman and Gang (1987, 1990), assumed several characteristics of developing countries that are implausible or contradicted by evidence. First, they used the Republic of Korea as an example of financial liberalization, but failed to provide data on relatively high rural interest rates and high urban wages. Amsden (1989, p. 202) however quoted evidence that the male wage rate in agriculture has been higher than the wage in modern industry at least up to the mid-1980s, slowing rural to urban migration. This also upset the condition for a stable equilibrium as stipulated by Feldman and Gang (1990, p. 352). According to their reasoning, the interest rate premium in rural areas has to be even higher to counteract these higher wages. Data are missing, however. Moreover, the Republic of Korea does not fit the traditional model of financial repression, nor is it a case of extensive financial liberalization (Amsden and Euh, 1990; Chung H. Lee, 1992).

Second, the Feldman–Gang model implies that the service sector is exclusively confined to the urban informal sector. The majority of the urban informal sector participants are indeed active in the service sector, but not exclusively. Manufacturing typically accounts for between 15 and 20 per cent and construction (usually considered a nontradable) for 4 to 8 per cent of informal activities (Charmes, 1990, pp. 26–7; Lubell, 1991, pp. 46–7, 51–4; Sanyal, 1991, p. 41). Moreover, services are not restricted to urban areas or to the informal sector. Trade, transport, storage, communication, repair, health care and education are all service activities common in rural areas as well. It is thus only to some extent appropriate to explain low service prices by focusing solely on the urban services.

Third, Feldman and Gang (1990, p. 345) assumed that wages are lower in the informal sector. This is not supported by the existing evidence which showed that the income of entrepreneurs in the informal sector is in almost all cases a multiple of the minimum wage and sometimes higher than average income in the formal sector (Charmes, 1990, pp. 28–39; Lubell, 1991, p. 12; Sanyal, 1991, p. 41; Sethuraman, 1981, pp. 38, 42–4). The urban informal sector is not the natural resort of recent immigrants to the city. On the contrary, many of them start with a job in the formal sector and later start a business after they have saved some capital (Lubell, 1991, pp. 111–12; Sanyal, 1991, p. 40).

Fourth, some assumptions are made about the effect of interest rates on migration patterns. It was assumed that financial repression causes higher interest rate in rural areas (Feldman, 1991, p. 1384; Feldman and Gang, 1990, p. 346). Although crucial for their argument, they do not make much effort to explain this result or corroborate this with empirical data. There is indeed evidence that interest rates in informal rural credit markets are higher than in formal rural credit markets and that consumption loans are largely met in the informal sector (Amsden, 1989, p. 76; Hoff and Stiglitz, 1990, p. 236), but higher rural interest rates need to be explained by higher risk premiums, associated with weather, limited collateral, monopoly power and screening and enforcement costs and not by financial repression (Hoff and Stiglitz, 1990). Moreover, there are theoretical reasons and empirical evidence that total saving is not much affected by the interest rate but rather by total income. Thus if financial liberalization leads to higher interest rates, borrowing for consumption and investment becomes more expensive while leaving savings unaffected (Desai and Mellor, 1993, chs 7, 8; Gibson and Tsakalotos, 1994, pp. 594–7; Killick, 1991, p. 299; Taylor, 1988, pp. 55–7). Indeed, higher interest rates are a primary objective of financial liberalization but financial liberalization is unlikely to change the interest differential between the rural and urban areas.

Demand Factors

Several authors have pointed out that associating services with luxuries can be fallacious (Fisher, 1939). Moreover, empirical studies have resulted in a wide range of income elasticities. Kravis *et al.* (1983, pp. 196–201) concluded from cross-section and time-series data that there is no strong basis for classifying final expenditures according to income elasticities (see also Summers, 1985, p. 41). Falvey and Gemmell (1991, p. 1304) however showed all income elasticities for services and nontradables to be significantly greater than one at the 5 per cent level and the ones for nontradables were all smaller than the ones for services.

2.3 EXPLANATORY POWER: REGRESSION ANALYSIS

If we assume the theoretical models to be valid, what can we say about their explanatory power? This section will give an overview of the econometric tests of the different models. The section will focus on cross-section analysis but will also discuss a few time-series studies.

Most authors test their models by using regression analysis – the major exception is Panagariya (1988). The respective models include the following proxies: for productivity differentials across countries: GDP per capita; for factor endowments: GDP per capita, mineral share in exports or GDP, agricultural land, literacy rate and school enrolment; and for financial repression: ratio of GDP to M2. GDP per capita is expected to have a positive sign as prices of nontradables are relatively low in poorer countries. (The sign expectations are summarized in Table 2.2.) Factor endowments can have different signs, depending on the size of the demand and supply effects. As discussed in section 2.1, Clague (1985; 1986a; 1988a) argued that countries rich in natural resources will have higher price levels. Officer (1989) contended, however, that a higher share of natural resource industries (such as agriculture and mining) in GDP reflects higher demand. In that case, the expected sign is reversed. In Falvey and Gemmell (1991; 1996), GDP per capita is endogenous and the effect of resource endowments on price levels can be positive or negative. The ratio of GDP to M2 measures the income velocity of money and a high velocity is argued to reflect financial repression, which in Feldman and Gang (1990) will lead to lower prices for nontradables. Hence the sign expectation for GDP/M2 is negative.

Other Structural Factors Affecting Price Levels

Some other factors are usually included because they influence the price level directly or indirectly. First, the international equalization of prices of tradables is argued to be influenced by the degree of exposure to international trade and tourism. Tourism fulfills the role Samuelson ascribed to rentiers: "If there were a tremendous number of footloose *rentiers* (as there are not), who would move between A and B whenever *their* cost of living was not equalized and would do so in such numbers as to force by their own shifts in demands enough changes in the regional price levels to bring about equality in their cost of living, we would have [free exchange rates being equal to purchasing power parities]" (1974, pp. 603–4; emphasis in original; the phrase within square brackets is the verbal equivalent of the formula in original). Hence, when only this demand effect is considered, tourism will have a positive effect on price levels (Balassa, 1964, p. 596; Clague, 1985; 1986a; Samuelson, 1964, p. 148). Officer (1989, p. 366) however postulated that a high share of revenues from tourism (and other international services) might reflect an abundant supply of tradable services and hence lead to lower price levels.

The Stolper–Samuelson theorem is used (implicitly) to clarify the effect of trade liberalization on prices. The theorem states that the price of the abundant factor will increase when a country reduces its tariffs. If the United States is the most capital-abundant country and all other countries are more labor-abundant and if nontradables are more labor-intensive, nontradable prices will rise when openness increases. Hence openness will have a positive effect on price levels in all countries other than the United States (Kravis and Lipsey, 1983, p. 15). However, the effect of openness on countries that are more capital abundant than the United States might be reversed. In other words, the effect might be "upward for poor countries and downwards for rich countries" (Kravis and Lipsey, 1988, p. 475), pulling price levels closer to a world average. On the other hand, if openness reflects more competition – as is often assumed in the burgeoning literature on the relation between trade orientation and growth – then openness might be correlated with low price levels (Kravis *et al.*, 1978, p. 221). Kravis *et al.*, in their different publications included in their regressions the variable openness, defined as the ratio of exports plus imports to GDP averaged for certain years. Clague called this variable the foreign trade ratio. Clague (1985; 1988b) disputed, however, that there is a theoretical explanation for the inclusion of this variable in the regression equation. Commenting on Kravis *et al.* (1978, pp. 221–2), who suggested that the degree of openness is likely to vary inversely with country size, Clague (1985) argued that the effect of the degree of openness should be analyzed separately from the size of the country but he did not think that openness will have an effect on price levels. He argued that

> as we go from autarky to free trade, the price of the abundant factor rises. But that proposition does not necessarily have anything to do with the factor prices of high-FTR [Foreign Trade Ratio] and low-FTR countries. ... Suppose a large country like Brazil were broken up into its states. ... [T]hese states would now have high FTR's. ... [O]bviously nothing would happen to factor prices or to service prices. (Clague, 1988b, p. 242)

The variable price isolation has also been used. This variable is based on effect rather than exposure and was measured by the squared difference between a country's implicit GDP deflator and a world average GDP deflator (Kravis *et al.*, 1978; Isenman, 1980).

Second, even if the prices of all goods and services, expressed in one currency by using exchange rates, were the same in all countries (the law of one price), the price level would not be equal to one if the weights of the goods and services differ across countries. If prices of nontradables differ across countries, their weight becomes particularly important. Kravis and Lipsey (1983, p. 15) argued that the expected sign for the share of nontradables is positive if high shares of nontradables are associated with high prices for nontradables, which is possible because the elasticity between tradables and nontradables is low. This effect exists independently of the fact that this variable is the mirror image of openness if tradables are equal to traded goods. Officer (1989, pp. 358–60) also followed this reasoning. However Clague (1989, pp. 375–6) argued that the interpretation of this variable is ambiguous and Desser (1994) showed that the regression equation hardly changes if a computed price level that excludes the arithmetical influences of the share of nontradables on the price level is used as a dependent variable and the share of nontradables is omitted as an independent variable.

Short-term Factors Affecting Price Levels

There are also some short-term factors that influence the price level and are often included in the regression equation to avoid biased results, although whether they should be included at all is also debated in the literature. Officer (1989, pp. 361–2) argued that there is no place for short-term variables in cross-section regressions. Clague (1986a; 1989, pp. 377–8) however disagreed (see also Kravis and Lipsey, 1983, pp. 17–20, 25–8). These short-term factors will be discussed first.

Flows of goods and services across the border make up only one part of the balance of payments and tradables account for only a portion of GDP. At the same time, all international payments (and not only payments for traded goods and services) affect the exchange rate and all components of GDP (and not only tradables) influence the purchasing power of a national currency. Therefore there are several factors that influence exchange rates, while leaving PPPs relatively unaffected, or vice versa. The factors that affect exchange rates but not PPPs are considered short-term factors (Dornbusch, 1987a; Kravis and Lipsey, 1983, p. 10; Marris, 1984, pp. 46–7; Officer, 1976a, p. 9; Samuelson, 1964; 1974).

The following short-term factors are sometimes included in the regression analysis. First, tariffs, import quotas, import licenses and export subsidies lowers the exchange rate necessary to maintain balance-of-payments equilibrium (and can also raise the PPP) of the country using these measures (Balassa, 1973, p. 1265; 1974, p. 612). There is also some evidence, at least for the United States, that appreciation of the real exchange rate fosters higher protection (Clifton, 1985). This all reinforces the positive relation between trade restrictions and price levels. However, Clague (1988b, p. 241) argued that the model of Bhagwati (1984) implied lower prices of services if the import-competing sector is capital-intensive and a tariff would raise the price of capital and reduce the price of labor.

Second, some have argued that, other things being equal, countries receiving transfers will have higher exchange rates to attain balance-of-payments equilibrium than capital-exporting countries. Phrased differently, a country with a trade balance deficit has expenditures in excess of income, which are spent on nontradables, increasing relative prices of nontradables (and higher price levels and lower relative prices of tradables) (Clague, 1985, p. 999; 1986a, p. 321; 1988a; 1988b, p. 240; Falvey and Gemmell, 1991; 1996). However, it is not clear why the excess of expenditures over income are spent to a larger extend on nontradables than on tradables. If this excess is spent on tradables the effect on the price level will be reversed.

Most authors argued that these two factors, tariffs and transfers, do not produce a systematic bias in international output comparisons between developing and developed countries. For example, Kravis and Lipsey (1983, p. 16) contended that "the currently accepted view of the transfer problem ... eschews any generalization about price-level changes." And Marris (1984, p. 41) wrote "[t]he evidence seems to suggest that tariffs and capital movements do not have biasing effects." Indeed, quantitative trade restrictions were more pervasive in developing countries in the 1980s but producer subsidies have been more widespread in developed economies (United Nations, 1988, p. 33; 1990a, p. 19). The total effect of trade restrictions on price levels would be hard to determine. The net transfer of financial resources does not produce a clear bias either. Between 1983 and 1990, Latin America and the four Newly Industrializing Countries had a negative transfer, as had Germany and Japan, while other developing countries, the United States and the United Kingdom had a positive transfer (United Nations, 1990b, p. 76; 1991, Table A.26). During the 1990s, this pattern changed. Most dramatic has been the change in Latin America, which has been a net recipient of financial resources since 1991 (United Nations, 1998, Table A.25).

Third, exchange rates are affected by speculation, expectations and confidence and PPPs are not. This is shown, for example, by Dornbusch (1980, pp. 202–5) who explained overshooting of the exchange rate by assuming a relatively slow adjusting price level in response to a monetary shock. Following Dornbusch (1980), monetary factors are included by Clague (1986a) and Kravis and Lipsey (1983) to account for this possibility. Exchange rates can also be influenced by the existence of multiple rates.

Fourth, transportation costs are sometimes considered short-term factors or it is argued that they do not change the conclusion of the model (Balassa, 1964, p. 585; Kravis and Lipsey, 1983, p. 17; Samuelson, 1964, p. 151). However, transportation costs are generally higher in low-income countries as infrastructure is still poor or economies of scale low. Moreover, it is not that easy to move an island onshore or create a port for a landlocked country. Hence we discuss these structural factors in Chapter 7.

Existing Regression Results

So far it has been assumed that the price level is the dependent variable. Some authors were indeed interested in explaining this variable, which has also been called the real price level and the (real) national price level, or its reciprocal, the exchange rate deviation index (Balassa, 1964; Clague, 1985; 1986a; 1988a; 1989; Clague and Tanzi, 1972; Kravis and Lipsey, 1983; Officer, 1976b; 1989). Others, however, wanted to predict PPP-converted GDP per capita when only exchange rate-converted GDP per capita was available (David, 1972; Kravis *et al.*, 1978; Summers *et al.*, 1980; Summers and Heston, 1984). Therefore they regressed PPP-converted GDP per capita on exchange rate-converted GDP per capita for a sample of countries for which both variables were known (see Table 2.2). Following the argument that the models are designed to explain the difference between prices of tradables and nontradables, some authors used the ratio of these two prices as the dependent variable in addition to the price level (Feldman and Gang, 1990; Kravis and Lipsey, 1983; Officer, 1989). Finally, Kravis and Lipsey (1983; 1988) also used the price level of nontradables as a dependent variable.

The data used for the dependent variable usually came from the subsequent phases of the United Nations International Comparison Programme (ICP) or from the Penn World Tables (PWT) (see Appendix 1). Only the early publications (Balassa, 1964; 1973; David, 1972) used data from other studies, such as those of Gilbert and associates (which included Irving B. Kravis) conducted at the predecessor of the OECD in the 1950s or from Maddison (1967). Officer (1974; 1976b) used also data from the German Statistical Office, which calculated purchasing power parities relative to Germany for a number of countries.

There are also a number of studies that tested the validity of the productivity model over time instead of across countries. These studies usually took as the dependent variable the ratio of a price index of nontradables to a price index of tradables and called it the real exchange rate. This terminology is somewhat confusing as the real exchange rate is usually defined as the nominal exchange rate multiplied by relative inflation rates compared to a base year (Maciejewski, 1983). Nonetheless, both definitions refer to changes over time, while the price level refers to a moment in time (Clague, 1986b, p. 155). Hence the real exchange rate can be seen as the reciprocal of the change in the price level (Kravis and Lipsey, 1983, p. 9), yet, some authors equated the price level with the real exchange rate (Bergstrand, 1991, p. 326).

The R^2 of the regressed equations as listed in Table 2.2 cannot be used to select a particular model because the dependent variables are different and therefore the R^2 cannot be compared properly. Nonetheless, in most studies the R^2 was higher than 0.75 and frequently higher than 0.9. More important is whether the estimated coefficients are significant. Almost all studies show that GDP per capita has an important positive effect on price levels, supporting the

Table 2.2 Survey of regression studies on structural determinants of price levels

Study	Data	Dependent variable	Independent Variables							
			(R)GDP/ capita	Openness	Share non tradables	Human capital	GDP/ M2	Natural resources	Tourism	Trade balance
Sign expectation for PL			+	+/−	+	−	−	+/−	+/−	−
Cross-country										
Balassa (1964)	various	PL	+							
		PNT/PT[a]	+[b]							
David (1972)	various	RGDP/C	+							
Balassa (1973)	various	PL	+							
Clague & Tanzi (1972)	Balassa	PL	+[c]	+(−)[d]		+(−)[f]		+[g]		
	ECLAC	PL	+[c]	+[-e]				+[g]		+[h]
Officer (1976b)	Germany	PL	+(+)(−)[i]							
	IMF	PNT/PT	+(+)(−)[i]							
Kravis et al. (1978)	ICP II	RGDP/C	+	+(+)[j]						
Isenman (1980)	ICP II	1/PL	−	(+)[j]		+[k]				
Kravis & Lipsey (1983)	ICP III	PL	+	+(+)(−)	+(+)	0				
		PNT	+	+						
		PT	+	(+)						
		PNT/PT	+	(+)						
Summers & Heston (1984)	ICP III	RGDP/C	+	+						
Clague (1986a)	ICP III	PL	+[l]		(+)[m]	(−)		+[n]	+[n]	−
Kravis & Lipsey (1988)	ICP IV	PL		(+)[o]	−(−)(+)[p]			+[n]	(+)[n]	
		PNT	+	+(+)[o]						
		PT	+	+(+)[o]						
Clague (1988a)	ECIEL[q]	PL	+	+		(−)		+[n]	(+)[n]	(+)

	Data	Dependent variable	(R)GDP/ capita	Openness	Share non tradables	Independent Variables Human capital	GDP/ M2	Natural resources	Tourism	Trade balance
Sign expectation for PL			+	+/-	+	-	-	+/-	+/-	-
Officer (1989)	ICP III	PL	+		+	-	-	-	+	
		PNT/PT	+		+	-		-	+	
Feldman & Gang (1990)	ICP III	PNT/PT	+							
Falvey & Gemmell (1991)	ICP IV	PNT	+			(-)(+)		(+)[r]		(+)
Bergstrand (1991)	ICP III	PNT/PT	+[ab]							
Clague (1992)	FAO	APL	+					+[t]		
Clague (1993a)	FAO	APL	+					+[t]		
	FAO	FPL	+					(+)[y]		
Lipsey & Swedenborg (1993)[v]	OECD	PL	+	+[u]						
	OECD	FPL	+	+[u]						
Falvey & Gemmell (1996)	ICP IV	PNT	-[z]					(-)[r]		
Time-series or pooled										
Bahmani-Oskooee (1992)[ah]		PL[y]	+							
De Gregorio et al. (1994)	OECD[y]	PNT/PT[w]	+							
De Gregorio & Wolf (1994)	OECD[y]	PNT/PT[wx]	+							
Asea & Mendoza (1994)	OECD[y]	PNT/PT	[aa]							
Zietz (1996)[ah]	BLS	PNT/PT[ac]	[ad]							
Canzoneri et al. (1996)	OECD	PNT/PT	[ae]							
Bahmani-Oskooee & Niroomand (1996)	IMF	[af]	(-)(+)[ag]							
Ito et al. (1997)	OECD	PNT/PT	( )[ah]							

Notes:

PL	Price level = PPP/exchange rate
APL	Agricultural PL
FPL	Food PL
RGDP/C	PPP-converted GDP (or GNP) per capita
GDP/C	exchange rate-converted GDP (or GNP) per capita
PNT	Price level of nontradables or services
PT	Price level of tradables or goods
PNT/PT	Ratio of price level of nontradables to price level of tradables
	or ratio of price index of nontradables to price index of tradables
+	positive significant coefficient
(+)	positive insignificant coefficient
−	negative significant coefficient
(−)	negative insignificant coefficient
()	insignificant coefficient, results not published

a   GNP deflator as a percentage of wholesale price index of manufactured goods.

b   Index of manufacturing output per man–hour is used as productivity proxy.

c   RGDP per capita and GDP per capita were used as independent variables and RGDP per capita was insignificant for 19 Latin American countries.

d   Import duties as a percentage of imports had significant positive effects and export duties as a percentage of exports had insignificant negative effects. These variables were used as proxies for trade barriers.

e   As proxies for trade barriers, import duties as a percentage of imports had significant positive effects and export duties as a percentage of exports had significant negative effects.

f   Significant positive effect in OECD countries and insignificant negative effect in Latin America. This is as expected if services are less skill-intensive than commodities in the OECD but more skill-intensive in Latin America.

g   The residuals of the regression of RGDP per capita on human capital were used as proxies for natural resource abundance. In the equations with the residuals, (R)GDP per capita was not included.

h   Ratio of imports to exports.

i   Three variables were used: GDP per capita, GDP per employed worker and the ratio of GDP per employed worker in the traded sectors (agriculture, mining, manufacturing) to GDP per employed worker in the nontraded sectors. PNT/PT was proxied by ratios of different price indices, such as consumer, wholesale and export price indices and GDP deflator. The construction of one ratio is unclear. Of the 159 equations with PL as dependent variable, only 4 equations gave a positive sign for productivity. Of the 18 equations with PNT/PT as dependent variable, 8 equations gave a positive sign for productivity.

j   Exposure to foreign prices was proxied by openness (Clague calls this the foreign trade ratio), measured as the ratio of exports plus imports to GNP (expected to have a negative sign) and as price isolation, measured as the mean squared deviation of the implicit GDP deflator from a "world average" implicit GDP deflator (expected to have a positive sign). In Kravis *et al.*, signs were mostly as expected but not always significant. In Isenman, signs were never significant and were not always as expected.

k   Isenman (1980) used enrolment ratios and teachers' wages as proxies for scarcity of skilled labor. Lower enrolment ratios and higher wages, signifying higher scarcity, have a positive effect on PL (and negative on 1/PL) if services are skill–intensive. Both estimated coefficients were confirmed.

l   Clague expected and confirmed in the text that RGDP per capita had a positive effect on PL. In the table, however, RGDP per capita had insignificant negative signs and (RGDP per capita)^2 had significant positive signs (same results as Kravis and Lipsey (1983, p. 22, fn. 2).With regard to both the sign and to the significance, these results are opposite to Kravis *et al.* (1978).

m   Clague (1986a, p. 321) argued that this variable "does not add to our understanding." The variable is highly correlated with PL but weakens the effect of other variables.

n   Mineral and tourist share in GDP, respectively, multiplied by a dummy for developing country. Clague (1988a) also included population density, which had a negative sign but was not always significant.

o   The coefficient for the term GDP * openness, used in addition to openness, was in almost all equations negative and often significant. The equation for PT gave weaker results than the equation for PNT.

p   Share of tradables in GDP.

q   Spanish acronym for Program of Joint Studies on Latin American Economic Integration, which from 1968 on continued the work of ECLAC on purchasing power parities.

r   Same variable as Clague used, that is, mineral share of GDP. Falvey and Gemmell (1991; 1996) considered GDP per capita endogenous, hence service prices are determined by a set of exogenous variables; that is, factor endowments such as agricultural land, mineral resources, (skilled and unskilled) labor and capital. The signs are ambiguous because they depend on the values of the marginal expenditures compared to the output increase. In Falvey and Gemmell (1991), agricultural land and the total labor force have significant coefficients (positive and negative, respectively) in most equations. In Falvey and Gemmell (1996), capital is also significant (and positive). Falvey and Gemmell (1991; 1996) also included PT in their equations, which had a positive and significant sign.

s   PPP defined as the ratio of each country's GNP deflator to the GNP deflator of the United States.

t   Mineral share in GDP and population per agricultural land (arable + permanent crops + half of pasture land) were used as proxies for natural resources. These two variables were always positive and were almost always significant, but population density slightly more often.

u   Protection measured by net producer subsidy equivalent and consumer subsidy equivalent.

v   Lipsey *et al.*, also included the indirect tax burden measured by indirect taxes on goods and services as a percentage of GDP and by value–added tax or sales tax rates. The first proxy performed better in the GDP PL equation (although it was not always significant) and the second in the food PL equation (always significant).

w   Ratio of deflator of nontradables sectors and deflator of tradable sectors. Total factor productivity differentials and GDP per capita and the ratio of government expenditures to GDP as a proxy for demand factors were included as independent variables.

x   The terms of trade was also added as an independent variable to capture its effect on changes in the real exchange rate.

y   OECD intersectoral database.

z   Falvey and Gemmell (1996) estimated sectoral total factor productivity (TFP) differences from the residuals from the regression equations with sectoral output as the dependent variables. These estimates were then introduced into the price equations. TFP in services is expected to have a negative effect on service prices because only a fraction of the increase in TFP in services (and, hence, of service output) is spent on services. An excess supply is the result. This is confirmed in the regression. TFP in tradables is expected to have a positive effect on service prices because only an income effect occurs in the service market. This is rejected in the regression.

aa   Asea and Mendoza (1994, p. 10) argued that the relative price of nontradables is not related to the GDP per capita, only to sectoral marginal productivity differences, which are in turn related to sectoral labor shares and sectoral capital–output ratios.

ab   Bergstrand (1991) used three independent variables: the ratio of labor productivity in commodities to labor productivity in services, capital–labor ratios and GDP per capita. All three coefficients are positive and significant, but for GDP per capita only at the 10 per cent level.

ac   Zietz (1996) used the ratio of the United States index of consumer prices for services and the index for goods prices as a proxy for the ratio of prices of nontradables to tradables. Data are from the Bureau of Labor Statistics.

ad   Zietz (1996) used as independent variables, for example, a nominal exchange rate index, the crime rate and health care and education costs. For a number of them he found significant effects.

ae   The relative price of nontradables and the relative productivities in the traded and nontraded sectors are cointegrated.

af   Ratio of GDP deflators of country *i* and United States (1985 = 100) to the exchange rate. Bahmani-Oskooee and Niroomand ran regressions for each year between 1974 and 1989 for about 100 countries. They are said to have used the same method as Officer (1976b) and called it a cross-section regression, but to call it cross-section they should have taken price levels (as Officer, 1976b, did) and for proper time-series regressions they should have taken the change in the nominal exchange rate (1985 = 100) and the change in GDP per capita (1985 = 100).

ag   Six different conversion factors were used to calculate the ratio of GDP per capita in country *i* to the United States.

ah   Only some Asian countries showed a positive relation between per capita GDP growth and an increase in the nontradable to tradable price ratio. This is ascribed to the development stage where countries at an early stage need a depreciated currency to promote exports and grow.

productivity model and the factor endowments model. This variable is almost always significant, often at the 1 per cent level. One of the exceptions is the study of Officer (1976b) where adjusted R^2 is frequently negative. Openness does not always fare as well. Although the estimated sign has mostly been positive – supporting the Stolper–Samuelson theorem if the openness variable can be used as a proxy for tariffs – it has not always been significant. Tourism yielded always a positive coefficient, supporting the demand interpretation, but was not always significant. The share of nontradables in GDP and the trade balance have produced mixed results. In support of the factor endowments model, natural resources have yielded in most cases a significant coefficient, but the signs have differed. The results for the human capital variable have been mixed as well. Finally, Feldman and Gang (1990) found significant coefficients with the expected sign for the ratio of GDP to M2, although the adjusted R^2 is below 0.4 when GDP per capita is not included. Feldman and Gang (1990, p. 350) did consider their model complementary to the factor endowments model but they did not consider any variable of this model to test for its relative strength. They included GDP per capita without mentioning it as a proxy for any factor. Regarding the short-term factors, the growth of the money supply had a negative sign in three equations (for price levels, nontradables price levels and tradables price levels) and was significant in two (the first two) in Kravis and Lipsey (1983).

One can of course ask whether the independent variables used are the proper proxies to account for productivity differences, factor endowments and financial repression. Human capital variables especially are notorious with regard to their validity and reliability (Brinkman, 1991). As mentioned, the interpretation has diverged among authors for variables like natural resources, foreign trade ratio, tourism and share of nontradables in GDP (Clague, 1986a; 1989; Desser, 1994; Officer, 1989). Most important, the validity of GDP per capita as a proxy for productivity differences and factor endowments can be questioned. This goes so far that Bergstrand (1991, p. 325) remarked, "*why* per capita GDP has such a robust empirical correlation to the price level and *what* economic factor(s) it represents have yet to be determined" (his emphasis).

Officer (1976b) was the first to address this issue by taking other proxies for productivity. He included GDP per capita, GDP per employed worker and the ratio of productivity in the tradables sectors to the productivity in the nontradables sectors, where productivity is defined as GDP per employed worker. But none of the three measures outperformed the others, except in the case of time-series (which is only partly relevant for our study) where the first two measures performed better.

Some recent publications have taken up the issue again. Bergstrand (1991) tested whether a proxy for productivity differences, factor endowments or demand factors is the best explanatory variable. To account for the productivity differences, he calculated the ratio of output divided by employment in commodities industries (equated to tradables) to output divided by employment in services industries (equated to nontradables). Moreover, capital–labor ratios from Leamer (1984) were included. Reduced-form estimation of prices (and quantities) showed that all three factors, namely productivity differences, capital–labor ratios and demand (GDP per capita), are significant at least at the 10 per cent level but that the t-statistic for GDP per capita is the lowest of the three.

Falvey and Gemmell (1991) argued that GDP per capita is only a proximate cause of price differences, while the underlying causes are factor endowments and technology. GDP per capita should therefore be endogenous and factor endowments, trade balance and population exogenous, as Clague (1986a, p. 320, fn. 3) suggested. An interesting aspect of this model is that factor endowments and population do not have an unambiguous effect on the prices of services. Additional assumptions have to be made with regard to whether increases in factor endowments increase the demand for services more than the supply of services and whether the average propensity to spend on services is greater or less than the marginal propensity. Hence relevant predictions of the model depend on empirical observations regarding these assumptions. Regression results generally showed that larger endowments of agricultural land, smaller populations, higher prices of tradables and smaller endowments of labor have a significant positive effect on the price levels of nontradables and services. Falvey and Gemmell (1996) extended their previous work by estimating sectoral differences in total factor productivity

(TFP) from the residuals from the regression equations with sectoral output as the dependent variables. These estimates were then introduced into the price equations. In this way they separated the effects of factor endowments from the productivity differences. Empirically, however, both were significant.

The time-series studies also used factors other than GDP per capita as a proxy for productivity. De Gregorio *et al.* (1994) and De Gregorio and Wolf (1994) calculated total factor productivity differentials for a number of developed countries. They also included GDP per capita and the ratio of government expenditures to GDP as a proxy for demand factors. All were statistically significant (see also Froot and Rogoff, 1994). Bahmani-Oskooee (1992) employed indices for productivity per man hour as a proxy for productivity differentials. This study, using cointegration, confirmed the productivity model for three out of four developed countries. Some other time-series studies focused on the relative version of the PPP theory of exchange rate determination – instead of price determination – and also used the productivity model to explain the exchange rate deviations from PPP. Here the evidence is mixed (Asea and Mendoza, 1994; Froot and Rogoff, 1994).

In conclusion, there is some empirical evidence in support of the three models subjected to empirical testing and none of the models can be rejected out of hand for empirical reasons although support for the financial repression model is rather weak. GDP per capita is a very consistent significant explanatory variable, but this variable is an imperfect proxy for both the productivity model and the factor endowments model.

2.4 SUMMING UP

The review of the literature has highlighted some deficiencies in the analysis of price levels across countries. First of all, aggregation masks the difference within sectors and in particular within the service sector, which is very heterogeneous. A distinction should be made between subsectors where labor productivity is relatively high and where it is relatively low (Baumol, 1985). Second, the factor endowments and economies-of-scale models do not stand up against the critique from economists at Cambridge, England of the concept of capital. The inclusion of average-cost pricing and economies of scale in Panagariya (1988) makes his model less traditional than the other models. However, the particular production function used in the model makes it unsatisfactory. Nevertheless, the difference in scale between a rich and a poor country is so large that investigating the implications of economies of scale might be worth pursuing while some aspects of Panagariya's average-cost pricing will also find its way into the model developed in Chapter 3. The productivity model faces the fewest theoretical challenges but the existing model does not include capital. The markup introduced in Kravis *et al.* (1983, p. 212) can in principle account for the presence of capital but different capital–labor ratios across industries and countries are inconsistent with the authors' assumption that the markup over unit labor costs is the same across sectors and countries (Semmler, 1982, pp. 48–9). Finally, the financial repression model is rather unsatisfactory for theoretical and empirical reasons.

NOTES

1. They included public utilities in the service sector; they are usually included in the industry sector. Construction (usually considered a nontradable) was included in industry. Productivity was measured by dividing sectoral employment shares into sectoral output shares.
2. Kuznets constructed labor productivity on the basis of sectoral shares of GDP and sectoral shares of labor force of 59 developing and developed countries (Kuznets, 1971, Tables 12, 14, 28 and 29) at GDP per capita benchmarks of 70, 150, 300, 500 and 1000 US dollars in 1958. Hence sectoral labor productivity is relative to the average for the country. He excluded, where possible, income from banking, insurance, real estate and dwellings from GDP. His industrial sector included mining and quarrying, public utilities and transport and communications.
3. Productivity was calculated – as by Kuznets (1971) – as the share of value added divided by the share of the labor force.

3. A post-Keynesian markup pricing model

This chapter will develop a markup pricing model that addresses some of the deficiencies of the explanations discussed in Chapter 2. The model will improve the productivity model by including intermediate inputs and the effect of the market structure on pricing and allow for a disaggregate analysis by (sub)sector. This chapter will outline the model and discuss the theoretical background. The following chapters discuss some aspects of the pricing model.

This chapter is organized as follows. Section 3.1 will discuss the theoretical assumption underlying the post-Keynesian markup model that prices are determined by costs and not by demand. Section 3.2 will outline the post-Keynesian markup pricing model and specify the price equation. This section will also summarize the most salient elements of Chapter 5.

3.1 THE KEYNESIAN DICHOTOMY

Economic theory has become a very abstract science over the past decades, in effect almost becoming applied mathematics. Many theoretical models are far removed from exigent economic problems or real-world phenomena and the assumptions many models rely upon are often devoid of empirical content or conflict with facts in order to make the mathematics manageable or elegant. Of course, fully controlled laboratory experiments do not exist in the social sciences and all their theories are abstractions from reality and have to focus on essential characteristics and stylized facts. Some economists think that simple and "silly" assumptions are absolutely necessary. "The reason for these [silly] assumptions is not that they are reasonable but that they seem to help us produce models that are helpful metaphors for things that we think happen in the real world" (Krugman, 1996, p. 227; see also Krugman, 1995).

Yet there are differences, albeit only in degree, in how far some theories are removed from the empirical world. Even more important, it is not only the extent of abstractions that matters but also what kind of abstractions are made when a model is formulated. Post-Keynesian economists have argued that neoclassical economics ignores or distorts some significant aspects of the real world, such as the existence of market power, unemployment, uncertainty and conflicts that dominate the wage determination process.[1] Post-Keynesians prefer theories with more realistic assumptions, more satisfactory explanations and better predictions that are based on phenomena that can be observed in the real world in real time (Arestis, 1992).

The neoclassical theory of price determination is one example of extreme unrealism. That prices are determined by demand and supply has intuitive appeal, but the theory underlying it is complex and has to make a number of far-reaching assumptions to ensure the continuity and differentiability of the curves and the existence and stability of an equilibrium (Debreu, 1959; Weintraub, 1979). Downward-sloping demand curves are derived from assumptions regarding the utility maximizing behavior of consumers. Likewise, upward-sloping cost curves are derived under the assumption that producers maximize profits. The price is where the demand and supply curve intersect and prices are thus determined by demand and supply. Prices are set and changed instantaneously by a fictitious Walrasian auctioneer who calls out a price, assesses whether demand is larger or smaller than supply and changes the price accordingly until equilibrium is reached. A number of assumptions are needed to ensure a solution: information is perfect and costless and time, uncertainty, economies of scale, externalities and power are ignored. Each producer and consumer is infinitesimal, so that it is not possible to influence the price. All firms are price takers and quantity makers and no firm has the power to set prices. Perfect competition is characterized by many producers and consumers, homogeneous products, freedom of entry and exit and perfect information (see, for example, Baumol and Blinder, 1982, p. 414). This situation is often approximated by markets that auction primary commodities such as oil and coffee or by financial markets. Yet financial markets are typically characterized by asymmetric information (Stiglitz, 1993) and "[m]arkets in which commodities are completely homogeneous – with respect to location and the date as well as other characteristics – are almost inherently sufficiently thin so that the postulate of perfect competition is inapplicable. Markets that are sufficiently 'thick' to be competitive are almost always nonhomogeneous" (Stiglitz, 1987, p. 25).

Most economists recognize that markets are often imperfect. Indeed, thinking about imperfect competition has a long history in economics, dating back to the nineteenth century, and really took off in 1933 with the publication of the books by Chamberlin and Robinson. This tradition gave the economic discipline two hybrid variants of imperfect competition between the two extremes of perfect competition and monopoly, namely monopolistic competition and oligopoly. Product differentiation is the defining characteristic of the first and the number of sellers – and thus entry barriers – that of the second hybrid. Most markets are somewhere in between perfect competition and monopolies (Baumol and Blinder, 1982, p. 480). Even when monopolies and monopolistic competition are ignored, Scherer and Ross (1990, p. 82) for example stated that "on the order of half of all U.S. manufacturing industry can be characterized as oligopolistic," which is quite remarkable for a country with strong antitrust laws. Oligopoly is considered by many economists as the dominant market form.

The neoclassical theory of the firm remains a powerful parable among economists despite the unrealistic assumptions, partly because it fits into a larger research program (Blaug, 1980, ch. 7) and because modeling imperfect competition has been so difficult that it has long eluded its incorporation into trade, growth and development theories (Krugman, 1995). Thus almost all explanations of price levels implicitly or explicitly assume a neoclassical model of price determination in a competitive environment – Panagariya (1988) is the exception.

The starting point in this book is the acknowledgement that nearly all markets in capitalists economies are imperfect and that this situation can best be described by a post-Keynesian markup model. A Walrasian auctioneer does not exist and firms are the institutions that set prices instead and they do this usually with considerable power either because the market is dominated by a few producers or products are differentiated. In effect, both textbook variants of imperfect markets, oligopoly and monopolistic competition, are incorporated in the post-Keynesian markup model. But its analysis is different from that of the textbooks and only the term "oligopoly" will be used.

The essential feature of the post-Keynesian markup model of price determination is that prices are determined by costs and that demand changes have no effect on prices but only on quantities. Firms set prices by adding a markup to costs; when demand changes the price is kept the same, with quantities being adjusted instead by varying delivery lags, inventories, hours of work, employment and so on. Quantity adjustments dominate over price adjustments (Malinvaud, 1985, p. 9; see also Blinder *et al.*, 1998, ch. 17 and pp. 310–12). Coddington (1983) called this situation, where quantities are determined by demand and prices by costs, the Keynesian dichotomy (see also Pasinetti, 1974, p. 33; 1981, p. 141). It might seem rather implausible that a firm would not raise its price when demand for its product increases. There are, however, several arguments in support of this behavior, such as the existence of constant costs, firms acting as if costs are constant as a result of fear for action by rivals and the reluctance to antagonize customers.

Normal Costs

Some economist have argued that marginal and average variable costs of a firm are constant up to full capacity. In that case, part of the supply curve of a firm will be horizontal, leaving prices unaffected when the demand curve shifts if the markup is also constant. This argument has been used by mainstream economists to support the phenomenon of rigid prices (Blinder *et al.*, 1998;

Hall, 1986). The argument has also been used by some post-Keynesian economists (see, for example, Bober, 1992, pp. 45–8; Coutts, 1987; Eichner, 1973, p. 1195). Post-Keynesians, however, usually employ a pricing model where a firm sets a markup above direct or variable costs, such as labor and raw materials, or above full (fixed and variable) costs without reference to marginal costs. Models along these lines were much inspired by the evidence from a survey conducted by Hall and Hitch (1939), which concluded that firms use average rather than marginal costs in pricing. Similarly, Blinder *et al.* (1998, ch. 12) found in a recent survey that, even when the concept of marginal costs was explained in plain English, business people had difficulty understanding it.

Average variable costs that are constant for an operative span of the cost curve are more likely under capitalist conditions where underutilization of capacity and unemployment are a normal state of affairs. Under such circumstances, producers can hire more workers without bidding up wages and increase capacity utilization when demand increases without an increase in marginal costs, keeping average variable costs constant. The existence of unemployment and excess capacity as a normal situation under capitalism, caused by demand deficiency, is at the core of post-Keynesian theory (Arestis, 1992; Coddington, 1983; Kornai, 1980, pp. 33–5, 1986, ch. 2; Malinvaud, 1980; Steindl [1952] 1976, ch. 2). Unemployment can occur even if all prices are fully flexible, a result not attainable within the neoclassical framework. Keynes (1936) argued that unemployment is normal because savings and investment are not equilibrated by the interest rate. Investment determines income and income determines savings. There is no mechanism that coordinates decisions to invest and to save, forcing demand to be equal to supply and all factors of production to be in full use, resulting in unemployment and excess capacity. When capacity utilization increases and approaches full capacity, profits and investment will increase and capacity expand.

Besides the macroeconomic reasons for unused factors of production, there are also microeconomic factors. A firm in an oligopolistic market, facing a continuing rivalry with other firms, has an incentive to maintain excess capacity. Excess capacity deters new entrants into the market and is used as a competitive weapon. This is particularly important when demand and the behavior of rivals are uncertain and when the costs of having no stocks and no excess capacity are high because of competition. A firm needs to keep unused capacity to jump into the market when a rival fails, when a boom occurs or when a price war is threatened. In sum, an oligopolistic entrepreneur wants to operate with unused capacity to keep the possibility open to increase its market share or production if possibilities reveal themselves, for example if demand rises (Arestis, 1992; Harcourt and Kenyon, 1976; Kenyon, 1978, p. 39; Rothschild, 1947; Steindl [1952] 1976, ch. 2; Thompson, 1992, p. 152).

In a capitalist system, companies have hard budget constraints and have to respond to costs increases or else face bankruptcy, while there is no such economic necessity to respond to a demand increase (Gordon, 1990, p. 1150; Silberston, 1970, p. 569). Firms therefore have an incentive to create a horizontal cost curve to prevent costs changing with every variation in output. This can be done by having excess capacity (Gordon, 1998; Kalecki, 1965). However, investment incurs expenses that do not stop when capacity sits idle – unlike labor, which could be fired (the costs of unemployment are external). A firm has to strike a balance between purchasing too many material inputs, installing too much capacity and hiring too much labor and not having any free capacity or no stocks to meet demand.

Even if each firm tries to use capacity at its fullest potential, underutilization of capacity can result if firms are subject to a prisoners' dilemma game. In such a situation, entrepreneurs could reach a global optimum if they cooperated and divided the market among them. They could thus install exactly enough capacity. On the other hand, if entrepreneurs do not cooperate, competing entrepreneurs will try to maximize their own market shares and will end up with excess capacity.

Some post-Keynesians allow for the possibilities that average fixed costs decline when capacity utilization increases, as fixed costs are spread over more units (economies of scale), and that marginal variable costs are higher for older vintages of equipment (Harcourt and Kenyon, 1976). These two countervailing tendencies could cancel each other out so that average total costs are still constant (Bober, 1992, p. 46).

In the end, empirical evidence could give some clues about the shape of the cost curve. The evidence, however, is mixed. Coutts (1987, p. 159) and Eichner (1973, p. 1195), for example, cited studies in support of constant costs, but the studies cited in Lee (1986) provided a mixed picture. Blinder *et al.* (1998) found that, assuming that the respondents to the survey understood the concept, 48.4 per cent answered that marginal costs are horizontal and 40.5 per cent that they are decreasing. Only 11.1 per cent thought that marginal costs are increasing. This reflects poorly on neoclassical theory, which argues that firms will produce on the upward-sloping part of the marginal cost curve as a firm could increase profits by producing more when it is on the downward-sloping part of the marginal cost curve.

The evidence on the shape of the cost curve becomes largely irrelevant in a post-Keynesian markup pricing model where firms act as if costs are constant or use the concept of normal costs, for example, because the informational requirements are too large and the exact shape of the cost curve is not known (Basile and Salvadori, 1984–5, pp. 251–2). Indeed, Blinder *et al.* (1998, pp. 101, 216–18, 302) found that business executives had trouble distinguishing between fixed and variable costs and understanding the concept of marginal costs. If that is the case, it makes sense for a firm to use the concept of average normal costs. Firms determine the desired or normal level of capacity utilization, independent of the state of the business cycle, calculate the average direct costs (of labor and intermediate inputs such as raw materials) associated with that level and add a markup (Coddington, 1983, pp. 12–15; Coutts, 1987; Eichner, 1973, p. 1195; Kenyon, 1978; Okun, 1975; Robinson, 1969, pp. 185–6; Sylos-Labini, 1984). With the concept of normal cost, marginal costs and the actual shape of the cost curve have become immaterial.

Rivals: Keep Prices Constant

Firms use the concept of normal costs and a markup rule of thumb. They act as if costs are constant because they prefer price stability in the face of uncertainty about rivals' behavior (Blinder *et al.*, 1998; Galbraith, 1967, ch. 17; Hall and Hitch, 1939; Rothschild, 1947; Scherer and Ross, 1990, pp. 261–5; Silberston, 1970, p. 522; Steindl [1952] 1976; Sylos-Labini [1969] 1993, p. 24; Varian, 1978, pp. 71–5). Oligopolistic markets are potentially unstable and oligopolists like to avoid price wars and keep prices constant.

> Price wars, while tending to occur infrequently, are a dominant feature of the oligopolistic situation. They may be caused by external or internal factors. The preparation for them, aggressive or defensive, leads to the adoption of measures which are peculiar to oligopoly. The outcome of a successful price war or the mere threat of one may be the complete annihilation of a rival's independence or the reduction of his status to that of a price follower. (Rothschild, 1947, p. 461; emphasis removed)

Price wars can be averted by following a markup pricing method that sets a markup over average costs at normal capacity. The rigid prices will deter rivals from starting a price war and newcomers from entering a booming market.

Oligopolists are basically engaged in a game where a mutually destructive outcome, a price war, should be avoided. Such an outcome is possible when firms do not cooperate. A failure to cooperate among firms can result in fixed prices in case demand rises. If demand rises, a firm might want to raise its price, but only if other firms will do that as well. This is again a prisoners' dilemma where the aggregate optimum situation for the firms would be a price increase, but because this is not coordinated and every firm fears that other firms will not raise their prices, the result will be that prices are unchanged. This argument was rather strongly supported in every industrial sector of the United States by the interviews Blinder *et al.* (1998) conducted among business executives. A similar coordination failure exists for the reverse case. However, in this case each firm has an incentive to cut prices because it could increase its market share, unless all firms cut their prices. The danger, of course, is then that a price war ensues. This asymmetry is also highlighted by the kinked demand curve which assumes that rival firms will match any price decrease but will not follow a price hike (Hall and Hitch, 1939; Sweezy, 1939). Blinder *et al.* (1998, pp. 264–5) found some evidence in support of this asymmetry.

The uncooperative solution to this coordination problem is consistent with the rigid prices that result from a markup pricing rule that sets prices over normal costs. A cooperative solution can be reached when a price leader is adopted or when firms collude. These two solutions are also consistent with markup pricing. The price leader will use markup pricing and the price will be copied by the followers (Eichner, 1973, p. 1195). Followers do not set prices autonomously but follow a "price minus' strategy of setting a target level of unit costs by deducting the required markup from the price set by the price leader (Coutts, 1987, p. 158). In case of collusion, the firms try to agree on a price that sets a markup, which depends on the combined market power of the colluding firms, over the average normal costs of the firms.

Oligopolists prefer stable prices but the markup does not have to be constant to reach that goal. If output increases in response to a temporary increase in demand, average costs could change. In order to keep prices constant, a firm could adjust the markup. This is clarified in Figure 3.1. It is assumed for the sake of the argument that the average variable cost curve (AC) is U-shaped. Assume normal utilization of capacity at q_n, which is before the lowest point of the average cost curve (AC) at q_1 (full capacity). The firm has excess capacity, which it can use for competitive reasons. At q_n, all normal intermediate and labor costs are C_n and the markup is μ_n. If the firm faces an increase in demand and the demand curve shifts from D_n to D_1, capacity utilization increases. At q_1, the price is set at the same level as before but actual variable costs have decreased and the markup is larger at μ_1. If average variable costs are constant up to full capacity, which is likely when there is excess capacity and unemployment, the markup does not change when the demand curve shifts but total costs (average and fixed costs) decline as average fixed costs decrease because they are imputed to more units when output expands (economies of scale). Thus the profit part of the markup increases.

A similar figure could have been drawn with a temporary or local (that is, firm-specific, not industry-wide) shift of the average cost curve. There is an economic necessity to increase prices when costs rise because of the risk of bankruptcy (Gordon, 1990, p. 1150) but small changes in costs can be borne by the markup. Of course, this effect is independent of the shape of the cost curve, although if the cost curve is not horizontal an increase in costs can result from a shift in the demand curve. Firms might want to maintain price stability when costs increases are small, temporary, or when they are local instead of global. A firm might not increase prices and lower the markup instead because of competition if only that firm faces a costs increase. A firm with monopoly power, however, is more likely to pass on any increase in the price of inputs. A cost increase can be local as a result of labor union strength at that firm or of the use of more imported inputs than its competitors while the exchange rate depreciates (Arestis and Milberg, 1993–4, p. 174; Faruqee, 1995). Hence the calculation of C_n not only incorporates a sense of where the demand curve normally is but also allows for small, temporary and local changes in costs, which will be borne by a change in the markup (see also Sawyer, 1992; Silberston, 1970, p. 522; Sweezy, 1939). Thus "neither *temporary* changes in prime costs, nor *temporary* changes in product demand directly influence to any significant extent output price" (Harcourt and Kenyon, 1976, p. 454; original emphasis). Generally, when costs of inputs (labor, intermediate inputs and imports) increase for all firms in the industry and when this is perceived as a permanent change, it is more likely that prices will rise proportionally. Cases where all firms face equal costs increases are collective bargaining agreements involving whole industries (as is the case, for example, in the Netherlands and the Nordic countries), rising commodity prices and depreciating currencies (if firms use similar amounts of imported inputs). Indeed, Blinder *et al.* (1998, p. 207) found "strong evidence that firms react more quickly to cost shocks that are large, and/or industry-wide, and/or permanent."

Yet short delays between costs and price changes at the level of the individual firm can compound to long delays when a product goes through many production stages as embodied in an input–output table, resulting in price stickiness (Gordon, 1981; see also Blinder *et al.*, 1998).

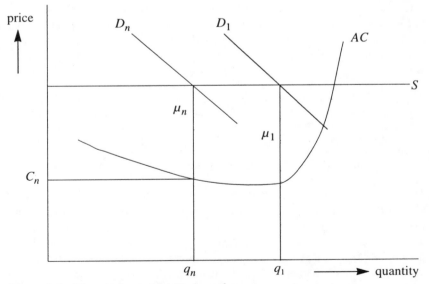

Figure 3.1   The markup under U-shaped average costs

Customers: Change Prices only when Costs Change

A firm needs to consider the reactions not only of its competitors to a price change but also of its clients. A post-Keynesian pricing model where a markup is set over normal costs corresponds well with the theory that firms want to keep steady relations with their customers and will therefore only increase prices when that is considered "reasonable", that is when costs increase. Okun (1975) called this the customer market, in contrast to a competitive auction market (see also Franciosi *et al.*, 1995).

> An established customer–supplier relationship introduces a bilateral monopoly surplus that can be split between the cooperating buyers and sellers. In the short run, most customers would pay a slightly higher price to their suppliers without shopping, and most suppliers would, if they had to, sell for a shade less to their customers. This interdependence puts a premium on maintaining the relationship and on limiting conflict over the sharing of the surplus to methods that will not impair its total value ... [thus constituting] an implicit contract. (Okun, 1975, p. 362)

Through this contract, consumers can reduce their search costs because yesterday's prices can be used as a guide for today's. By keeping prices rigid, a firm can eliminate the uncertainty about the reaction of consumers to price changes. Moreover, the supplier has the possibility to create customer loyalty by pledging continuity. By doing so, a firm can reduce the elasticity of demand even if it does not know its exact magnitude (see also Gordon, 1990, p. 1149). Thus the short-run elasticity of demand is likely to be low and Blinder *et al.* (1998, p. 99) indeed found that 84 per cent of the respondents thought that the price elasticity was smaller than one, indicating that total revenues would decline if prices were reduced, and 41 per cent thought that the price elasticity was zero. Yet

> [a] change in costs ... is a presentable reason for a change in prices; but a change in demand is not a presentable reason. To say that price has been raised because demand has gone up amounts to saying to the customer "I am charging you more because I can get more out of you." That would not make for good relations! So one can understand that a firm of this sort will maintain steady prices, *except when costs change*. (Hicks, 1982, p. 311; original emphasis)

The existence of such an implicit contract is supported by empirical evidence. One of the strongest conclusions Blinder *et al.* (1998, pp. 307–9) drew from their survey in the United States is that firms have a strong reluctance to antagonize their customers by raising prices (60 per cent of the firms say this at least once). Moreover, 64 per cent of the respondents thought that their firm has an "implicit understanding with their customers – who expect the firms not to take advantage of the situation by raising prices when the market is tight"

(p. 95) while 71 per cent of the firms believed that their customers tolerate a price increase when costs rise (see also Kahneman *et al.*, 1986). Blinder *et al.* (1998, p. 94) also concluded that for about 25 per cent of GDP prices are fixed in written contracts. Other evidence comes from Conigliani *et al.* (1997) who found that, in case of monetary tightening, it was less likely that banks would raise interest rates for Italian firms that have longer relations with their banks. Yet Blinder *et al.* (1998) found no correlation with the share of repeat costumers, which indicates that search costs probably do not play a large role. The overall evidence nonetheless showed that "our survey results contain clear direct support for Okun's view" (p. 150).

A customer market encourages a pricing strategy that involves setting a markup over normal, average costs. Customers are willing to accept a higher price if costs are permanently raised, not when costs are temporarily higher or when marginal costs are higher.

Apart from the desire to avoid antagonizing customers, firms might not change prices because of the costs associated with changing prices. These costs have recently been emphasized by neo-Keynesians to explain price stickiness in the face of demand changes even if marginal costs are not constant. Firms have to do market research, renegotiate contracts, instruct employees and print menus, price lists and catalogues (Blinder *et al.*, 1998, p. 234; Gordon, 1990, p. 1145). These costs are often labeled menu costs, after the costs a restaurant has to incur to print new menus when it changes its prices. It is argued that the costs of adjusting prices might be high compared to the additional revenues yielded by a lower price (Romer, 1993, p. 8). However, the costs of price adjustments need also to be compared to the costs of output adjustments. It is (implicitly) assumed that the former is smaller than the latter but this is only the case when uncertainty is ignored because uncertainty about the reaction of rivals and customers to price changes is much larger than the reaction to output changes (Greenwald and Stiglitz, 1993, p. 37). Indeed, Blinder *et al.* (1998, p. 243) found that the adjustment costs of output are typically smaller than the adjustment costs of prices, despite the fact that 43 per cent of the firms had non-trivial menu costs, and when asked about the nature of these costs nearly as many mentioned the loss of future sales as a result of antagonizing customers.

Prices are Rigid

The pricing model as presented here results in rather rigid prices. Demand changes will not lead to price adjustments and only substantial, industry-wide or permanent changes in costs will have an effect on prices. Rigid prices, in contrast to the instantaneous price adjustment of the neoclassical model, are indeed quite common. Blinder *et al.* (1998), Carlton (1986) and Silberston (1970, p. 569) provided evidence that the degree of price rigidity in nearly all industries is substantial (see also the discussion in Gordon, 1990, pp. 1126–8). Carlton (1986) showed that in some industries in the United States prices remain unchanged for several years and that rigidity is strongly correlated with concentration. Blinder *et al.* (1998, p. 84) found that nearly 50 per cent of nonfarm, private, for-profit, unregulated GDP in the United States is repriced once a year or less frequently and 78 per cent quarterly or less often. They found a clear mode at once a year, indicating that annual price changes are by far the most typical (39 per cent). About 10 per cent of GDP is repriced less than once a year and an equal share of GDP is repriced more than once a week. Blinder *et al.* (1998, p. 84) concluded that "there is an auction market sector. But it is pretty small."

Moreover, several studies found empirical support for the thesis that prices are not adjusted or are adjusted only a little in response to changes in demand. Semmler (1984, p. 81) concluded from several studies that "coefficients for the demand variables are generally very low. ... Thus in the long run prices seem to be regulated by cost of production and some kind of target rate of return on capital (markup)." Coutts (1987) pointed at the importance of distinguishing between normal and actual costs and concluded that "influence of demand on price over the cycle is almost completely offset by the decline in actual, relative to normal unit costs and hence that demand effects are probably small compared with costs in determining industrial prices" (p. 159). (See also Okun, 1975, p. 365.) Recent empirical evidence in support of the insignificance of demand factors has been provided by Andersen and Hansen (1995),[2] Arestis (1986), Bhaskar *et al.* (1993), Blinder *et al.* (1998, p. 240), Geroski (1992) and Haskel *et al.* (1997) for developed countries and, for example, by Ros (1980) and Taylor (1988, pp. 38–41) for developing countries.

In summary, firms set prices as a markup over average variable costs at a normal, desired level of capacity utilization, which is less than full capacity, because of uncertainty with regard to the behavior of competitors and consumers. Firms prefer stable prices and want to avoid a price war and refrain from antagonizing customers. Firms will keep prices unchanged when demand increases (they will boost output instead) but will raise prices when costs rise, particularly when the increase is large, industry-wide or permanent.

Applicability

Can this model of price determination be applied to primary commodities? In that case, demand factors play a role because the most important factors of production, land and natural resources, are scarce and prices are more flexible (Kurz, 1978). Supply is constrained in the short term and prices adjust so that demand will be equal to supply. Several authors have made a distinction between the price determination of manufactured goods and primary commodities. Hicks (1965, ch. 7; 1982, pp. 310–12) differentiated between fixprice and flexprice goods, Kalecki (1965) between cost-determined (raw materials) and demand-determined (finished) goods and Okun (1975) between customer goods and auction goods (see also Sylos-Labini, 1984). This pattern of sectoral price determination was also adopted by Bober (1992), Dornbusch (1987b, p. 95), Kaldor (1980, p. xxvi), McKinnon (1979), Robinson (1962; 1969, pp. 360–62) and Taylor (1988, p. 33). Kaldor (1980) argued that competitive conditions prevail in agriculture and most types of mining, oligopolistic conditions in manufacturing and "polypolistic" (small-scale businesses, free entry and a limited market for each business) in much of the tertiary sector. Yet cartels and oligopolies in primary commodities are also common (see section 5.2 and Chapter 7).

In the longer term, however, when technical change plays a role, supply constraints in the primary sector are less of an issue, as the decline in commodity prices over the long term and the falsifications of Malthusian predictions have shown. Moreover, all primary commodities are inputs into the production of other goods and services, and supply constraints become less important when one examines prices of expenditure components, because before primary commodities reach the consumer, value has been added, products have been processed, differentiated, advertised, packaged and distributed and market power has been applied in the separate stages of production. This reduces the importance of the prices of the underlying commodities. The cost of the primary commodity as a share of the final product is usually smaller than 15 per cent. It can be as low as 4 per cent in the case of cotton, but as high as 47 per cent in the case of tea sold in the United Kingdom (World Bank, 1994a, p. 41). Small and temporary changes in primary commodity prices might be partly countered by changing the markup to keep retail prices constant in order not to antagonize consumers (see, for example, Bettendorf and Verboven, 1997). Large and permanent changes, even if demand-induced, will lead to higher output prices. Thus, in the case of prices of expenditure categories, demand might have an impact on prices but only through its effect on primary commodities, and this is taken into account in our model through higher prices for inputs. In the case of prices of output by industry of origin, demand might have a direct impact on output prices only in the commodities-producing sectors (agriculture and mining).

Andersen and Hansen (1995), Arestis (1986; 1996, p. 126), Beckerman and Jenkinson (1986), Silberston (1970, p. 569) and Sylos-Labini (1979; 1984) found evidence that changes in prices of imported primary commodities partly explain prices of final output in developed countries. And Yang and Hwang (1994) showed that Korean manufacturers change domestic prices on a one-to-one basis in response to changes in prices of imported raw materials within three months and argued that the domestic market is oligopolistic.

Another question that might be asked is whether developing countries are demand-constrained. Many authors have pointed out that small and open developing economies in particular are constrained by foreign exchange (Taylor, 1988; 1991). This creates a situation where output is limited not only by demand but also (or primarily) by foreign exchange. In our model, a foreign exchange shortage means higher prices for imported inputs, which will lead to higher output prices when the shortage is deemed permanent and imports are limited. Thus only if there is a supply constraint caused by a foreign exchange shortage will higher demand lead to higher prices. Bilginsoy (1997) confirmed this for Turkey.

3.2 THE PRICING MODEL

Let us take, for exemplary purposes, a four-sector economy. The first sector is agriculture and the second manufacturing, ignoring mining, utilities and construction. Services are divided into intermediate producer services and final demand consumer services. Consumer services include personal and social services (for example, retail trade, hotels, restaurants, domestic and repair services, barbers, health, education and government) and producer services include wholesale trade, transportation, communications, finance, insurance, real estate and professional and business services. This classification, which partly follows others (Elfring, 1988, pp. 102–6), is largely based on production techniques (capital–output ratio and productivity) as will be discussed in Chapters 4 and 5.

To jump from the firm level to the industry level, one can assume that the firm is the industry, that there is a price leader, that firms act similarly without interacting and that they all follow a markup pricing rule and can just be aggregated, or that they collude. The post-Keynesian pricing model looks as follows:[3]

$$\mathbf{p} = \mathbf{ts}\, \mu\, (l\, \mathbf{w} + \mathbf{A'}\, \mathbf{p} + \mathbf{m})$$ (3.1)

where
$\mathbf{p}$ [4,1] = column vector of the prices per unit of domestically produced output;
$\mathbf{ts}$ [4,4] = diagonal matrix of indirect taxes minus subsidies; 1 + rates;
μ [4,4] = diagonal matrix of markups; 1 + markup rate;
l [4,4] = diagonal matrix of direct labor requirements per unit of gross output;
$\mathbf{w}$ [4,1] = column vector of wage rates;

A [4,4] = matrix of interindustry technical coefficients, that is the amount of intermediate inputs from sector i used in the production of a unit of output of sector j; **A′** is the transpose of **A**; and

m [4,1] = column vector of imported intermediate inputs in national currencies

= **M**e $(1 + \textbf{t}_m)$ = imported quantity used per unit of output multiplied by the price in dollar terms (**M**) multiplied by the exchange rate (e) and multiplied by one plus the tariff rate on imported intermediate goods ($\textbf{t}_m$).

Manipulation gives

$$\textbf{p} = (\textbf{I} - \textbf{ts}\,\mu\,\textbf{A}')^{-1}\,(\,\textbf{ts}\,\mu\,l\,\textbf{w} + \textbf{ts}\,\mu\,\textbf{m}) \tag{3.2}$$

where $\textbf{I}$ [4,4] = the identity matrix.

In this system there are four prices and four equations. Each price is determined by a markup added to the costs of inputs, that is the intermediate inputs from the different sectors (**A**), labor ($l\,\textbf{w}$) and imports (**m**). In addition, taxes are added to and subsidies subtracted from these costs. Prices can change as a result of changes in net taxes, intermediate costs, labor costs or the markup. Intermediate costs, wages and labor requirements can all be influenced by economies of scale. All these cost components have a rather distinct pattern across countries and sectors, which will be described in Chapter 4 (labor productivity), Chapter 5 (wages) and Chapter 6 (economies of scale). Foreign market power and international trade barriers can affect the markup and costs, as will be discussed in Chapter 7.

This system shares some elements with Sraffa (1960). In the Sraffa model and the post-Keynesian pricing model, prices are determined without any recourse to demand factors or marginal analysis, distinguishing them from the neoclassical model. Another similarity is the inclusion of an input–output matrix that can account for capital as heterogeneous produced intermediate goods and is thus able to withstand the capital critique. Yet the post-Keynesian model also differs from Sraffa (1960) in an important way. Prices in Sraffa (1960) cover costs of production with a uniform rate of profit across sectors. These prices should prevail in the long run, otherwise the reproduction of the system cannot exist. Sraffa was concerned about prices of production, the long-term centers of gravity around which market prices fluctuate. Deviations from prices of production are influenced by uncertainty, harvest failures, monopolies and so on (Eatwell, 1977, pp. 63–4). However, Sraffa was not concerned about the process of market price formation (Arestis, 1992, p. 139). That is exactly the focus of this book. We are particularly interested in some of the factors influencing market prices (including trade and transportation margins), notably market power. In contrast to Sraffa, the markup model allows differential markups (and profit rates for that matter) across sectors. Our model, however, does not necessarily yield an economically meaningful solution, that is positive prices, because the Perron–Frobenius theorems are not applicable as the equation cannot be stated as an eigenvalue problem because there is not a uniform profit rate but a diagonal matrix of markups. This is in contrast to Sraffa's system, where the (ir)reducible and nonnegative matrix **A** and the uniform wage rate are given, and the relative prices and the uniform rate of profit are solved by using the Perron–Frobenius theorems.

The price equation (3.2) is rather empty (tautological or nothing more than an accounting exercise) without a behavioral explanation of the markup. The model does not establish the size of the markup and it therefore does not determine prices without an explanation of the process by which the markup is set. Indeed, the most important behavioral function behind this identity is the determination of the markup, which will be discussed in more detail in Chapter 5. But let us run ahead a little. There are basically three factors that affect the markup: the need to finance investment, the market structure and the power of organized labor.

In oligopolistic markets, sellers determine their investment plans, calculate the markup needed to generate finance for the planned investments and add the markup over unit labor costs and unit intermediate costs at normal capacity utilization, while consideration is taken of rivals' and consumers' behavior and expected output.

The extent to which a firm will be able to generate the internal earnings to finance investment depends in part on the market power of the firm. Market power is determined by concentration, product differentiation, foreign market power and trade barriers. In markets with fewer competitors (increasing the likelihood of collusion) or with a price leader, prices are likely to be higher. Concentration is determined by economies of scale compared to the size of the market and by barriers to entry. By differentiating products, firms can create brand loyalty and change the shape of the demand curve. Even in markets with many competitors, product differentiation creates market power. Product differentiation is particularly prevalent in markets for services in developed countries, as will be argued more fully in Chapter 5, and can thus explain to some extent the prevalence of relative high prices for services in developed countries.

Finally, labor union power is determined by the degree of unionization and has a negative effect on the markup. However, if labor power leads to higher wages and lower markups, the total effect on prices is not immediately clear because wage costs also enter directly into the price equation. The total effect depends on the market power of the firm and whether all firms face higher wages. These two factors determine to what extent higher wages are passed on to consumers by way of higher prices. Thus the total effect of labor power on prices is either zero (when the markup takes the burden) or positive (when at least part of the higher wages is translated into higher prices).

NOTES

1. Even more fascinating is the proposition that neoclassical economics, being the dominant ideology in economics, is able to shape the conduct of economies because it influences actions of economic agents in such a way that it confirms to the models that describe "how economies should behave." This is particularly relevant in financial markets where psychological factors are important and where the role of self-fulfilling prophecies is large (Eatwell, 1997).
2. Andersen and Hansen (1995) confirmed that demand has no impact in the long run but they did find evidence of a demand effect in the short run.
3. This formulation is partly owed to Ednaldo da Silva, former Assistant Professor at the New School for Social Research.

4. Productivity in an input–output framework

As the discussion in Chapter 2 showed, productivity differences between countries are likely to remain an important determinant of price levels across countries even if additional factors such as market power are accounted for. However, in an input–output framework, as in the price equation (3.2), the traditional productivity measures are inadequate. This chapter will develop a method to measure productivity when produced intermediate inputs (such as capital goods) are present, although the preferred method has to be adapted because of data limitations. Moreover, this framework accounts for the fact that goods (for example, a tradable) use other goods (for example, a nontradable) as intermediate inputs that are produced with different productivity. For example, some goods have a large service component, like the meal enjoyed at a local restaurant. Some services, like transportation, have a large good component, transportation equipment. On the other hand, some services, like a haircut, have a very small good component.

Productivity is measured by dividing a quantity of output by a quantity of inputs, which in growth terms is approximated by subtracting the input growth rate from the output growth rate. If the input is labor (capital), one speaks of labor (capital) productivity. If both labor and capital are taken into account, the measure is called joint, multi- or total factor productivity. It has also been referred to as "technical change" (although it includes more than that), the residual or "the measure of our ignorance" (Denison, 1967). Usually, productivity measures are used to explain output, in growth accounting. But the reciprocals, the amount of inputs used per unit of output, are of course important determinants of prices, as discussed in Chapter 3.

Traditional sectoral productivity estimates do not account for productivity increases in the production of intermediate inputs. Traditional measures of total factor productivity are not able to identify the responsible industries in any causal sense, even if price and value data were accurate and double deflation could be used for all industries (Denison, 1989, p. 13). More specifically, they are not able to differentiate between advances in knowledge and increased input use.

48

Suppose new knowledge permits more capital goods, unchanged in design, to be produced with no increase in the amounts of labor, capital, or land used in their production. The usual procedure will show the capital stock increasing as the extra capital goods enter the stock and will credit capital (and total input) with the resulting gains in national product. This occurs even though the increases in output per unit of input in producing capital goods result from advances in knowledge, not from saving in the fundamental sense of consumption forgone. (Denison, 1989, p. 30; see also pp. 13, 25, 62; and Griliches, 1992, p. S30)

These advances of knowledge are part of the real externalities described in Chapter 6. This is one of the reasons why, at least in the United States, "several aspects of the methodology tend to assign too much of the productivity increase to manufacturing (and commodity-producing) industries and too little to nonmanufacturing (and service-producing) industries, and the size of this bias has increased over time" (Denison, 1989, p. 12).

4.1 THE HARROD–ROBINSON–READ MEASURE OF PRODUCTIVITY

As was argued in detail by Rymes (1972; 1983), the proper measure of total factor productivity, which distinguishes between advances in knowledge and input use, has to take account of the fact that capital is not a primary good but is produced with increasing productivity. Rymes developed a measure that incorporates this fact and attributed it to Harrod and Robinson, who developed the concept (Robinson, 1969, pp. 117–25), and to Read, who made the concept operational (Read, 1968). This measure has also been attributed to Peterson (1979) and Pasinetti (1973; 1981). Rymes argued that the productivity gains in the production of intermediate inputs should be subtracted from these inputs before they are subtracted from output to get the Harrod–Robinson–Read (HRR) measure of total factor productivity growth. As a result, the Harrod–Robinson–Read measure tends to indicate a larger total productivity increase than the traditional measure (Read, 1968; Rymes, 1983). In other words, owing to the increase in productivity in the production of intermediate goods (including capital), consumption forgone is smaller while producing the same net output. This is empirically confirmed by Gowdy and Miller (1990), Miller and Gowdy (1992), Peterson (1979), Rymes (1983) and Wolff (1985). Besides the fact that the HRR measure incorporates the effect of productivity gains in one sector on the productivity in another sector, an additional advantage of the HRR measure is that it gives sectoral productivity changes in terms of direct and indirect input requirements per unit of each sector's final demand (Gowdy and Miller, 1990, pp. 591–2, 601).

The HRR measure looks as follows (Gowdy and Miller, 1990; Ochoa, 1986; Rymes, 1983). From the standard Leontief framework we have

$$\mathbf{X} = (\mathbf{I} - \mathbf{A})^{-1} \mathbf{Y}, \tag{4.1}$$

$$l\,\mathbf{X} = l\,(\mathbf{I} - \mathbf{A})^{-1} \mathbf{Y} = \mathbf{L}, \tag{4.2}$$

$$\mathbf{BX} = \mathbf{B}\,(\mathbf{I} - \mathbf{A})^{-1} \mathbf{Y} = \mathbf{K}, \tag{4.3}$$

where, in addition to the definitions in Chapter 3,
$\mathbf{Y}$ = column vector of final demand by industry;
$\mathbf{X}$ = column vector of gross output by industry;
$\mathbf{L}$ = column vector of employment by industry;
$\mathbf{B}$ = matrix of capital stock (capital produced by industry i used by industry j per unit of output); and
$\mathbf{K}$ = column vector of capital stock by industry.

If $\mathbf{B}$ is divided into capital consumption and capital services of the net stock and final demand is divided into consumption and net investment we get

$$\mathbf{AX} + \mathbf{DBX} + \mathbf{C} + \mathbf{gK} = \mathbf{X}, \tag{4.4}$$

where
$\mathbf{C}$ = column vector of consumption goods;
$\mathbf{D}$ = diagonal matrix of depreciation coefficients by industry (which allows for replacement investments); and
$\mathbf{g}$ = diagonal matrix of growth rates of the net capital stock.

Manipulation of (4.4) gives

$$(\mathbf{I} - \mathbf{A} - \mathbf{DB})^{-1}\,\mathbf{C} + \mathbf{g}\,(\mathbf{I} - \mathbf{A} - \mathbf{DB})^{-1}\,\mathbf{K} = \mathbf{X}. \tag{4.5}$$

Multiplication of (4.5) by l and $\mathbf{B}$ yields, respectively,

$$l\,(\mathbf{I} - \mathbf{A} - \mathbf{DB})^{-1}\,\mathbf{C} + l\,\mathbf{g}\,(\mathbf{I} - \mathbf{A} - \mathbf{DB})^{-1}\,\mathbf{K} = \mathbf{L} \text{ and} \tag{4.6}$$

$$\mathbf{B}\,(\mathbf{I} - \mathbf{A} - \mathbf{DB})^{-1}\,\mathbf{C} + \mathbf{Bg}\,(\mathbf{I} - \mathbf{A} - \mathbf{DB})^{-1}\,\mathbf{K} = \mathbf{K}. \tag{4.7}$$

Equation (4.6) shows the direct and indirect labor requirements for the production of final demand and equation (4.7) the direct and indirect capital requirements for the production of final demand. Because capital is considered a produced input, equation (4.7) is rewritten as

$$K = (I - Bg [I - A - DB]^{-1})^{-1} B (I - A - DB)^{-1} C \qquad (4.8)$$

and substituted into equation (4.6). We get

$$L = l (I - A - DB)^{-1} C +$$
$$l g (I - A - DB)^{-1} (I - Bg [I - A - DB]^{-1})^{-1} B (I - A - DB)^{-1} C. \qquad (4.9)$$

The first term of equation (4.9) shows the amount of direct and indirect labor required to produce consumption goods, including capital consumed in the production of consumption goods. The second term of equation (4.9) shows the amount of labor required to produce the consumption good equivalent of the net addition to the capital stock, both in the consumption good and in the capital good sector. Dividing equation (4.9) by C gives the input requirements per unit of consumption good. This is equal to Pasinetti's hyper-indirect labor (Pasinetti, 1973). Changes in the column sums of the two matrices that are the premultiplicators of C in equation (4.9) are the HRR measures of productivity growth per sector. Thus one needs for each country more than one input–output matrix that are comparable (same size) to be able to calculate the HRR measure of productivity growth.

A disadvantage of this method is that it is difficult to apply across countries, not least because of the need for input–output tables. There are only less than a dozen developing countries with more than one input–output table. Moreover, many are dated, not all tables are published, nor are they all comparable (UNIDO, 1985a; United Nations, 1987b). More burdensome is the requirement of a complete set of sectoral purchasing power parities, for inputs and outputs, in order to be able to compare the HRR productivity measures across countries. Sectoral PPPs for developing countries have only begun to appear recently (Maddison, 1990; Pilat, 1994), but they are not using double-deflated productivity measures with separate price indices for outputs and inputs (Szirmai and Pilat, 1990). But the most important constraint on the application of this method to a developing country is the requirement of a matrix of the capital stock, that is, capital stock produced by sector i that sector j has to employ per unit of output (Leontief, 1986, p. 30). For these reasons, the Harrod–Robinson–Read measure of total factor productivity is modified.

4.2   ADAPTATION OF THE HRR MEASURE OF PRODUCTIVITY

For developing countries the data requirements are frequently too large to calculate the HRR productivity measures and an alternative method is called for. In this kind of model, where production is vertically integrated and where labor is the only primary input, technical progress is by definition ultimately equal to labor productivity growth. Any decrease in input use can be attributed to a decrease in the use of labor, directly, indirectly or hyper-indirectly (Pasinetti, 1973; 1981). If we first start with only circulating capital, following Pasinetti (1973), we define

$$\mathbf{v} = l\,(\mathbf{I} - \mathbf{A})^{-1}. \tag{4.10}$$

If l is a vector, $\mathbf{v}$ is also vector and v_i is equal to the quantity of labor directly and indirectly used in the production of a unit of final output i. The vector $\mathbf{v}$ is equal to the column sums of $\mathbf{v}$ if l is a diagonal matrix. Technical progress in sector i thus means smaller $\mathbf{v}$. Let us introduce fixed capital, like the model discussed above, and assume that $\mathbf{A}\mu^a = \mathbf{A} + \mathbf{DB} + \mathbf{gB}$; that is, a markup over the interindustry matrix is equal to the interindustry matrix plus depreciation and net growth of the capital stock (which is similar to Pasinetti, 1973, pp. 3–4). Equation (4.4) now becomes (remembering that $\mathbf{K} = \mathbf{BX}$)

$$\mathbf{A}\mu^a\,\mathbf{X} + \mathbf{C} = \mathbf{X}. \tag{4.11}$$

Manipulation of (4.11) gives

$$(\mathbf{I} - \mathbf{A}\mu^a)^{-1}\,\mathbf{C} = \mathbf{X} \text{ (analogous to equation (4.5)) and} \tag{4.12}$$

$$l\,(\mathbf{I} - \mathbf{A}\mu^a)^{-1}\,\mathbf{C} = l\,\mathbf{X} \text{ (analogous to equation (4.6)) or} \tag{4.13}$$

$$\mathbf{v}^a\mathbf{C} = l\,\mathbf{X} = \mathbf{L}, \text{ where} \tag{4.14}$$

$$\mathbf{v}^a = l\,(\mathbf{I} - \mathbf{A}\mu^a)^{-1}. \tag{4.15}$$

The markup μ^a accounts for depreciation and the net increase in capacity. In other words, a markup μ^a will generate the internal finance needed for depreciation and the expansion of capacity. However, μ^a is not necessarily equal to μ in equation (3.2) because it does not take account of the effect of the market structure and labor union power on μ. This deviation between μ^a and μ is similar to the distinction Harcourt and Kenyon (1976) made between the expected price and output to be catered for by new investment and the price needed to generate a flow of retained earnings to fund the investment. It is also comparable to the analysis in Eichner (1973, pp. 1193–4) of the situations where demand and supply for additional investment funds are not equal. (See Chapter 5.)

If productivity increases in the production of capital or if capital productivity rises, the markup μ^a could decline; that is, a producer could set the markup lower because a smaller amount of capital needs to be financed. It is likely that the markup is reduced when capital goods become cheaper because that will affect its competitors as well. When the capital productivity increases in one firm only, the markup could remain unchanged and profits increase instead. In general, whether a producer actually reduces the markup or takes in more profit depends on market structure variables such as concentration and entry barriers (although as far as entry barriers are associated with the capital–output ratio, entry barriers will decline as capital productivity increases).

As μ^a is not known, and as such also less interesting, we have calculated $\mathbf{v^*} = l\,(\mathbf{I} - \mathbf{A}\mu)^{-1}$ and called this the marked-up direct and indirect labor requirements per unit of output.[1] This will give an indication of the combined effect of labor and capital directly and indirectly used in production. Before some estimates of $\mathbf{v^*}$ are presented, we will make some general remarks about the labor requirements and the input–output matrix, the two major components of $\mathbf{v^*}$. The direct labor requirements per unit of output (l) are by definition equal to the reciprocal of labor productivity. Let us first look at what can be said a priori about the sectoral pattern of labor productivities.

From the discussion in Chapter 2 we already know that the labor productivity of manufacturing generally increases faster than the labor productivity of several services. Moreover, among the goods-producing sectors, labor productivity growth is relatively low in agriculture; among the services, labor productivity growth is relatively low in consumer services. Baumol (1985) classified services in three categories. The first group is the stagnant personal services. The quality of these services is directly related to the amount of labor time spent, and direct contact between producer and consumer is often essential. Examples are hotels and restaurants, education, recreation (for example, live concerts) and personal services (for example, barbers and beauty salons). Progressive impersonal services form the second group. Little or no contact between producer and consumer is required and the record of and the prospects for productivity growth are among the highest in the economy. Telecommunications is the typical example, but trade and transportation are also included. Finally, asymptotically stagnant impersonal services, such as research and development (R&D), broadcasting, computation, finance and insurance, combine elements of the two other categories. This subsector can show periods of very rapid productivity growth but which are self-extinguishing because the personal component in the production process is not able to increase productivity as fast as the technology involved.

Baumol's stagnant personal services correspond with our consumer services and progressive impersonal services and asymptotically stagnant impersonal services correspond with our producer services. Thus one can expect labor productivity growth in the producer services to be larger than in the consumer services. Several authors have indeed confirmed that productivity increases in the distributive services and several producer services are larger than in the consumer services and larger than some manufacturing sectors (Baumol *et al.*, 1989, ch. 6; Elfring, 1988, p. 65; Faini, 1984, pp. 309–10; Gershuny and Miles, 1983, pp. 138, 144; OECD, 1996a). These productivity increases are often related to the supply of new and/or cheaper intermediate manufactured products, such as computers and communication technology (OECD, 1996a).

The expectations for sectoral productivity growth rates are summarized in Table 4.1. The last column of the table shows that the growth rate of labor productivity is highest for manufacturing and lowest for consumer services. Across sectors (second and third column of Table 4.1), the level of labor productivity will be highest in manufacturing and producer services and lowest in agriculture. For consumer services, the level will be relatively high in developing and relatively low in developed countries, resulting in a level of labor productivity that is about equal across countries (see first column of Table 4.1). For all other sectors, the productivity level will be lower in developing countries (see first column of Table 4.1).

Table 4.1 Labor productivity differences

	Level of Labor Productivity			Growth Rate
	Across countries	Across sectors		
		Developing countries	Developed countries	
Agriculture	−	− −	−	+
Manufacturing	−	+	+	++
Consumer services	=	++	−	−
Producer services	−	++	+	+
Aggregate	−	na	na	na

Notes: −, +, = refer to negative, positive or neutral effect in developing country relative to developed country for the first column and one sector relative to the average in the last three columns; na = not applicable.

This can be compared with the original labor productivity model. Balassa (1964) for example only considered labor productivity in goods- and services-producing sectors. Using the same method of presentation as Table 4.1, Balassa's model would look like this:

level of labor productivity
across countries

goods	−
services	=
total	−

The second major component of **v*** is the input–output matrix. Input–output coefficients change because of technical progress, economies of scale or changes in the output mix because outputs are used as weights for aggregation (Leontief, 1986; Pasinetti, 1973; 1977; 1981; OECD, 1992a). Technical progress and economies of scale, which are both positively related to GDP per capita, will lead to different input–output coefficients. The input–output coefficients do not necessarily decline with technical progress because more inputs can be associated with less labor (that is, higher labor productivity). For example, the green revolution in agriculture led to higher use of inputs, such as hybrid seeds, fertilizer, pesticides, mechanical equipment and irrigation services, as well as higher labor input while labor productivity increased (Hayami and Ruttan, 1985). Progressive filling up of input–output tables during the process of development (see also Chapter 6) will cause larger input–output coefficients. This is related to the aggregation problem. Higher aggregation can be viewed as integration of sectors, while the increase of specialization and the division of labor during development can be viewed as disintegration of sectors. Relative magnitudes of input–output coefficients across sectors and across countries are therefore hard to predict. However, progressively filling up the input–output table or vertical disintegration is technical progress if a smaller amount of labor is used directly and indirectly in the production of intermediate inputs. Empirical evidence is all that is left.

Table 4.2 presents some schematic input–output data for four broad categories of economic activities. The data for the low-income country are based on the table for Kenya (Van der Hoeven, 1988), the middle-income country's data on the tables for some countries in south-east Asia (UNIDO, 1985b) and the high-income country data on the tables of Japan and the United States (UNIDO, 1985b).

*Table 4.2   Schematic input–output data for four broad sectors in low-,
middle- and high-income countries (percentages)*

	Low-income country				Middle-income country				High-income country			
Agriculture	40	35	0	0	20	25	0	0	25	15	0	0
Manufacturing	40	50	65	65	55	53	50	55	35	58	35	40
Consumer services	1	1	3	3	3	3	5	5	5	5	10	10
Producer services	19	14	32	32	22	19	45	40	35	22	55	50
Inputs as % of output	10	70	20	20	20	65	30	25	55	60	35	35

Sources: Author's assessment, based on UNIDO (1985b, Table 8) and Van der Hoeven (1988).

A number of observations can be made about Table 4.2. The input content of agriculture rises significantly during the development process (from 10 to 55 per cent). The input content of manufacturing, however, is likely to decline

Table 4.3 *Direct labor requirements (l) and marked-up direct and indirect labor requirements* ($v^* = l (I - \mu A)^{-1}$) *per million US dollars by sector in the Republic of Korea and Japan, 1985*

Sector	Republic of Korea		Japan	
	l	v^*	*l*	v^*
Agriculture, forestry	461	900	276	457
Mining	113	262	24	77
Food & beverages	15	710	10	257
Textiles & leather	44	364	20	112
Lumber & wood products	79	612	48	221
Paper, print & publishing	31	248	13	77
Chemicals	19	271		
Industrial			5	75
Petroleum & coal			1	77
Rubber & plastic			8	73
Nonmetal mineral products	19	224	12	74
Primary metal manufacturing	9	236	9	70
Metal products & machinery	26	229		
Nonelectrical			7	64
Electrical			11	74
Miscellaneous manufacturing	100	343	13	77
Construction	31	213	31	93
Public utilities	12	220	8	74
Wholesale & retail trade	145[a]	322[a]	45	81
Transport, wrhs & communication	31	196		
Transportation & warehousing			30	70
Communication			20	49
Finance, insurance & real estate	20	154		
Finance, insurance			18	54
Real estate			28	81
Public administration & defense	21	155	16	16
Other services	41	143	46[a]	115[a]

Note: [a] Including restaurants & hotels.
Source: Author's calculation, see Appendix 2.

somewhat during the development process, mainly because the share of sectors that process agricultural commodities, which have a high input content, declines. The percentage of inputs from agriculture falls from 35 to 15 per cent. Finally, the importance of producer services increases considerably during development, indicating increasing specialization and division of labor.

The schematic input–output data of Table 4.2, the expected pattern of labor productivity of Table 4.1 and a typical pattern of a markup across sectors and countries can be used to predict marked-up direct and indirect labor requirements per unit of output (v^*). But, rather than doing that, we have calculated the l and v^* for a developing and a developed country.

Table 4.3 gives the calculated values of the direct (l) and marked-up direct and indirect labor requirements (v^*) for the Republic of Korea and Japan in 1985. A number of facets of these calculations are striking. First, productivity is generally higher in Japan than in the Republic of Korea, as we would expect (see Table 4.1). The marked-up direct and indirect labor requirements are all clearly smaller in Japan, but the difference in the direct labor requirements is much smaller. In primary metal products, construction, finance, insurance and real estate and other services, Korean direct productivity is actually matching or better than the Japanese. Consumer services are not a separate category, but some components, such as public administration and other services, suggest that the direct productivity level is indeed similar between the Republic of Korea and Japan, conforming to the expectation expressed in Table 4.1. Second, the difference between l and v^* is of course determined by the input–output relations. The more inputs a sector uses, the larger the difference between l and v^*. For food and beverages, for example, this difference is the largest and Table 9.1 shows that this sector was (at least in 1980) the sector where intermediate inputs took up the largest share of total costs. Consumer services (part of other services) use fewer inputs and the difference between l and v^* is smaller. Third, l and v^* are highest in agriculture. Thus agriculture is in both countries the sector with the lowest productivity, confirming the expectation expressed in Table 4.1. For other sectors, the patterns conform less to the predictions made in Table 4.1 (second and third columns). Consumer services (other services, retail trade) in Japan are indeed among the sectors with the lowest direct productivity, but services in the Republic of Korea are not uniformly among the sectors with the highest direct productivity.

NOTE

1. If l is a vector, $(l (I - A\mu)^{-1})'$ is equal to $(I - \mu A')^{-1} l$ in equation (3.2), because a diagonal matrix $\mu = \mu'$ and for any matrices C and D, $(C')^{-1} = (C^{-1})'$ and $(CD)' = D'C'$. Taxes and subsidies are ignored here. They can be thought of as being included in the markups; that is, a new matrix $\mu^* [4,4] = ts [4,4] + \mu [4,4]$. But for simplicity's sake we omit the *.

5. The determinants of the markup

Much has been written about the determination of the markup (Arestis, 1992; Basile and Salvadori, 1984–5; Coutts, 1987; Eichner, 1973; Harcourt and Kenyon, 1976; Kenyon, 1978; Kotz, 1987; Semmler, 1982; 1984, pp. 58–63; Sylos-Labini, 1979; Taylor, 1988, pp. 38–41; 1991, pp. 43–4; Thompson, 1992). Different authors referred to different factors. As already indicated in Chapter 3, there are basically three factors that affect the size of the markup: the need to finance investment, the market structure and the power of organized labor. In oligopolistic markets, sellers determine their investment plans, calculate the markup needed to generate the retained profits to finance the investments and add the markup over variable costs at normal capacity utilization, while consideration is taken of the market structure and the power of labor unions (Arestis, 1996, p. 119; Bober, 1992, chs 3 and 4; Eichner, 1973; Harcourt and Kenyon, 1976; Kenyon, 1978; Lavoie, 1995; Sylos-Labini, 1984; Taylor, 1995).

This chapter will analyze these three factors and describe how they differ across sectors and countries. In section 5.1, the need to generate internal earnings to finance investment and the relation between the markup and the capital–output ratio will be examined. Section 5.2 is devoted to the structure of markets and how its two major interrelated determinants (concentration and product differentiation) affect the markup. In section 5.3, the effect of labor union power on the markup is addressed. The final section presents an overview of the arguments.

5.1 INVESTMENT FINANCE AND THE CAPITAL – OUTPUT RATIO

One determinant of the markup is the need to generate profits to finance investment. The relation between the markup and the funds needed for depreciation allowances and the growth of capacity was spelled out in more detail in Chapter 4. There we defined $\mathbf{A}\, \mu^a = \mathbf{A} + \mathbf{DB} + g\mathbf{B}$, where μ^a is the markup that will generate enough profits to finance depreciation and net additions to the capital stock. The depreciation allowances (matrix $\mathbf{D}$) and the growth rate of investment (matrix $\mathbf{g}$) are calculated over the capital stock per unit of output (matrix $\mathbf{B}$). Thus μ^a is related to the depreciation allowances, the growth rate of investment and the capital–output ratio. A larger capital–output ratio, a higher growth rate of investment or larger depreciation allowances will lead to a higher markup because more funds are needed to finance gross investments, that is net investments plus replacement investments. If the growth rate of gross investment is the same, a higher capital–output ratio requires more finance and thus a higher markup. On the other hand, if two sectors are completely identical, including their capital–output ratio, except that one sector faces or anticipates rising demand for its products and the other sector has to cope with stagnant demand, the first sector will invest more and needs a higher markup to finance the investment. The capital–output ratio only relates to past investment, but the growth rate of investment is more forward looking. Thus the markup is influenced by the growth rate of gross investment and the capital–output ratio and both variables will be included as independent variables in the regression equation.

The capital–output ratio is also associated with the investment–output ratio. The variation of investment, however, varies more from year to year as a result of the bulky character of fixed investment and the business cycle. Investment planning would allow the financial requirements to be spread out over several years. Hence the markup is more likely to be correlated with the capital–output ratio than with the investment–output ratio.

Adding the growth rate of investment also makes it possible to differentiate between the capacity utilization effect and the finance requirement effect of the capital–output ratio. Taylor (1991, p. 43) suggested that the output–capital ratio measures capacity utilization, which is a demand factor. A higher output–capital ratio indicates increasing demand and upward pressure on prices and markups. Hence the demand interpretation and the finance interpretation of the capital–output ratio have contrary effects on the markup. It is, however, possible that, in cross-country or cross-sector studies, like this one, the finance interpretation is more prevalent and in time-series studies, as in Taylor (1991), the demand interpretation. Including another proxy for the finance requirements, namely the growth of investment, allows the regression to pick up the demand effect of the capital–output ratio.

A larger capital–output ratio also increases entry barriers, partly because of the finance requirements and partly because of economies of scale (see Figure 5.1, p. 66). A larger capital–output ratio is thus associated with higher concentration, which also has an upward pressure on the markup (Semmler, 1984, p. 97; Sylos-Labini, 1984, pp. 124, 128).

Eichner (1973) was one of the first to analyze the relation between the markup and investment finance. He argued that the markup is determined by the demand and supply for internal investment funds by the firm. The firm's demand curve is the "familiar marginal efficiency of investment curve" (p. 1190). The firm's supply curve is characterized by declining marginal revenues when the markup is raised. The declining marginal revenues result from the fact that customers switch to competitors' products when the price is raised, from the entry of new firms and from government intervention (Eichner, 1973, p. 1190). The markup is determined by the point where the demand and supply for internal investment funds are equal. Harcourt and Kenyon (1976) presented a similar model, one that does not rely on the marginal efficiency of investment curve. In their model the markup is determined by the point where two sets of expectations coincide: the expected price and output to be catered for by new investment and the expectations concerning the flow of retained earnings to fund the investment associated with a certain price. In other words, expectations about the demand for its product should be compatible with the expected retained earnings to finance the investment. In sum, in both models the demand for finance is balanced by the supply of finance which is constrained by the structure of the market for the firm's output, which is the topic of the next section.

If the "costs" of raising internal revenues become too large (in terms of declining marginal revenues), it might become beneficial to raise funds externally. The share of funds that will be raised externally is determined by comparing the market interest rate with the implicit interest rate for internal funds. The implicit interest rate can be calculated by taking the funds lost as a result of the substitution and entry effects and government action as a percentage of the extra funds generated by the higher markup (Eichner, 1973, p. 1192).

Recent theoretical insights on capital markets imperfections were obviously not taken into account by Eichner (1973) and Harcourt and Kenyon (1976). Asymmetric information, which leads to moral hazard and adverse selection problems, cause rationing of lending and give additional reasons for the reliance on internal earnings for the financing of investment (Levine, 1997, p. 715; Stiglitz and Weiss, 1981; Van Ees *et al.*, 1997). Moreover, recent research has found evidence that constraints on external financing affect pricing decisions because they raise the need for generating retained earnings (Hubbard, 1998). On the other hand, it is easier and cheaper for large firms than for small firms to raise external funds, thus lowering the need for retained earnings to finance investment (Kaldor, 1949–50, p. 127; Scherer and Ross, 1990, pp. 126–7; Sylos-Labini, 1984, p. 124).

There is substantial evidence that a large share of investment is financed by retained earnings in both developing and developed economies, although institutional and historical factors have to be taken into account to explain some of the variation across countries (Athey and Laumas, 1994; Carpenter *et al.*, 1994; Cobham and Subramaniam, 1998; Eichner, 1973, p. 1196; Fazzari *et al.*, 1988; Hermes and Lensink, 1998; Hubbard, 1998; Jenkins, 1998; Levine, 1997, p. 720; Shafik, 1992; Singh, 1995a; 1998; Singh and Weisse, 1998; Stiglitz, 1993; Taylor, 1995, p. 701; Van Ees *et al.*, 1997). The share of internal finance is even likely to be larger in developing countries than in developed countries because the financial sector is less developed, the reputation of firms is poorer and price volatility is higher. However, Singh (1995c, p. 18) showed that large corporations in developing countries usually finance less than 30 per cent of investment from internal sources. But this percentage is likely to increase steeply when the size of the firm declines as the lack of finance usually tops the list of factors inhibiting growth of small- and medium-sized companies in developing countries (Morrison *et al.*, 1994). Singh (1997, p. 777; 1998) and Singh and Weisse (1998, p. 612) offered three possible explanations for the unexpected high share of external finance for large corporations in developing countries. The fast development of stock markets and heavy reliance on equity finance is not an evolutionary process but the result of government actions (such as privatizations). Second, internal and external financial liberalization led to a relative decline in the cost of equity capital while the cost of debt was relatively high in the 1980s as a result of the high interest rates. Third, retained earnings might have been insufficient to finance the fast growth of corporations in countries such as Japan and the Republic of Korea, while their market power was insufficient to raise prices.

Thus, because a large share of investment is financed by retained earnings, a firm that has higher finance requirements will raise prices as long as labor unions and its market power allow.

Capital–Output Ratios across Sectors and Countries

There are no a priori reasons for a particular pattern of the growth rate of investment across sectors and countries. On the other hand, the capital–output ratio – and thus the markup as far as it is determined by the need to finance investment – shows a rather distinct pattern across countries and across sectors. This pattern will be the focus of the rest of this section.

The relative size of the capital stock is a result of the choice of techniques. The neoclassical production function assumes that there is a wide variety of choices and that these choices are known and freely available. In all countries, firms in a given industry have the same set of techniques to choose from. The selection of the capital–labor ratio is determined by the wage–rental ratio, which in turn is determined by the relative factor endowments. The neoclassical production function establishes a monotonically increasing relation between the wage–rental ratio and the capital–labor ratio. A developing country with the same available techniques as a developed country and a relative abundance of labor will have a relative low wage–rental ratio and hence a relative low capital–labor ratio (Pack and Westphal, 1986, p. 108; Pasinetti, 1981, p. 196).

Garegnani (1970) has refuted this reasoning. When there is no uniform capital–labor ratio across sectors, there is no smooth monotonically increasing relation between the wage–rental ratio and the capital–labor ratio. Hence no monotonic increase in the capital–labor ratio can be expected a priori when GDP per capita increases and relative labor abundance declines. Only if the choice of technique is restricted to labor and land, as is the case in agriculture to a certain degree, can a monotonically increasing relation between the wage–rental ratio and the land–labor ratio be established. This is the case because both land and labor can be expressed in physical terms and hence neither the value of land nor that of labor depends on the wage–rental ratio. The production technology underlying the markup model, in contrast to the neoclassical model, does not yield any specific relation between the capital–labor ratio and factor prices (Sraffa, 1960).

Yet there is a choice of technique in the post-Keynesian markup model. This choice might be influenced by wages and rentals, inter alia, despite the fact that there is no monotonically increasing relation between the wage–rental ratio and the capital–labor ratio. But the choice is rather limited. Many techniques are imported and possibilities for adaptation are in many cases limited. "Much of the potential substitution of labor for capital stems from use of labor-intensive methods in 'peripheral' production activities," such as packaging, handling, transporting and storage (Pack, 1984, p. 352; see also Bhalla, 1985; Lall, 1978, pp. 237–41; Morawetz, 1974, p. 520; Nixson, 1984, pp. 108–14). Developing countries also choose similar techniques as used in developed countries because they produce products of higher quality or because it saves on scarce factors such as management or skilled labor in general (Bagachwa, 1992; Hirschman, 1958). Capital-intensive methods are often favored for prestigious reasons in developing countries, particularly when governments are involved in the production of goods and services. Tying of aid can also lead to more capital-intensive methods of production. For all these reasons, technology is largely product-specific at the level of the core production process. To take two extremes: chemicals are typically produced with a high capital–output ratio and a haircut with a low ratio.

At the sectoral level, each capital/output ratio is essentially determined by *technology*. In more practical terms, if, at any given point in time, the capital/output ratio in a sector such as "house renting" is of the order of 100 times larger than in a sector such as "clothing", the reason simply is that *technology* is such that the minimum-cost production processes require, in the house renting sector, a capital/output ratio which is 100 times larger than in the clothing sector. ... [T]raditional economic theory, by its emphasis on the rate of profit, has led us to overlook them – namely to neglect the role played by factors accounting for differences of the order of 1 to 100 – and to concentrate on factors of uncertain influence and in any case of negligible importance. (Pasinetti, 1981, pp. 216–7; original emphasis; see also pp. 193–4)

As a result, the variation of capital–output ratios across products is much larger than across countries for the same products. Indeed, many writers have observed that, for the same product, the capital intensity in developing countries is not much different from the intensity in developed countries (Baer and Hervé, 1966; Morawetz, 1974; Oshima, 1971; Teitel, 1978; Thirlwall, 1983, pp. 217–20).

So far we have ignored the question of how to measure factor intensities (see Bhalla, 1985, ch. 1 for a general overview). First of all, there is the problem of measuring capital (Pasinetti, 1981, pp. 177–9). Measurement in physical terms does not make sense for most purposes because aggregation would be impossible. Another possibility is to reduce capital to the amount of labor required to produce it. This method is particularly appropriate for productivity measurements (see Chapter 4). The most common method is to measure capital at current prices, that is, physical units multiplied by the corresponding prices (Maddison, 1991, app. D; 1993). This method is more relevant when techniques are (internationally) compared or when the determination of prices in a markup model is studied. However, which prices should be used? Pasinetti (1981, p. 185) gives an example where India imports in dollars from the United States a chemical factory with exactly the same characteristics as it has in the United States, hence the physical capital to labor ratio will be exactly the same. If in India the wage is one-quarter the wage in the United States (at the same efficiency and in dollars), the capital–output ratio will be four times greater in India because output is four times cheaper, although exactly the same. (If capital is expressed at current prices and produced in India, the capital–labor ratio will be four times smaller in India.) The capital–output ratio should therefore be measured at local prices for price determination because, if profits and the profit rate (profits as a percentage of capital) need to be the same in India and the United States, the markup (calculated with gross output) needs to be larger in India as well, to compensate for the lower gross output. However, for international comparisons, capital and output should be measured at purchasing power parities (Pasinetti, 1981, pp. 180–83).

Kaldor (1961) suggested that a constant capital–output ratio is one of the stylized facts of economic development. However, the data from Summers and Heston (1991) indicate a positive correlation between the capital–output ratio and GDP per capita across countries (all converted at PPPs). But this might be partly a result of sectoral transformation, as will be discussed below. Maddison (1991, pp. 66–8; 1993, p. 8) showed also a (small) increase in the capital–output ratio during the twentieth century for four western European countries and Japan. For the United States, the capital–output ratio only rose until about 1933. The data of Summers and Heston (1991) show that in 1988 the highest capital–output ratio (Japan) was only about 5.5 times larger than the lowest (Guatemala), but typically this ratio is two to three times larger in developed countries (see also Simon, 1990). Assuming that the rate of profit is more or less equalized across countries,[1] the markup will be two to three times larger in developed countries, ceteris paribus. As will be discussed in Chapter 11, capital goods are relatively expensive compared to GDP in developing countries, which means that the capital–output ratio at PPPs will be lower than the capital–output ratio at national prices. Investment compared to GDP is about 50 per cent more expensive in the poorest countries (see Table 8.2). We assume that the capital–output ratio at national prices is also about 50 per cent higher in the poorest countries. Thus, at purchasing power parities, the capital–output ratio is typically two to three times larger in developed countries, but at national currencies, which is more relevant for price determination, the capital–output ratio is typically less than two times larger.

As argued above, the variation of the capital–output ratio is smaller across countries than within a country. Capital stock estimates by sector are less readily available and not always comparable, hence conclusions should be tentative. However, some evidence exists. For Kenya, for example, the capital–output ratio in mining was about 27 times larger than the capital–output ratio in small–scale agriculture in 1976. The ratio was relatively small in large–scale agriculture, traditional construction, trade and services and education and health, and relatively large in transport and communications, general government services and ownership of dwellings (Van der Hoeven, 1988, p. 275). In the Republic of Korea, the ratio is also relatively large in transport and communications, services and ownership of dwellings (Khan, 1985, p. 366). In Japan, in 1975, the largest capital–output ratio was 38 times larger than the smallest and in the United States 14 times. In both countries, the capital–output ratio was smallest in other services and finance and insurance, and largest in agriculture, mining and public utilities. The ratio was also high in transport and communication in the United States (Pilat, 1991b, pp. 33, 37).

There is some similarity between the capital–output ratios for the different sectors across countries, except for agriculture. In manufacturing, for example, the ratio is 2.2 in Kenya, 2.4 in Japan and 2.7 in the United States (although manufacturing includes public utilities in Kenya). For other sectors there is some variation across countries, but this variation does not seem to be associated with the level of GDP per capita. Agriculture is the only exception. Data from Hayami and Ruttan (1985, Table A.4) reveal, for example, that the capital–output ratio of agriculture was 47 times smaller in India than in the United States in 1980. Moreover, the capital–output ratio of agriculture in India increased by 19 times between 1960 and 1980. (Capital was proxied by Hayami and Ruttan by tractor horsepower.)

With these large differences in agriculture, the gap in the aggregate capital–output ratio between developed and developing countries should partly be explained by the relative size of the agricultural sector (see Pasinetti, 1981,

p. 214 on a similar argument). When at low GDP per capita a large share of the labor force is employed in agriculture, where the capital–output ratio is low, the overall capital–output ratio will be small as well. But when GDP per capita rises, more labor moves into sectors with higher capital–output ratios, pushing the aggregate capital–output ratio up. This process also occurs on a less aggregated level. With development, the sectors with higher capital–output ratios, such as chemicals, will become larger at the expense of sectors with lower capital–output ratios, such as textiles. This process can be influenced by government intervention, as for example has been the case in the Republic of Korea (Amsden, 1989).

5.2 MARKET POWER

The extent to which firms have the power to set prices is determined by the market structure, which has two principal interrelated determinants: concentration and product differentiation. Concentration and product differentiation are the two proximate determinants of the markup and they will be the main focus of this section. Both display a distinct pattern across sectors and countries. Concentration is in part determined by economies of scale, which are discussed separately in Chapter 6 because they also have direct and indirect effects on other components of the price equation (3.2). Concentration is also partly a result of barriers to entry, which are in part determined by economies of scale, capital–output ratios and product differentiation, and are discussed in the sections that cover these factors (Scherer and Ross, 1990, pp. 360–61; Semmler, 1984, chs 2 and 4).[2] One set of barriers to entry, namely those associated with transportation costs and external borders, will be examined separately in Chapter 7. Constraints on the financing of investment can also act as a barrier to entry and larger firms might find it easier to finance investment – or other expenditures, such as on advertising and research and development, that determine product differentiation – either from retained earnings or from capital markets (Sylos-Labini, 1984, pp. 124, 128). This barrier to entry is associated with the capital–output ratio and is discussed in section 5.1. The interrelation between these variables is presented in Figure 5.1.

Concentration

A higher degree of concentration of sales increases the discretionary power to set prices. The smaller the number of firms, the less they can ignore effects of their pricing and output decisions on competing firms and the larger the likelihood of collusive behavior and higher prices. The larger the number of firms, the more the difficulty of coordinating action increases. With more firms,

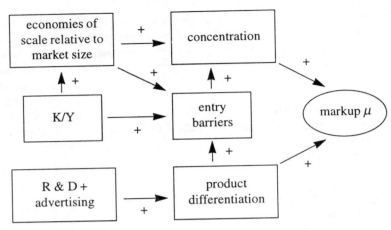

Figure 5.1   Interrelation between several determinants of the markup

it is also more likely that one maverick will start a price war. Moreover, with an unequal distribution of sizes, say with one large price leader, it is more likely that coordination will take place and that price wars will be avoided or ignored (Scherer and Ross, 1990, pp. 277–8, 315; Shepherd, 1987).

The extent to which a concentration ratio, as measured for example by the share of the market of the largest four firms, reflects the power to raise prices depends on the proper definition of the market (Rothschild, 1987; Scherer, 1987; Scherer and Ross, 1990, pp. 73–9, 424–6; Shepherd, 1987). If the market is defined too broadly, the concentration ratio will underestimate market power; if it is defined too narrowly, the ratio will be too high. The scope of the market is essentially limited by the number of close substitutes and the geographical region. Of course, concentration and the extent to which the power can be used to raise prices are also constrained by government intervention. In the United States, for example, collusion is prohibited under the law (Blinder *et al.*, 1998).

What are close substitutes? "Are Post Toasties corn flakes a meaningful substitute for Kellogg's famous corn flakes? Is oatmeal part of the same market? Toasted bread? Ham and eggs? Appetite-suppressant pills? Relevant again is the question, by how much can the seller(s) raise prices before consumers shift in large proportions to what appear to be more distant substitutes?" (Scherer, 1987, p. 343). The larger the relevant market is, the larger the possibilities for substitution, the larger the price elasticities and the lower the concentration (see also Sylos-Labini [1969] 1993, pp. 90–92).

The scope of the market is also determined by geographical distances. Geographical distances and transportation costs result in market power (spatial monopoly). As pointed out by Capozza and van Order (1987, p. 428), "perfect competition is only a limiting case when fixed or transport costs go to zero and demand density becomes infinite. ... Space implies that suppliers at each location *always* have monopoly power" (original emphasis). Firms will be able to create market power for themselves by moving away from competitors as long as they do not move away from their customers. In cases where there are more than two sellers and evenly distributed consumers, sellers will locate themselves at equidistant points (Kaldor, 1935, p. 68; Lancaster, 1987; Varian, 1978, p. 68). (This is in contrast to duopoly, which is the famous Hotelling location game of two ice-sellers on a beach who will end up selling ice next to each other. See Arnott, 1987; Chamberlin, 1960, app. C; Hotelling, 1929.) By implication, sparsely populated areas might suffer from a scarcity of suppliers of goods and services, but the ones that are there have considerable market power. We would therefore expect variables like population density, urbanization and "GDP density" (GDP per km^2) to have a negative effect on the price level. Geographical distances are particularly important for services that need direct contact between provider and consumer and for goods with relatively high transportation costs.

The relation between concentration and prices, as part of the structure–conduct–performance paradigm, has been the topic of numerous studies. These studies generally confirm a positive relation between concentration and prices. Semmler (1982; 1984, ch. 4) surveyed the evidence on the relation between concentration and profit rates and concluded that almost all studies show a positive significant relationship. Higher profit rates should translate into higher prices if entry barriers are important. Leff (1978, p. 672) quoted evidence from developing countries in support of a positive relation between concentration and prices. Shepherd (1987, p. 564) reported that "a broad and significant correlation did emerge, enough to establish a presumption that the theoretical effects of oligopoly market power on pricing activity do occur in practice." Scherer and Ross (1990, pp. 422–3) however emphasized that time-series studies show that this relation is not continuous and not symmetric. They found that, when the four-firm concentration ratio is below a threshold level of about 50, there is little evidence of any effect on profits. Moreover, when concentration is rising over time the threshold level is even higher before an effect is discernible. Recent evidence points to the importance of market share of individual firms, rather than concentration in an industry (Scherer and Ross, 1990, p. 429; Shepherd, 1987, p. 563). However, the aggregation level makes it impossible to use market share data in our analysis.

Concentration across countries

Concentration of firms is likely to be higher in developing countries because smaller markets need fewer firms (Lai, 1991). If, for a certain level of output, average costs reach a minimum (costs per unit of output are not declining infinitely) and this minimum is at a level of production closer to the size of the market in smaller countries, then the optimum number of firms is smaller and concentration is higher. In other words, "[t]hough the establishment sizes are typically smaller in LDCs [less developed countries] than in DCs [developed countries] the general level of seller concentration will still be higher in LDCs ... provided that the markets are proportionately smaller still" (Lee, 1984, p. 70). For example, one oil refinery or one steel plant in a small country can serve the whole market and still have excess capacity (Leff, 1979, p. 719; Scherer, 1987, p. 344). Concentration is likely to be related to the capital–output ratio because a high capital–output ratio in a certain industry means high fixed costs and an average cost curve that reaches a minimum at a large level of production (see Figure 5.1). In sum, economies of scale in comparison to the size of the market determines concentration (Needham, 1978, pp. 151–4; Scherer, 1987; Scherer and Ross, 1990, p. 87).

Concentration can still be larger in bigger economies if average costs are decreasing. Pressure to concentrate will then continue to operate until there is only one firm per market (Sraffa, 1926). Moreover, concentration is determined by a number of factors, not only by economies of scale in relation to the market size. Other factors, such as entry barriers and product differentiation, can also play a role (see Figure 5.1). If economies of scale are the only factor influencing concentration and if they are increasing faster than the size of the market, concentration will increase. But, if average costs do not decline as fast as the market size increases, the concentration ratio might decrease if entry barriers are low and more firms move into the market.

There are four additional factors contributing to concentration, particularly in developing countries: transnational corporations, business conglomerates, public enterprises and weak antitrust legislation. Transnational corporations (TNCs) account for a significant share of GDP in many developing countries (Lee, 1984, p. 53; UNCTAD, 1997). The stock of inward foreign direct investment (FDI) amounted in 1995 to about 9 per cent of GDP in developed countries and to about 15 per cent in developing countries, but in small countries the stock of inward FDI is often larger than 25 per cent of GDP, even reaching more than 100 per cent in certain cases (UNCTAD, 1997, pp. 339, 341). The size of transnational corporations compared to the size of the host developing countries leads to the expectation that, in markets where TNCs are present, the concentration is higher. TNCs benefit from economies of scale on global operations, such as management, marketing, internal finance, transportation, information and production of intermediate inputs. Nixson (1984, pp. 98–101) reviewed the evidence and concluded that "TNC involvement is likely to increase the level of industrial concentration in any given LDC" (p. 101) although there was some evidence that TNCs follow each other into an important developing market, creating a "miniature replica" in the smaller market and reducing concentration in the short run, despite the fact that

TNCs often enter markets where entry barriers and concentration are relatively high. In the longer run, however, higher levels of concentration can be expected because of the entry barriers created by, for example, the higher capital–labor ratios and higher degree of product differentiation of many TNCs, because of the acquisition of local firms by TNCs or because TNCs are able to force local firms out of business. UNCTAD (1997) reviewed the evidence more recently and found that in developing (and in smaller developed) countries the presence of TNCs led to higher concentration (see also Blomström and Kokko, 1997; Lall, 1978, pp. 226–31; Lee, 1984, pp. 73–5; Willmore, 1989).

The second factor that has led to higher concentration in developing countries is the existence of business groups. Hikino and Amsden (1992) argued that the characteristics of late-industrializing countries make the formation of business groups more likely. Late-industrializing countries typically borrow technology at a medium level of complexity because the lower level is vulnerable to low-wage competition and the higher level is not easily available or adaptable. But medium-level technology can be obsolete overnight when a high-tech substitute is developed. Diversification into often technologically unrelated fields of activity covers against this uncertainty. Similarly, Leff (1978) argued that large diversified and vertically integrated economic groups are more dominant in developing countries because groups appropriate monopoly rents, internalize externalities and minimize risk and uncertainty, which are all more prevalent in developing countries. While the presence of diversified business groups will increase the overall concentration in an economy, it does not necessarily increase concentration within a particular product market or industry. Moreover, governments could intervene. Despite very high industry and aggregate concentration, the power of *chaebols* in the Republic of Korea, for example, has been restricted by some price controls, competition on the basis of quality and supplementary services and competition for government subsidies and licenses which were allocated on the basis of performance (Amsden, 1989; Singh, 1994; 1995b; 1998).

The third factor that has contributed to higher concentration in developing countries is the presence of large public enterprises. It is not clear, however, whether higher concentration caused by public enterprises contributes to higher prices if certain prices are subsidized for political or social reasons. On the other hand, Bilginsoy (1994) argued that public enterprises have higher markups to finance budget deficits.

In the 1950s and 1960s, many developing countries established public enterprises, often by nationalization, to foster development. Following the writings of economists such as Hirschman (1958), Kaldor (1967), Rosenstein-Rodan (1943) and Scitovsky (1954), public enterprises were expected to correct market failures (financial, for example), economize on scarce entrepreneurial talent, overcome large indivisibilities, realize economies of scale, induce positive externalities and linkages and increase the power of the state over the "commanding heights" of the economy. This development strategy was often combined with or a result of import substitution (Hirschman, 1981; 1987, p. 207; Krueger, 1997).

As a consequence, public enterprises have accounted for a significant share of total GDP. For a sample of five Latin American, six Asian and 12 African countries, this share was 12, 6 and 18 per cent, respectively, in the late 1970s and early 1980s (World Bank, 1983, p. 50). For subsectors these percentages were much larger, however. Public utilities have been dominated by public enterprises (as in developed countries). Second in rank was the transport and communication sector, where public enterprises typically accounted for at least 50 per cent of the sectoral GDP. Mining was also often controlled by public enterprises, but there are some exceptions. Public enterprises were least significant in agriculture, trading and other services, typically contributing less than 25 per cent to sectoral GDP. The importance of public enterprises varied widely in manufacturing. Their contribution to sectoral GDP was often larger than 25 per cent, but varied between 5 and 60 per cent (Kirkpatrick, 1984, pp. 152–6). Given the wave of privatizations in recent years in developing countries, these percentages are declining. It is not clear, however, whether this also means lower concentration ratios, as in certain cases public monopolies were just transformed into private monopolies.

Finally, antitrust legislation and competition policy in general that curb concentration or its effect on prices are generally weaker in developing countries (Leff, 1979). Developing countries have at times actively promoted mergers and large business groups for economic reasons. However, the number of developing countries that adopted competition laws has increased, from 14 in 1986 to 38 in 1996 (compared to about 25 developed countries in both years), many existing laws have been strengthened and in an additional 25 developing countries a competition law is under preparation (UNCTAD, 1997, p. 189). Moreover, the coordination of competition laws internationally has recently gained attention among policy makers and economists (see Chapter 7).

What is the empirical evidence of concentration across countries? Cross-section data of developed countries, largely restricted to manufacturing, reveal that "the aggregate degree of concentration is related in some way to the overall market size, rather than level of economic development," with lower concentration ratios in larger markets, confirming our argument (Pryor, 1972, p. 134; see also Scherer and Ross, 1990, pp. 62–5, 85–9). The data for the United States show that concentration in the manufacturing sector had probably risen up to 1950, but the increase after 1950 was small, partly owing to the antimerger law adopted in 1950. Weaker laws in Europe might have played a role in the increase in concentration there (Mueller and Hamm, 1974; Scherer, 1987, p. 344; Scherer and Ross, 1990, pp. 60, 65, 82–5; Simon, 1990, p. 154;

Sylos-Labini [1969] 1993, pp. 6, 221–4).

More important, how does this compare to concentration in developing countries? Now the data problems are even larger. Besides the usual problems of where to delineate a market with regard to geography and products, data on sales per firm are available for only a few developing countries. Lee (1984, p. 70) surveyed the literature and found that smaller markets generally have higher concentration levels. This is confirmed by Lai (1991, pp. 46–7) who presented data for the manufacturing sector in four developed countries and six, rather large, developing countries: Brazil, Chile, India, Mexico, Pakistan and Taiwan. The data revealed that concentration is in general higher in developing countries. For all countries, the concentration measure is rising over time, although for Taiwan not monotonically. UNCTC–UNCTAD (1991, pp. 44–5) also showed, using in part the same numbers, that the concentration ratios in Brazil, Chile, India, Mexico, Pakistan and Turkey are higher than in the United States and France, despite the fact that the ratio is biased upwards in the United States as a result of the larger disaggregation (see also Frischtak *et al.*, 1989).

Concentration by sector
The differentiation of concentration by sector is particularly relevant for the explanation of prices. The average cost curve is determined by the technology typical of the particular sector, which is reflected in the proportion of fixed costs in total costs. This proportion is correlated with the capital–output ratio and the discussion in section 5.1 about the variation of the capital–output ratio across sectors is relevant here as well. Hence whether, or at which level of production, a sector reaches a minimum of the average cost curve differs more across sectors than across countries (Scherer and Ross, 1990, pp. 115, 140). In sum, economies of scale in comparison to the size of the market determines concentration in a particular sector.

Research has indeed found a remarkable stability of the ranking of concentration ratios of equally defined sectors across countries, both in developed and in developing countries (Lee, 1984, pp. 70–75; Pryor, 1972, pp. 135–7; Scherer, 1987, p. 343; Scherer and Ross, 1990, pp. 85–9; Schmalensee, 1989, p. 992; Sutton, 1997, p. 42). Most of the available evidence is, however, restricted to the manufacturing sector (Lai, 1991; Scherer, 1987).

As will be argued in Chapter 6, internal economies of scale are very important in the manufacturing sector, but might be partly unrealized in developing countries because of the limited size of the market. If economies of scale are increasing less rapidly than the size of the market, concentration is likely to be larger in the manufacturing sector in developing countries. Economies of scale are particularly important in manufacturing sectors where the proportion of fixed costs is high, such as in chemicals and metals, but less so in, for example, textiles (Nolan, 1996; Scherer and Ross, 1990, pp. 115, 140).

In agriculture, economies of scale are usually small or negligible in the production process (see section 6.2) although larger in complementary services, such as extension, irrigation, transportation and marketing. Hence it can be expected that concentration in agriculture is not significantly determined by the size of the market compared to economies of scale. However, the degree of sellers' concentration is significantly influenced by colonial settlements and other historical factors and varies very much for different commodities (Binswanger *et al.*, 1995; Leff, 1979, p. 728). Export crops are usually much more concentrated than food crops (Brinkman and Gabriele, 1992, pp. 12–14). Moreover, government intervention in pricing, marketing and acreage limits competition in many countries. In general, agriculture is often characterized by oligopsony or monopsony (Scherer and Ross, 1990, p. 79).

In sand and stone mining, concentration is very low, but high transportation costs compared to product value limits competition. In other areas of mining, such as fuels and minerals, economies of scale are very important because of large fixed investments, although pockets of informal or illegal small-scale mining sometimes exist parallel to large-scale mining, for example in gold and diamond mining. In addition, world markets in several commodities are dominated by cartels (for example, diamonds, oil) and large TNCs. In sum, oligopoly prevails in mining (Scherer and Ross, 1990, p. 80).

Economies of scale are important in such producer services as transportation, warehousing, wholesale trade, communication and utilities. Hence these sectors are generally dominated by either natural monopolies (that is, the minimum average costs are larger than the size of the market) or oligopolies. However, these markets are often subject to government regulation. On the other hand, concentration is rather low in construction (Scherer and Ross, 1990, p. 80).

Concentration in the financial sector in developing countries can be quite high because of government involvement, transnational corporations or merger and acquisition activity. In developed countries as well, concentration can be high, for example in local markets (*The Economist*, 2 May 1992; 12 April 1997; 31 October 1998; Gershuny and Miles, 1983, pp. 137–9; Hikino and Amsden, 1992, p. 25; World Bank, 1993b, p. 252).

Consumer services are dominated by small-scale enterprises, although hard evidence is missing for most developing countries because censuses are usually restricted to the manufacturing sector and typically exclude establishments below a certain number of workers, the cutoff ranging from five to 20 (Lee, 1984, p. 50; see, on the United States, Fuchs, 1968, pp. 190–92; Scherer and Ross, 1990, pp. 80–81; Stigler, 1956, pp. 53–60). There are some reasons to expect that concentration will be low in consumer services. First, economies of scale are not important in most consumer services. Second, public enterprises and transnational corporations are least active in these services (UNCTC, 1991, pp. 15–22, annex). Third, the producer–consumer relation of services, frequent usage and high transportation costs (in travel time for the consumer) result in close proximity of producers to consumers and in a large number of producers of services. You can buy many goods at one supermarket, but for each service you have to go to a different supplier. Hence transportation costs play a larger role for services than for goods. In the absence of economies of scale, only a small number of consumers are usually needed for a service provider to settle in certain areas. Examples are groceries, barbers, restaurants, schools and physicians in neighborhoods or small towns. On the other hand, the necessary producer–consumer relation also bestows market power on the provider (see below).

Similar to the case of the capital–output ratio (in section 5.1), structural change accompanying development is also a factor behind the difference in concentration between the developed and the developing countries. As concentration is likely to be higher in the manufacturing sector in developing countries, when the manufacturing sector grows during the development process, concentration declines (if economies of scale are increasing less rapidly than the size of the market). The same process also takes place within each sector. Oliveira Martins (1993) for example characterized wood products and furniture, textiles, apparel and leather and nonmetallic mineral products as subsectors with low product differentiation and low concentration. Yet, concentration in these subsectors is still expected to be larger in developing countries than in developed countries. These subsectors are usually relatively large in developing countries and become relatively smaller with development (Balassa, 1981). Thus, while the total manufacturing sector expands and concentration declines with development, the manufacturing subsectors with relatively low concentration become smaller as a country develops and each subsector is expected to have higher concentration at a lower level of development. These subsectors, however, are often oriented towards exports and should be excluded from the calculation of domestic market concentration.

Product Differentiation

The other principal determinant of the markup is product differentiation. Product differentiation makes a similar product or service really or apparently different from a competitor's. Product differentiation refers to the variation of some or all of the characteristics that similar products share. It does not refer to the differences between a car and a table but between the different characteristics of different cars or tables (Lancaster, 1987). The characteristics of, for example, a car can vary dramatically. A car can have two but also 16 cylinders, carry two people or a large family, be black but also purple and the possibilities of varying the appearance and accessories of a car are almost infinite. Products can also be differentiated by means of branding, quality variation, packaging, labeling and supplementary services such as guarantees. With each permutation of the characteristics of a product, a manufacturer tries to appeal to a different group of consumers and create brand loyalty. By varying the characteristics of its product or service, a firm can create market power independent of its share of the market. Moreover, the effectiveness of public policy instruments is more limited for price discrimination than for concentration. Product differentiation changes the shape of the demand curve. That is, when products are more differentiated, the substitutability smaller and the brand loyalty larger, the demand curve becomes more inelastic, which increases the market power of the firm (Kaldor, 1949–50; Lancaster, 1987).

Product differentiation is similar to the market power derived from location (Chamberlin, 1960; Lancaster, 1987). Products are perceived as a bundle of characteristics and consumers buy those products that have characteristics that are closest to their tastes. Variation in the characteristics determines the product differentiation. Similarly, in the locational variant, consumers position themselves not only in characteristics space (comparing their tastes – their ideal mix of characteristics – with the characteristics of the goods offered) but also in physical space (Capozza and Van Order, 1987; Lancaster, 1987). Again, firms can influence their market power by positioning themselves in characteristic space and physical space to maximize their market power and their sales volume. More product differentiation gives firms more scope for setting markups independently from each other and increases entry barriers. Competition will be lower and the markup higher.

Product differentiation is achieved in particular by advertising and research and development (R&D) activities (Needham, 1978, ch. 4; You, 1995, p. 452). Research and development is needed to change physical characteristics of a product and advertising is used to convince consumers that a product is indeed different and better. Advertising and R&D expenditures are also important entry barriers, as new firms may have to spend substantial sums to make an attempt to enter a new market, for example because these expenditures are subject to economies of scale (Scherer and Ross, 1990, pp. 131, 360, 436; Schmalensee, 1987; Sylos-Labini, 1984, p. 124). Scherer and Ross (1990, pp. 598, 646) summarized the evidence as pointing to a positive or U-shape relation between advertising and R&D, on the one hand, and concentration, on the other hand (see also Cohen and Klepper, 1996; Sutton, 1996). Schmalensee (1987, p. 35) however found the relation between advertising and concentration less straightforward. But he concluded that " [t]he clearest empirical regularity to emerge ... is the strong, positive cross-section correlation between industry-level measures of advertising intensity ... and accounting measures of profitability." And high profitability will translate into higher markups.

Product differentiation across sectors and countries

The degree of heterogeneity of products is much smaller in developing than in developed countries, because of the level of development, the importance of the primary sector (which produces rather homogeneous goods), the relatively high share of low-tech and low-quality manufacturing goods and the small expenditures on advertising and R&D in developing countries (Barker, 1977; Gordon, 1998; Murphy and Schleifer, 1997). When income per capita increases, the demand for higher-quality goods and services and product differentiation rise and with that the willingness and ability to pay higher prices. Thus Amsden (1997) argued that market failures related to production increase when economies develop because firms become more knowledge-based and brand names, product differentiation and patents become more prevalent. There is some evidence in support of this postulate. Van Ark (1992, p. 21) for example noted that, when manufactured goods are compared across countries to calculate PPPs, "relatively high matching percentages of output were achieved in countries such as Brazil, Mexico and Korea." Similarly, "supermarkets in the United States carry from 10,000 to 20,000 items and brands, while in many countries the number would be under 1,000" (United Nations, 1992a, p. 30; although this of course also reflects product variety, not just product differentiation).

The scope for product differentiation increases with development, but the scope is the highest for consumer services and some producer services and the smallest for such goods as raw materials, water, gas, fuels and electricity because they are rather homogeneous. It can thus be expected that product differentiation is lowest in the primary sector and public utilities. Manufactured products are somewhere in between primary commodities and services (see, for example, Oliveira Martins, 1993). However, many products that originate in the primary sector are fairly homogeneous at the production stage but become differentiated at the retail stage, for example through packaging and supplementary services by retail outlets (Chamberlin, 1960, p. 63; Lancaster, 1987) and this differentiation of primary goods occurs increasingly when a country develops. Transportation, storage and communications is also a rather homogeneous sector within but not across countries. In transportation, for example, there are different classes in trains and planes within countries, but one passenger mile by train in western Europe is quite a different service from one passenger mile in India. Likewise, a telephone call in the United States is different from one in Nigeria, where malfunctions are very common.

Product differentiation among many producer and consumer services is quite large and increases fastest with the level of development and could thus explain to some extent the relatively high prices for services in developed countries. Product differentiation among services is partly a result of the direct contact between the consumer and the producer of several services. Yotopoulos and Floro (1992, p. 305) argued that

> [t]he *differentia specifica* that fixes a point in the continuum between goods and services in this case is trust. Transactions in goods establish rights over objects and the appropriability of these rights may be possible with relatively small transaction costs. Transactions in services, on the other hand, involve the obligation by a party to deliver according to certain specifications. This means that services are usually more "customised" than goods, i.e., the product is intrinsically differentiated so that the market invariably is imperfect.

Gaynor (1994) for example contended that professional services are inherently heterogeneous, nontradable and subject to asymmetric information between consumer and producer and therefore subject to market power (see also Satterthwaite, 1985).

Product differentiation by way of varying the quality of the service provided plays an important role in consumer services such as the retailing sector, restaurants and hotels (Baumol and Blinder, 1982, pp. 413, 481). The Russian Tearoom is altogether a different service provider from the coffee shop around the corner, just as Harvard University is different from a community college and an urban specialty store from a street vendor. While quality might be an essential aspect of services, it is also very difficult to assess (Holmstrom, 1985, p. 197). Moreover, the costs of switching from one producer of services to another can be quite high, for example in the case of a bank, architect, school or doctor (Thompson, 1992, p. 155). Thus information is asymmetric and trust and reputation are crucial.

Akerlof's market for lemons has shown that there is a danger that low-quality services will drive out high-quality services in the case of asymmetric information as sellers (the only ones who know the true quality) will only offer those services with their value below the price (Akerlof, 1970; Holmstrom, 1985). But firms can differentiate their services by providing information on their quality. Services, partly because of direct contact between consumer and producer, have ample opportunities to establish consumer goodwill and brand loyalty, which are important means to differentiate services from competitors, and create entry barriers and market power. Holmstrom (1985) discussed, for example, how a firm can reduce the information asymmetry. He mentioned contracts contingent on the outcome of the service provided, reputation in the form of communication among consumers and improved signaling through advertising. Several aspects of his models create the possibility for significant market power, such as when the price acts as a signal for quality, when the incentive for reputation building is dependent on the rent and when reputation is related to the size of the seller.

Trust is particularly important in the financial sector. Diaz-Alejandro (1985) for example argued that banks are not butcher shops. Banks want loans to be repaid, hence they do not lend to just anyone and they do not lend all a customer wants at the prevailing interest rate. Trust and the borrower–lender relation play a crucial role. A customer with a track record at one bank cannot easily switch to another bank. Nor will banks lower interest rates to attract borrowers from other banks because they will only attract the customers that are "bad risk" as a lower interest rate for a "good risk" customer will be matched by the present lender. Asymmetric information necessarily creates market power for lenders. Credit is therefore rationed and the market invariably imperfect (Stiglitz and Weiss, 1981; Yotopoulos and Floro, 1992). Hence more banks do not mean more competition and a higher concentration ratio might not be related to interest rates. It is therefore less surprising that the evidence on the relation between structure and performance (profit or interest rates) for the financial sector (mostly in the United States) is mixed (Osborne, 1992; Savage, 1992; Shaffer, 1992).

In conclusion, the potential for product differentiation increases with development but is particularly prevalent for services. Product differentiation is therefore possibly an important factor in explaining the relative high prices for services in developed countries.

5.3 WAGES AND LABOR POWER

One particular important determinant of prices is the wage rate. Wages enter directly into the price equation (3.2) as a cost component but also influence the markup. The total effect of wages on prices thus depends on the extent to which the positive relation between wages and prices is compensated by the negative relation between wages and markups. Higher wages can lead to lower markups and still have a positive effect on prices.

The traditional models often assume that wages are equalized across sectors through labor mobility, but this assumption is clearly contradicted by the facts (see section 2.2). Wages differ across sectors and across countries. Some of the reasons suggested in the literature for interindustry wage differentials are education or skills of the worker, productivity, profitability, plant or firm size, technology, capital intensity, institutions (such as minimum wages), market power and union membership or the bargaining power of labor (Amadeo, 1994; Dickens and Katz, 1987; Gibbons and Katz, 1992; Lewis, 1986; Morrison, 1994; Rebitzer, 1993; Velenchik, 1997; Wood, 1978).

Across countries, wages could be equalized through trade or migration. Yet "factor price equalization [across countries] has not been tested: we know it isn't so" (Leamer, 1992, p. 2). Increased imports have had only a small effect on wages in the importing countries, despite all the talk of globalization (Cline, 1997; *The Journal of Economic Perspectives*, **9** (3), 1995 and **12** (4), 1998).

Moreover, labor is not very mobile and can therefore be considered a part of the nontradable component of prices (Wei and Parsley, 1995). Wages might differ across countries for similar reasons as they might differ across sectors. The educational attainment and skills of the worker, labor productivity and union membership are especially important. Most of the factors explaining wages across sectors and countries are discussed in the other chapters in this book as direct or indirect determinants of prices, except labor power and the effect of the costs of living.

A factor that becomes important when wages across countries are compared is the effect of the price level of consumption on wage determination. For example, wages are higher in New York than in rural areas partly because the costs of living are higher. This can be extended to cross-country comparisons. Employers do not pay United States wages in Bangladesh, nor are Bangladeshi wages comparable to those of the United States because the costs of living are different. To compare wages across countries, nominal wages need to be deflated by the PPP of the consumption component of GDP to get real wages – parallel to deflating wages by the consumer price index to compare wages over time. In this regard, social institutions and historical factors play an important role (Arestis, 1996, p. 125). In the United States, for instance, there seems to be less of a concern about people falling to the bottom than in Scandinavian countries. "Swedish citizens regard the social value of the welfare state and related wage compression and other egalitarian policies to be worth their total social costs" (Rosen, 1996, p. 740). Hence the real wage rate is partly determined by a minimum bundle of consumption goods, in addition to factors such as labor productivity. This bundle is not further defined but is largely determined by institutional and historical factors. The point is that this bundle is larger in Sweden than in the United States and larger in the United States than in Bangladesh.

This argument is related to the effect of wage relatives. Workers compare their wages to those of other workers and set a target real wage that they try to reach in the bargaining process with employers (Arestis, 1992, pp. 164–9; Wood, 1978). The extent to which this comparison will have an effect on the wage rate also depends on the institutional and historical circumstances that influence the solidaristic character of the wages. For example, wages might be relatively high in consumer services in certain developed economies, despite low labor productivity, so that wages in this sector will at least allow for the necessities to survive. This minimum will probably be close to the official minimum wage in many countries. Yet in many developing countries (enforcement of) a minimum wage is restricted to the formal sector. Moreover, wages in agriculture can be below a socially accepted minimum because agricultural workers, who live in rural areas, are usually able to cultivate some food. This is especially important in the developing world, where the agricultural sector is large.

The effect of wage dispersion on price levels has been investigated by Lipsey and Swedenborg (1996). They argued that, if the possibilities for substitution among skilled and unskilled labor are absent, the country with large wage differences will have lower prices for services intensive in unskilled labor and high prices for services intensive in skilled labor. "The country with a 'solidaristic' wage policy, on the other hand, should face high prices for low-skill services and low prices for high-skill services" (Lipsey and Swedenborg, 1996, pp. 2–3). Their regression results confirmed that lower dispersion among wage levels leads to higher overall prices.

Institutional factors also play a role in explaining why wages are rigid (even when unemployment exists). Wage rigidity is one reason why prices are rigid because it is an important cost component. Multi-year labor contracts and collective bargaining agreements that cover a number of years are institutions that lead to rigid wages. These contracts can be in nominal or real terms. Wages can also be rigid because the productivity of workers depends on the real wage they receive and consider fair (efficiency wages) or because the costs of hiring and training unemployed workers (outsiders) outweigh the lower wages that would be paid to the unemployed while the hiring and training costs could increase as a result of harassment and the noncooperation of current workers (insiders) (Gordon, 1990). In developing countries, however, the existence of multi-year real wage contracts is less common and real wages have been more flexible downward, particularly in countries with high inflation rates.

The model emphasizes a distributional conflict between employees and employers and thus incorporates elements of the conflict theory of inflation, which emphasizes the real income targets of workers and capitalists (Kotz, 1987; Rosenberg and Weisskopf, 1981; Rowthorn, 1977). The extent to which workers can meet their targets is dependent on the power of unions while these targets are determined, for example, by skills and past income. Powerful labor unions can reach a good bargain for workers and limit the profits and the markup in an industry (Arestis, 1996; Thompson, 1992). The extent to which employers are willing to meet workers' demands depends on the ability of firms to pass wage increases on to consumers, which is dependent on the structure of product markets. The combined effect of a lower markup and higher wages on prices is not immediately clear. If all firms in a sector face the same wage increase it is more likely that they will pass it on to consumers. This is the case, for example, when there are strong labor unions in an industry. If one firm faces a strong union, that firm may keep its price constant and suffer a lower markup (Arestis and Milberg, 1993–4, p. 174; Levine, 1986). Thus higher wages can lead to lower markups and higher prices and the total effect of labor power on prices is either zero (when the markup is cut proportionally when wages increase) or positive (when at least part of the higher wages are translated into higher prices).

The nonmanufacturing sectors and developing countries (except the public sector) have typically lower degrees of unionization than the industrial sectors and developed countries, respectively. The reason is that organizing the labor force is easier when larger numbers of workers with the same interests are concentrated, which is the case in urban areas, in the public or formal sector and in the manufacturing sector (Lewis, 1986, pp. 8, 125–6, 134–6). Of course, the freedom of organization and legal requirements are also important factors (Fuchs, 1968, ch. 6; ILO, 1985, pp. 10–12).

5.4 OVERVIEW OF THE PATTERN OF THE DETERMINANTS OF THE MARKUP

To summarize the arguments, Table 5.1 presents the four factors and their differential impact on the markup. This table reads as follows. The first column under each heading shows the relative effect across countries of the factor affecting the markup and the second column the relative effect across sectors within a country. The "aggregate" row is the effect of the factor on the markup at the aggregate (economy-wide) level across countries. The plus and minus signs refer, not to a sign expectation for the regression analysis, but to the value of the variable; that is, a negative sign indicates that the variable has a relatively small value.

The total capital–output ratios are one to two times larger in developed countries than in developing countries, hence a minus sign on the "aggregate" row under the capital–output heading in the table. (But the capital–output ratio in all sectors and in all countries has an expected positive sign on the markup in a regression equation.) The low capital–output ratio in developing countries is caused by a relative low capital–output ratio in agriculture (a minus sign in the first column for agriculture). The capital–output ratios in the non-agricultural sectors are basically similar across countries (although probably slightly smaller in developing countries). Across sectors, the highest capital–output ratios are found in transport and communication (part of producer services, hence a positive sign in the second column for producer services) and public utilities, and the lowest are found in consumer services. Manufacturing does not have the highest capital–output ratio in the economy, but the ratio is higher than in consumer services in both groups of countries and agriculture in developing countries (a positive sign in the second column for manufacturing).

There is less scope for product differentiation in developing countries for all sectors (minus signs in the first column under the heading product differentiation) except for primary commodities, where the scope will be about the same across countries (equal sign for agriculture in the first column), although at the retail level the scope is considerably larger. The scope for

Table 5.1 *Sectoral effects of markup determinants on prices in developing and developed countries*

	Capital–output		Product differentiation		Concentration		Unions	
Agriculture	−	−/+	=	−	=	−	−	−
Manufacturing	=	+	−	+	+	+	−	+
Consumer services	=	−	−	++	=	−	−	−
Producer services	=	+	−	++	+	+	−	−
Aggregate	−	na	−	na	+	na	−	na

Notes: First column under a heading refers to relative effect across countries; second column refers to relative effect across sectors; −, +, = refer to negative, positive or neutral effect in developing country relative to developed country for the first column and one sector relative to the average in the second column; na = not applicable.

product differentiation is largest for services (plus signs in the second column). Thus, if the markup were solely determined by product differentiation, product differentiation alone could explain the fact that prices in general and service prices in particular are lower in developing countries (see, for example, Table 8.3) because the scope for product differentiation is lower in developing countries, particularly for services in developing countries.

Compared to other sectors, concentration is expected to be the highest in manufacturing and some producer services (plus signs in the second column under the heading concentration). Smaller countries have higher concentration ratios, particularly in manufacturing and producer services (plus signs in the first column), if it is assumed that the size of the market increases with GDP per capita, which is reasonable because only the GDP of the largest developing countries (Brazil, China, India, Mexico and the Republic of Korea) is larger than that of the smallest developed economies.

Unions are likely to be less powerful in developing countries (minus signs in the first column under unions). Across sectors, unions are most powerful in the manufacturing sector (a plus sign in the second column under unions).

Adding up, the variation of the markup will be greater across sectors than across countries. The largest markups will be in manufacturing and producer services, owing to a high capital–output ratio, high product differentiation and high concentration. Agriculture in developing countries will have the lowest markup because the three factors have a small effect in this sector. For consumer services, the three factors have opposing effects and the markup will therefore probably be somewhere in between the extremes, although the effect of product differentiation is likely to outweigh the effect of concentration (particularly in developed countries). Across countries, the markups for agriculture and consumer services are likely to increase when GDP per capita increases, because the capital–output ratio in agriculture and product differentiation in consumer services increase. For manufacturing and producer services, the behavior of the markup when GDP per capita increases is not unambiguous: product differentiation has a positive effect, but concentration a negative, although here as well the effect of product differentiation is likely to outweigh the effect of concentration.

NOTES

1. This might be a plausible assumption given the mobility of capital across borders. Clague (1991, p. 514) cited a study by A.C. Harberger who found that annual rates of return to capital do not differ in a systematic way across countries. See also Pasinetti (1981, p. 143).
2. Patents as a barrier to entry will not be examined directly. The number of patents is likely to be correlated to research and development expenditures which are discussed as a determinant of product differentiation. See, for example, Scherer and Ross (1990, pp. 126–7, 360, 625–6) for a discussion of this issue. It is likely that enforcement of patents is less intense in developing countries and hence barriers to entry are lower. The importance given by developed countries to trade-related intellectual property rights (TRIPs) in the Uruguay Round multilateral trade negotiations exemplify this.

6. Economies of scale

We will start with some methodological issues. In contrast to many other authors, we will distinguish between returns to scale and economies of scale, following the entries in *The New Palgrave: A Dictionary of Economics* (Baumol, 1987; Eatwell, 1987; Silvestre, 1987). Returns to scale refer to the situation where all inputs are multiplied by a positive scalar and output increases by the same or by a larger amount than the value of the scalar while the output and input proportions are kept constant. The scale is just replicated. Increasing returns to scale can only result from area–volume relations. Classic examples are pipelines and warehouses. Increasing returns to scale are most prominent in transportation and storage, but they are also important in the chemical industry. By definition, only constant or increasing returns to scale can exist because decreasing returns can only derive from a fixed input that cannot be replicated (land for example) but then we speak of diseconomies of scale.

Economies of scale mean that costs per unit of output decrease when output is expanded while output proportions are kept constant. Likewise, diseconomies of scale indicate that average costs increase when output expands. Economies of scale can result from area–volume relations, indivisible inputs, fixed costs, sunk costs, set-up costs or division of labor. An indivisible input, such as machinery or management, can be interpreted as a fixed cost, a set-up cost or a sunk cost and the increase in output means that the cost of this input is spread over more units of output. Diseconomies of scale result from substitution between inputs as a fixed input prevents replication. Finally, economies of scope refer to cost reductions as a result of changes in the output mix while the input proportions are kept constant. In this case, cost reductions result, for example, from a fuller use of capacity when more than one output is produced at a plant or farm.

Economies of scale can affect different components of the price equation (3.2). The input–output coefficients, labor requirements, wages and the markup can all change as a result of economies of scale. For input–output coefficients and labor requirements, the effect is very direct: the variable costs of inputs per unit of output decline by definition when these two factors are subject to economies of scale. If a firm is operating at less than full capacity and output expands, the markup can be higher because the fixed costs, which are financed by the retained earnings that are part of the markup, are spread out over more units of output (see Figure 3.1). If in a larger economy different technology is installed that enjoys economies of scale, total (variable and fixed) costs are lower but the share of fixed costs in total costs could increase as a result of a larger capital–output ratio and the markup could therefore increase as well, although prices can be lower. The relation between scale and wages is ambiguous. Wages can decline in the case of economies of scale because a larger company may have more bargaining power, forcing wages to decline. Yet there is evidence that wages are higher in larger firms, perhaps because of higher productivity and profits of which workers extract a share (see, for example, Anderson Schaffer, 1998; Green *et al.*, 1996).

6.1   EXTERNALITIES

Externalities can cause economies of scale but not increasing returns to scale. Costs fall if inputs are not enumerated or prices of inputs decline. A distinction is usually made between real or technological and pecuniary externalities (Bohm, 1987; Scitovsky, 1954; Stewart and Ghani, 1991). Real externalities refer to a situation where the production function of one economic agent is affected by the activities of other economic agents, without being accounted for in inputs purchased or in prices. Examples are technology transfers or research and development (R&D) spillovers (Geroski, 1991; Griliches, 1992; Scherer, 1982; Stewart and Ghani, 1991), human capital formation (Rosenstein-Rodan, 1943; Schultz, 1961) and environmental effects (usually negative) from which is abstracted here.

Pecuniary externalities refer to situations where prices faced by one economic agent are affected by the activities of others. Pecuniary externalities are transmitted through the market. Typical is the situation where an investment in industry A leads to lower prices of the output of A (for example, as a result of internal economies of scale). If products of A are used by industry B as inputs, profits of B will increase or prices could be reduced. A classic example is railroads (Fishlow, 1965; Justman and Teubel, 1991). The development of the iron industry reduced the price of rails, stations and trains and the development of railroads reduced transportation costs for all kinds of industries. These positive externalities, however, were not included in the decisions to develop the iron or railroad industry.

Externalities exist because they are not (or cannot be) internalized through the market. Externalities occur when an incomplete set of Arrow–Debreu–McKenzie markets exist (Datta-Chaudhuri, 1990, p. 27).[1] In particular, pecuniary externalities occur when there are no future markets accounting for future price reductions that result from the activities of others, as in the case of railroads.[2] Externalities are a subset of market failures. However, this is not to suggest that noncompetitive pricing causes externalities. When real or pecuniary externalities exist, agents benefit whether prices are set at marginal cost or not. "If the producer does not have complete monopoly power over the invention, the price received will not reflect all of the social benefit, since part of it will be passed on to consumers in the form of lower prices per equivalent quality or performance unit" (Griliches, 1988, p. 18; see also Scherer, 1982, pp. 627, 632). (This assumes that the monopolist knows the social benefits and can set the price accordingly, which is rather farfetched.)

Real externalities affect several components of the price equation. Observed input–output coefficients, labor requirements or capital stock are smaller than the true size because inputs are not accounted for. Pecuniary externalities will result in lower input prices, whether capital rentals, wages or prices of intermediate goods.

Linkages

Externalities are sometimes compared with Hirschman's linkages (Bohm, 1987; Hirschman, 1987; Stewart and Ghani, 1991). The example of pecuniary externalities between the iron and railroad industry makes the comparison clear. With regard to real externalities, linkages between users and producers are an important source of productivity increases (Pack and Westphal, 1986, p. 110; Stewart and Ghani, 1991, p. 575). Even between competitors, real externalities can be important because knowledge can often not be kept secret, labor moves and information is exchanged, for example through journals and meetings (Bartelsman *et al.*, 1991; Griliches, 1992, pp. S36–7; Justman and Teubel, 1991, pp. 1170–73; Stewart and Ghani, 1991, pp. 574–5).

Real or pecuniary external economies can also result from the expansion of the economy. When the size of the market grows, specialization within and among firms becomes possible, often resulting in vertical disintegration. New firms can be founded by individuals who learned the trade from their former employers (a real externality) (Bohm, 1987; Gershuny and Miles, 1983, pp. 49, 56; Hansen, 1990, p. 469; Pack and Westphal, 1986, p. 110; Stewart and Ghani, 1991, p. 578; Weiss, 1984, pp. 40–47; Young, 1928, pp. 537–9). When goods and services are contracted out and are now bought by everybody, while previously they were only available to the producer, externalities result from the fact that the costs of acquiring the skills and capabilities are not borne by all prospective buyers. This phenomenon takes place at every stage of development. At early stages, farmers market their own products. But when the market grows, economies of scale resulting from the division of labor can be realized and (wholesale and retail) traders take over the task of marketing. Indeed, "the division of labor is limited by the extent of the market" (Smith [1776] (1986), bk 1, ch. 3). This is similar to the development of new goods and services that involve fixed set-up costs and therefore generate internal economies of scale and pecuniary externalities as well. (Although it is controversial whether new markets and new goods should be considered real or pecuniary externalities. See Dixit and Stiglitz, 1977; Pack and Westphal, 1986; Romer, 1986, p. 1005; 1989, pp. 5–6.) This process can be visualized "in terms of an input–output matrix ... whose cells ... progressively fill up, in large part because of backward and forward linkage effects" (Hirschman, 1987, p. 206).

6.2   ECONOMIES OF SCALE ACROSS SECTORS

The relative importance of internal and external economies of scale cannot be solved without addressing the aggregation problem. "External economies become internal as the aggregation level rises" (Caballero and Lyons, 1989, p. 2). We are interested in prices on a rather aggregate sectoral level, increasing the relative importance of internal economies of scale.

Economies of scale are specific to a sector because technology is specific to a sector (see section 5.1). Several authors have emphasized the importance of economies of scale within the industrial sector. Marshall (1920), Smith [1776] (1986) and Young (1928) have all underscored the significance of economies of scale, "but as far as I can see, none ... paid enough attention to the fact that the relationship is peculiarly associated with industrial activities" (Kaldor, 1967, p. 15; see also Kaldor, 1972). Both internal and external economies of scale are important in manufacturing. Indivisibilities and fixed costs associated with machinery give rise to internal economies of scale in certain subsectors but differences among the subsectors within manufacturing are substantial (You, 1995). The chemical industry faces large economies of scale but textiles, leather and wood processing show only small economies of scale (Nolan, 1996). External economies of scale result, for example, from the fact that capital goods branches are important in transmitting technical progress and from the fact that the possibility for specialization and division of labor among different branches or firms is greater within manufacturing than within other sectors of the economy and they thus have high intrasectoral linkages (Weiss, 1984). Moreover, despite the likely underreporting of R&D expenditures in the service sector, a large share of total R&D is spent in the manufacturing sector (UNCTC, 1989, pp. 14–16). Hence R&D spillovers originate to a large extent from the manufacturing sector (Griliches, 1992; Nadiri, 1993; OECD, 1996a). There is indeed evidence that economies of scale at the level of total manufacturing are largely the result of external economies within manufacturing (Caballero and Lyons, 1989; Khan and Bilginsoy, 1994; Weiss, 1984).

Agriculture has few economies of scale inherently internal to the farm because land can be tilled with a hoe and with a tractor and plow and inputs such as labor, land, fertilizers, seeds and pesticides are highly divisible (Hayami and Ruttan, 1985, pp. 147, 157). However, economies of scale in agriculture exist because of R&D spillovers, access to credit and economies of scale in such areas as processing, extension, irrigation and transportation (Griliches, 1992; Binswanger *et al.*, 1995). These activities are partly outside the agricultural sector and thus refer to externalities from other sectors. External economies of scale originating in agriculture are particularly important when food prices decline, allowing higher real wages in other sectors.

Public utilities involve huge capital expenses to generate and distribute electricity or deliver water and gas and economies of scale are therefore important in this sector. Some services and public goods are inherently producing externalities. A public good is a good that can be used by any agent if it is available to one (nonexcludable) and its use by one does not preclude the use by others (nonrivalness or joint consumption). Hence an individual cannot adjust the level of consumption of a public good unilaterally and this inflexibility effectively destroys the possibility of a market for a public good (Samuelson, 1954; Varian, 1978, pp. 197–200). Examples of pure public goods are defence and sea-defence walls. However, the criteria of nonexcludability and nonrivalness do not have to hold strictly to generate externalities. For example, the producer can exclude some consumers (or consumers can exclude themselves) from using bridges or public education or charge a price for access. Charging a price or exclusion can be expensive or difficult and access can be given at zero (or close to zero) marginal costs, as Dupuit already showed in 1844. Indeed, because of large indivisibilities and decreasing average costs, infrastructure involves pecuniary external economies, even if infrastructural services were private "goods." Many public goods are free of charge and do not enter into the profit calculations of firms. As long as there is some degree of nonrivalness and nonexclusivity, external economies exist. Of course, economic agents can be taxed by the government to cover the costs of building and maintaining infrastructure, but then the familiar free-rider problem operates. In the case of public goods, individuals have no incentive to reveal the price they are willing to pay because they can consume the public good anyway, while the costs are borne by others. In sum, public goods generate economies of scale external to the firm (or industry). Many studies have indeed confirmed the contribution of public inputs to productivity increases (Aschauer, 1989; Gramlich, 1994; Munnell, 1992).

Many services have public good characteristics and therefore generate externalities. Services from infrastructure (such as bridges, roads, ports, communication systems and irrigation systems), public education, research and development, extension services and health care have public good characteristics. A lesser known example is the financial sector. The liquidity, mobility and acceptability of bank-issued transaction accounts and the monitoring and selection functions of the financial sector have the characteristics of public goods and therefore generate externalities (Diaz-Alejandro, 1985; Stiglitz, 1993).

Several services are also likely to generate externalities for other reasons than public good characteristics. In contrast to Eatwell (1982, ch. 3), Kaldor (1967) and Khan and Bilginsoy (1994), who assign primary importance to the manufacturing sector as a source of externalities and an engine to growth, we attribute additional significance to the producer services. First of all, there is the problem of accurate measurement of the prices of services because units and quality are more evasive concepts for services than for commodities (Gershuny and Miles, 1983, pp. 33–40; Inman, 1985). Griliches (1992, p. 30) described the case where a new hybrid corn variety is supplied by the public agricultural research sector at marginal cost but the officially measured seed input price index is not adapted for quality change. In that case, the measured productivity growth will show up in agriculture. But if hybrid corn is supplied by the seed industry at marginal cost and input prices are adjusted downward because of higher quality, then the nominal value of the seed output will be deflated by a smaller number and the real output will be higher and the productivity increase will show up in the hybrid seed industry. This is a normal pecuniary externality for agriculture. (See Denison, 1989, and OECD, 1996a, for the same problem with regard to computers.) If competition forces the price to decrease, the benefit will shift. Hence "how it [a particular innovation] actually will show up in our national product accounts will depend on the competitive structure of the industry and the ingenuity and energy of the 'price' reporting agencies" (Griliches, 1992, p. S30). And as noted in the introduction of Chapter 4, this energy might be too low to correct for the bias, favoring the productivity growth measures of the manufacturing sector (Denison, 1989).

Second, some service sectors face large indivisibilities, causing internal economies of scale that become pecuniary external economies if prices decrease. The transport, storage and communication sectors especially have relatively large fixed costs. Moreover, transport, storage and wholesale trade also enjoy returns to scale resulting from area–volume relations. In the financial sector there are also several (peculiar) reasons for economies of scale (Baumol, 1992). Some authors have suggested that investment in human capital and R&D is also subject to fixed costs and therefore generates economies of scale, and that knowledge is almost by nature subject to externalities. Edwards and Starr (1987) argued that labor in general experiences indivisibilities, because of set-up cost, training time and switching cost, and will therefore generate scale economies. The higher the skills, the higher the indivisibility, especially affecting the professional and business services.

Urban Externalities and Intermediate Service Inputs

The importance of externalities originating from services has recently attracted significant attention in the literature. Some new growth theorists have argued that, even if sectors such as business services, education and research do not enjoy economies of scale, their real externalities generate economies of scale in other sectors, particularly in manufacturing (Lucas, 1988; Romer, 1986). Others emphasized the importance of internal economies of scale in intermediate service inputs and the lower prices for the input-using sectors they yield (pecuniary externalities). In fact, this is an argument underlying some new growth theoretical models that focus on multiple equilibria with one equilibrium at a low output level. In this underdevelopment trap the market is too small to develop the intermediate service inputs that are subject to pecuniary externalities (Francois, 1990; *Journal of Development Economics*, **49** (1), 1996).

Externalities originating from intermediate services have also been used in models to explain phenomena such as industrial agglomeration, industrial structure and divergence of growth rates. Abdel-Rahman and Fujita (1990) developed a model in which intermediate services are subject to economies of scale to explain industrial agglomeration. Cities are associated with a larger variety of intermediate services, such as repair, maintenance, engineering, transportation, communication and legal, financial and advertising services. Higher variety causes larger economies of scale and lower prices of these services. Hence "the larger the variety of intermediate services the higher is the productivity of the traded-good industry" (Abdel-Rahman and Fujita, 1990, p. 165). Similar arguments have been made by Faini (1984), Hansen (1990), Krugman (1991) and Rodríguez-Clare (1996), and Clague (1991) found some empirical support for them.

One determinant of the size of the market and therefore of economies of scale is population density (Abdel-Rahman and Fujita, 1990; Vassilakis, 1987). Transportation costs are generally smaller for any good if geographical distances are smaller. This is especially important with regard to the services that require close or frequent contact between the producer and the consumer. Moreover, some have argued that most innovations originate in cities and that real externalities are often dependent on physical proximity (Jacobs, 1969). People get ideas from each other and this process is greatly stimulated by geographical proximity. Indeed, many industrial districts have benefitted from a high concentration of different kinds of manufacturing and services companies (Krugman, 1991; Lucas, 1988, pp. 35–9). Likewise, Miyagiwa (1991) argued that scale economies in education result from externalities made possible by close geographical proximity.

The importance of geography is supported by evidence (Quigley, 1998).

Jaffe (1989) and Jaffe *et al.* (1992) showed, for example, that real externalities, proxied by patents, are inversely related to geographical distances, and Ciccone and Hall (1993) showed that density of economic activity is positively related to productivity. Deckle and Eaton (1994) found that externalities diminish with geographical distance. Agglomeration thus more than offsets congestion effects.

At this point it is possible to make some general observations based on the above analysis. This is partly summarized in Table 6.1, which displays the information as in Table 5.1. Let us first look at the last two columns, which compare sectors relative to each other. Internal economies of scale are more prevalent in manufacturing than in service sectors with the exception of transport, communications and storage and wholesale trade, which are part of producer services (plus signs in the third column). Second, externalities originate to a large extent in the manufacturing and the producer services (plus signs in the fourth column). Pecuniary externalities mainly result from the manufacturing, transportation, storage, communication and trade sectors and real externalities from the manufacturing and producer services. Third, as far as economies of scale are present within the service sector, they are mainly within the intermediate producer services and generate externalities. Fourth, population density and degrees of urbanization are associated with both internal and external economies of scale, because they influence the size of the market and create externalities.

Table 6.1 Economies of scale across sectors and across countries

	Across countries		Across sectors	
	Internal	External	Internal	External
Agriculture	0	=	–	–
Manufacturing	– –	+	++	+
Consumer services	=	0	– –	0
Producer services	– –	++	+	+
Aggregate	– –	+	na	na

Notes: –, +, = refer to negative, positive or neutral effect in developing country relative to developed country for the first two columns and one sector relative to the average in the last two columns; 0 indicates effect is nonexistent or negligible; and na = not applicable.

The first two columns of Table 6.1 compare economies of scale across countries. In developing countries, external economies from manufacturing and producer services are relatively large compared with internal economies (plus signs in the second column) while in developed countries the reverse is more likely (that is, internal economies of scale are relatively large in manufacturing and producer services; minus signs in the first column). Indivisibilities are relatively large in small economies and these occur especially in services, such as education, research, extension, roads, railroads, airports and telecommunications. "[T]he size of indivisibilities necessary to create such [pecuniary] externalities is relative to the size of the market. The smaller the market the greater the likelihood of such externalities. Pecuniary externalities, therefore, may be particularly relevant to less developed economies" (Stewart and Ghani, 1991, p. 577). Psacharopoulos (1994) estimated, for example, that in Africa, where educational attainment is the lowest in the world, the social returns to primary and secondary education in Africa are the highest in the world. The role of intermediate services in the creation of a development trap also highlights the importance of externalities generated by services. Another reason for relatively large externalities in developing countries is the relatively large potential for technological spillover effects from developed countries (or multinationals) (Hikino and Amsden, 1992).

NOTES

1. General equilibrium analysis has a great many problems dealing with economies of scale and externalities. In fact Sraffa (1926) showed that perfect competition is incompatible with (dis)economies of scale. Debreu (1959, p. 49) explicitly abstracted from them. Varian (1978, pp. 203–7) pointed out that creating a full set of markets and assigning property rights will not be able to account for public externalities. Some argued that perfect competition is still possible if economies of scale are internal to the industry but external to the firm. But when economies of scale are internal to the firm, competition has to be imperfect (Silvestre, 1987).
2. According to Rosenstein-Rodan (1943) and Scitovsky (1954), this is an important impediment to economic growth and they argued therefore for investment coordination by the government. This idea has recently been revived by Murphy *et al.* (1989).

7. International trade

Taking account of international trade does not fundamentally change the markup pricing model developed in Chapter 3. Prices are still basically determined by costs and market power. In a way, international trade just expands the size of the market, except that geographical distances lead to additional transportation costs and that borders are associated with trade barriers.

It has long been argued that prices of tradables would be equalized across countries by competition if there were no barriers to trade. Underlying all traditional explanations for the price level is the assumption that these barriers are large or even infinite for nontradables and small or even zero for tradables. Nearly all authors, after recognizing that trade barriers exist for tradables, ignore them and focus on the main point of their model. This is partly a result of the neoclassical gist of most traditional models, emphasizing price flexibility. By implication, trade barriers are an easy excuse when price differences for tradables across countries – or within countries for that matter – do occur.

Trade barriers have received little attention in the theoretical and empirical literature on price levels; an exception is Lipsey and Swedenborg (1993). But trade barriers are quite important. Equalization of prices of tradables can be impeded by natural barriers (international transportation costs), policy-induced barriers (protective measures) or other barriers associated with borders. All these barriers enhance market power for the domestic firms operating behind them, similar to the effect of geographical distances within a national economy (see section 5.2), but can also enhance the market power of foreign companies. Yet market power of domestic and foreign firms still exists even if these barriers are zero and is a major explanation for differences in price levels across countries.

Empirical evidence again and again fails to support the law of one price, which is an essential building block of the purchasing power theory of exchange rate determination and states that the domestic price of a good should be the same as the foreign price expressed in the same currency (Dornbusch, 1987a; Engel and Rogers, 1995; Faruqee, 1995; Froot and Rogoff, 1994; Goldberg and Knetter, 1997; Isard, 1977; Ito *et al.*, 1997; Rogoff, 1996). Isard (1977, p. 942) looked, for example, at a number of the most detailed categories of highly traded goods, including some which were rather homogeneous, and concluded that "the law of one price is flagrantly and systematically violated."

All the discussions and concerns about globalization notwithstanding, the evidence shows that, at least for the market of goods and services, this process has not advanced far enough to talk about a global economy, despite a doubling in the ratio of world exports to GDP between 1980 and 1997, from 0.10 to 0.20. International markets are not well integrated and do not show spatial arbitrage, rejecting the law of one price (Faruqee, 1995, pp. 856–7). Thus two recent surveys concluded that "[i]nternational goods markets, though becoming more integrated all the time, remain quite segmented" (Rogoff, 1996, p. 655) and that "[n]ational markets for goods are better viewed as segmented than integrated" (Goldberg and Knetter, 1997, p. 1270).

This chapter will argue that the impact of international trade on domestic prices is smaller than traditional theory contends because of foreign market power or because domestic firms increase output rather than prices in response to tariffs on final goods. If there is an effect it will largely be on the markup, not on costs. Tariffs on intermediate goods are considered cost increases and will translate into higher domestic prices.

7.1 FOREIGN MARKET POWER

Even if all transportation costs, tariffs and the like are zero, prices are unlikely to be equalized for all goods because of different market structures. When international markets are considered, a distinction needs to be made between primary commodities and other internationally traded goods and services, as primary commodities play a larger role in international trade than in domestic markets, accounting in 1996 for 22 per cent of world exports. McKinnon (1979, pp. 74–7, 133) distinguished tradables I and tradables II. He defined tradables I as manufactured goods whose prices are controlled by their producers and have a sizeable service component in the final product, but here tradables I will cover all goods and services except primary commodities. Producers of tradables I are price setters, prefer constancy and are able to set the price fairly independently of similar (although not identical) products owing to product differentiation. Tradables II are homogeneous primary commodities whose prices are set on international markets, such as commodity exchanges. Producers of tradables II are price takers. As long as price discrimination and preferential arrangements are not dominant, the prices of tradables II should be rather uniform as a result of arbitrage across international borders. Hence if the law of one price holds for any product category it is for tradables II (Isard, 1977; Rogoff, 1996).

Price determination of internationally traded goods and services follows the price equation (3.2) as discussed in Chapter 3. However, for tradables II, the markup is not endogenously but exogenously determined. The markup is a residual category, given the price on the world market, transportation costs and production costs.

Prices in the markup pricing model of Chapter 3 refer to domestically produced goods and services. Intermediate imported inputs are included in the input–output matrix or accounted for separately, as indicated in equation (3.2). Final demand imports are treated as competitors. The markup of domestic producers is partly determined by the extent of competition from final demand imports, similar to domestic competition from domestic producers. A firm would assess its market power vis–à–vis its domestic and foreign competitors and set the markup. Hazledine (1990) presented a model in which domestic prices (p_d) respond to a weighted average of import prices (p_m) and domestic production costs (c_d):

$$p_d = \gamma p_m + (1 - \gamma) c_d. \tag{7.1}$$

Here c_d is comparable to ($l\,\mathbf{w} + \mathbf{A}'\,\mathbf{p} + \mathbf{m}$) in equation (3.1). Hazledine hardly discussed the determinants of the weight γ but, in our model, γ – and the markup – are partly determined by trade barriers, such as transportation costs and tariffs, and by concentration and product differentiation of imports in comparison to domestic goods. In general, γ could be zero for goods and services that are absolutely not tradable and γ could be close to one for tradables II.[1]

Market power plays a role in international markets, just as in domestic markets. Barker (1977) was one of the first to examine the implications of product differentiation for international trade, but research has progressed only slowly since then. Similar to the domestic market structure, the more imports are differentiated and the larger the market share of imports, the higher the market power of foreign producers. Domestic producers will compare their market power with the market power of foreign producers and assess price elasticities and substitutability of its products for domestic and foreign products. In our model γ would generally be (close to) zero as domestic firms prefer price stability and are less likely to react to a price change of a competitor, domestic or foreign, unless it is a permanent price increase such as a tariff (see below). Feinberg (1996, p. 42) argued that imports in general are likely to be less closely substitutable for domestic products and that domestic firms have therefore less need to cut prices in response to imports. Foreign firms, like domestic firms, would like to avoid price wars. Yet the international equivalent of a price war, dumping, has been a source of international trade disputes, partly because antidumping measures are among the few protective measures allowed under the World Trade Organization rules. Foreign firms, similar to domestic firms, can dump goods and services at low prices on the domestic market in order to increase market share or eliminate domestic producers. However, again similar to the domestic case (the threat of) an international price war can lead to collusion and price fixing. There is, indeed, evidence that (the threat of) antidumping measures has had exactly that effect (*The Economist*, 7 November 1998; Graham and Richardson, 1997, p. 27).

Foreign market power is indeed rather important, even for tradables II. A few countries, transnational companies or some traders control the prices of many commodity markets (for example, cocoa, diamonds, oil and uranium), permitting manipulation, as the Hunt silver case of 1979–80 and the Sumitomo copper case of 1996 exemplify (Helleiner, 1979; Helpman and Krugman, 1989, p. 1; Morisset, 1998; Sylos-Labini, 1984, pp. 160–61). For example, three to six transnational corporations handle more than 70 per cent of global exports of almost all commodities (World Bank, 1994a, pp. 40–41). Moreover, Yeats (1990a) showed that former French colonies in Africa pay about 20 to 30 per cent more for their imports of iron and steel (homogeneous tradables!) from France than for imports from other countries. Similar premia were found for former colonies of Belgium, Portugal and the United Kingdom on imports from their former colonial powers. A number of variables measuring market power and market size were correlated with these premia. Yeats also discussed, but did not test, some other factors, such as the tying of aid, transfer pricing, the extent and variability of government intervention and the weak infrastructure compared to the market size, which makes startup costs relatively high.

Foreign market power has also proved critical in explaining the relation between exchange rate fluctuations and import and export prices. The literature on these subjects, which has emerged over the last decade or so, has provided ample evidence that foreign market power reveals itself in pricing-to-market behavior and incomplete exchange rate pass-through, two sides of the same coin. Exchange rate pass-through refers to the response of import prices to exchange rate movements and pricing to market refers to price discrimination across export markets that is induced by exchange rate variation. Knetter has extensively researched this topic and argued that exporters might reduce a markup when a currency depreciates to maintain constant prices in local currencies. Evidence supported this hypothesis, particularly among German, Japanese and United Kingdom exporters (Knetter, 1992a). Several other researchers have confirmed incomplete pass-through of exchange rate changes and pricing-to-market behavior (Arestis and Milberg, 1993–4; Athukorala and Menon, 1994; Feenstra *et al.*, 1996; Feenstra and Kendall, 1997; Froot and Rogoff, 1994; Knetter, 1989; 1992b; Malueg and Schwartz, 1994; Naug and Nymoen, 1996; Rangan and Lawrence, 1993; Rogoff, 1996, p. 654).

Some authors confirmed a relationship between the pass-through or pricing to market and measures of market power. Feenstra *et al.* (1996) for example found evidence that pass-through depends on market share. Similarly, Campa and Goldberg (1995) showed that industries with a low markup absorbed a lower proportion of an exchange rate change than industries with a high markup. Two other studies showed that the extent of pass-through is significantly related to measures of market structure: concentration in Lee (1997) and product differentiation in Yang (1997).

The extent of foreign market power depends partly on international trade barriers. Menon (1996) found a strong significant negative effect of nontariff barriers on pass-through in addition to a negative significant effect from foreign control of imports and a positive significant effect from the elasticity of substitution between domestic and imported goods. Knetter (1994) showed that nontariff barriers allow an exporter of a differentiated product to reap rents. He found that German exporters charge higher prices (measured at the port of exit) for exports to Japan, a market where nontariff barriers are prevalent, than for products exported to Canada, the United Kingdom and the United States. Aw (1992) found evidence that Taiwanese footwear exports into the United States enjoyed a markup as a result of the voluntary export restraint (VER) imposed by the United States. (See also Feinberg, 1996, p. 43; Goldberg and Knetter, 1997.)

Elimination of trade barriers could reduce foreign market power but would not eliminate it. Foreign market power is one important reason why an increase of international trade and a reduction of policy-induced trade barriers do not necessarily lead to more equal prices across countries. Van Wegberg *et al.* (1994) argued that a reduction in trade barriers might actually decrease competition because the likelihood of collusion across markets (countries) among firms increases as the frequency of contact increases. A similar argument was made by Rothschild in 1944 (King, 1994, p. 432). The formation of the Single European Market in 1992, for example, did indeed lead to a wave of mergers and acquisitions and an increase in concentration. Moreover, competition policies within countries are more strict than across countries, allowing, for example, export cartels to dominate international trade (Graham and Richardson, 1997). Indeed, the issue of internationally coordinated competition policies has reached the agenda of the international community and a working group within the World Trade Organization has been set up to explore the matter, although the work program and terms of reference are heavily contested. Some have argued that the World Trade Organization should obtain jurisdiction over competition laws. In the meantime, coordination of competition laws is increasing within regional trade agreements (Hoekman, 1998).

7.2   POLICY-INDUCED BARRIERS

In a post-Keynesian model a distinction is made between barriers imposed on final good imports and on intermediate good imports as their effect on prices of domestically produced goods is different (Norman, 1996). In addition, the effect of trade barriers on imported goods has to be separated from the effect on domestically produced goods. The imposition of a tariff on final goods is similar to a price increase by a rival firm. As discussed in Chapter 3, a domestic firm with excess capacity is likely to increase its market share and expand production, rather than change prices, to accommodate the shift in demand towards domestically produced goods if a tariff is imposed, but the effect depends partly on price elasticities (Norman, 1996; Ocampo and Taylor, 1998). This is also the case when non-tariff barriers are imposed as they will also lead to a demand shift toward domestic producers.

On the other hand, a tariff on intermediate imports is a cost increase and is likely to lead to higher final goods prices, particularly when rival firms face the same price increase.[2] Norman (1996, p. 523), thus stated that

> under the PKTP [Post Keynesian Theory of Protection], the effect of protection on the prices of finished products is small and arises entirely from materials tariffs, while the production effects depend entirely on demand factors. In the standard neoclassical tariff theory, the results are quite obverse: product prices are fully (or mostly) reflected in finished-goods prices, and materials tariffs never are, while the production effects are entirely supply determined.

There are some cases where a domestic firm is more likely to raise prices and not to increase output in response to higher tariffs on final demand imports. When tariffs are considered permanent, domestic firms can experience tariffs as a form of reduced competition. With fewer imports, the concentration and the market power of domestic firms are increased and they are likely to increase the markup. Moreover, if the exporting foreign firm is a price leader, a higher tariff might be followed by domestic producers raising prices as well; that is, γ being closer to one (an effect that is likely for both final and intermediate imports). On the other hand, higher tariffs on final goods can lead to foreign exporters cutting their markups to keep prices in the export market constant, an effect similar to the pricing-to-market behavior. If import prices remain the same, there is no reason for domestic producers to react to a tariff increase. In oligopolistic markets as for tradables I, higher tariffs are more likely to lead to higher prices for imports than for tradables II because the substitutability for tradables II is higher unless there is a supply constraint on the production of tradables II.

Neoclassical theory argues that policy-induced barriers can lead to higher prices in two ways. First, tariffs, nontariff barriers and foreign exchange shortages raise the domestic price of imports (Leff, 1979, p. 719; Norman, 1996, p. 515). As argued, post-Keynesians disagree. Second, when domestic firms are less exposed to international trade, whether through imports or exports, they are supposedly less efficient and show lower productivity growth. Reducing protectionism and allowing competition through imports will force firms to reduce costs and increase productivity. Exports also force firms to keep costs and prices low, otherwise they will lose market share.

The theoretical case for the second argument rests largely on the argument that allocative efficiency will increase when prices are market-based and controls on prices of goods, services, finance and foreign exchange are lifted. This argument has several limitations. Efficiency gains are static and can only be realized once, that is as long as productive factors are relocating. Moreover, the theory of the second best has shown that it is only possible to predict an increase in efficiency if all controls are totally removed. If competition is imperfect the increase in efficiency is more dubious. Imperfect competition means that domestic prices can be larger than marginal costs and protection allows domestic prices to be above international prices. Hence it is possible that marginal costs are below international prices, which makes the efficiency gains from squeezing the import-substituting sector, resulting from import liberalization, doubtful. In sum, the effects of liberalization are likely to be small in contrast to what adherents of neoclassical theory often assume (Rodrik, 1992b; 1995).

Another argument in favor of liberalizations pertains to the dynamic effects of learning and technical change. The theoretical foundations for this argument are weak, however. Some argued that imports increase the variety of goods, the availability of intermediate goods and technology and can facilitate the transfer of know-how. Others, however, argued that technology is only tradable up to a certain degree and that the existence of dynamic benefits associated with externalities and learning by doing constitute a case for protection (Dornbusch, 1992; Liang, 1992; Miyagiwa and Ohno, 1995; Pack and Westphal, 1986; Rodrik, 1992b; 1994, p. 39). Empirical evidence is inconclusive. For example, it is not always clear in which direction causality runs. Do governments tighten restrictions when economic growth declines? (Rodrik, 1995; World Bank, 1992, pp. 23–4).

Tariffs on final demand imports generally lead in our model to higher domestic output (or higher markups) and in the neoclassical model to higher costs. There is, however, one mechanism through which exposure to international trade can directly lead to lower domestic costs (and prices) that is consistent with the markup pricing model. That is the case when economies of scale exist. If production is subject to internal economies of scale and the domestic market is small, exports allow firms to expand production to levels where they benefit from lower costs per unit of output. Likewise, if foreign firms benefit from economies of scale, imports of intermediate inputs and capital goods allow domestic firms to use cheaper inputs.

In conclusion, while the neoclassical economists argue that protection leads to higher costs, post-Keynesians contend that protection on final demand leads to higher output. Domestic firms will increase output when tariffs are raised on final demand imports because of shifting demand but will increase their prices if tariffs are leveled on intermediate imports because it is a cost increase. However, higher tariffs could leave import (and thus domestic) prices unchanged and lead to lower foreign markups if pricing-to-market behavior is prevalent. They could also lead to higher domestic markups if higher tariffs are considered a permanent reduction in competition or if foreign firms are price leaders. The arguments are summarized in Table 7.1.

Table 7.1 Effects of a tariff

	Import price	Import volume	Domestic output	Domestic price	Domestic markup	Foreign markup
			Effect of tariff on:			
Tariff on final demand						
PKTP: demand shift	+	–	+	0	0[a]	0
if permanent tariff (less competition)	+	–	0	+	+	0
if foreign price leader	+	?	0	+	+	0
if pricing to market	0	0	0	0	0	–
Tariff on intermediate imports						
PKTP: cost increase	+	?	?	+	–/0	0
if permanent tariff (less competition)	+	–	0	+	+	0
if foreign price leader	+	?	0	+	+	0
if pricing to market	0	0	0	0	0	–

Note: [a] Unless average costs decline (see Figure 3.1).

As discussed in Chapter 2, Kravis *et al.* in their publications included the variable openness, defined as the average ratio of exports plus imports to GDP, in their regressions. This is consistent with the neoclassical contention that exposure to trade, whether exports or imports, will lead to costs cutting and lower prices. Clague (1988b) argued – as also mentioned in Chapter 2 – that there is no theoretical explanation for the inclusion of this variable in the regression equation. We argue that the ratio of intermediate imports to GDP and the tariff rate on intermediate imports are better candidates for inclusion in regression equations. Moreover, final demand imports and tariffs on them affect domestic output and markups rather than costs.

7.3 TRANSPORTATION COSTS

The effect of transportation costs on prices is somewhat different from the effect of policy-induced barriers because natural barriers like this change only slowly and affect all imports, though some potential imports disproportionately (nontradables).

As discussed in the introduction to Chapter 2, equating nontradables with services (and construction) is problematic. Many services, such as restaurants and hotels for tourists, banking, accounting, insurance, transport and communications, are traded and to an increasing extent, amounting to 20 per cent of world exports of goods and services in 1996. In fact, there is no good or service that is absolutely nontradable – even the stereotypical haircut is tradable (Marris, 1984, pp. 42–3). Paradoxically, transportation costs for certain services, such as information services, that are exported by way of telecommunications technology are relatively low. The increase in the trade in services, ranging from travel services to data processing in the Caribbean and software development in India, has been partly a result of the convergence of computer, telecommunications technology and the internet (Hoekman and Primo Braga, 1997; Messerlin and Sauvant, 1990; United Nations, 1987a, pp. 64–9; 1993, pp. 74–5; 1996, ch. XII; UNCTC, 1989, pp. 27–8). The increasing trade in services has demanded the attention of policy makers and has led to the General Agreement on Trade in Services at the conclusion of the Uruguay Round of multilateral trade negotiations. Construction is also traded in many cases and international construction companies often bring employees of all levels to foreign projects. Moreover, many goods have large service components, such as trade and retailing, and some services have important goods components, for example transportation. Engel and Rogers (1994) even consider all final goods nontradable because of the retailing and marketing services that bring goods to the market. Finally, there are some goods, such as certain perishables, coarse grains and rootcrops, that are hardly traded internationally (Brinkman and Gabriele, 1992, pp. 17–19; Delgado, 1992; Kyle, 1992; Kyle and Swinnen, 1994).

In sum, the strict dichotomy between tradables and nontradables should be abandoned and replaced by a continuum of tradability determined by transportation costs and input–output relations (De Gregorio *et al.*, 1994; Marris, 1979, p. 55). Even when transportation costs are relatively large, it does not mean that prices of nontradables are determined in isolation from international competition as foreign direct investment can provide nontradables to another country. A significant share of TNCs are indeed active in the service sector (UNCTC, 1990; United Nations, 1996, p. 289). Yet, as argued in section 5.2, TNCs probably have significant market power in the host country, especially in developing countries.

Homogeneous primary commodities (tradables II) are at one end of the continuum and their prices could be equalized across countries as a result of competition if transportation costs and other trade barriers are zero (and if market power is absent). However, once transportation costs and tariffs are taken into account, price equalization of tradables II across countries becomes problematic again. Costs to move a good from one place to another include handling, loading and unloading, physical moving, insurance and the like. These costs can become prohibitively high when the price in the place of destination is lower than the price in the place of origin and transportation costs are added. This is especially likely in developing countries where infrastructure such as roads and ports is scarce or in poor repair.

The extent to which transportation costs can be added to the final sales price of an imported good or instead are borne by a lower markup depends on the market power of the producer. For tradables I, higher transportation costs are more likely to lead to higher import prices, while for tradables II it is more likely that higher transportation costs will lead to lower markups. In a landlocked country, prices are higher because transportation costs are high for all imports. But two identical products (tradables II) are likely to have identical prices even if one is imported from far away and the other from close by and the markup will bear the transportation costs (unless foreign market power is significant; see section 7.1). On the other hand, similar but not identical products (tradables I) imported from two different places, one far away and one close by, will have more of their transportation costs added to the production costs when the products are more differentiated and the producers have more market power. Hence, even in the same country, similar but differentiated products can have different prices.

The prices of domestically produced goods and services are affected by transportation costs in two ways: first through the use of intermediate imported inputs, just like the case of tariffs; second, domestic firms, say, in a landlocked country set higher markups because final goods imports are more expensive as a result of high transportation costs and they therefore face less competition from abroad and have more market power. This is similar to the case where tariffs have been in place for a long time and are unlikely to change, just as transportation costs do not vary much over time and can be considered a structural factor.

Export data are reported "free on board" (f.o.b.; value at customs frontier, including export duties) and imports are in the majority of countries reported including "costs, insurance, freight" (c.i.f.; excluding duties and subsidies) (IMF, 1990a, p.v; United Nations, 1968, p. 116). Hence the difference between c.i.f. and f.o.b. are transport, insurance and sometimes finance charges (Yeats, 1990b, p. 137). The International Monetary Fund (1990b) published annual c.i.f. to f.o.b. ratios, which are of course always greater than one, to calculate the balance of payments on an f.o.b. basis. The variation of these ratios across countries is quite large and partly determined by distances to western Europe and North America, which have had the lowest ratios in the world (between 1.01 and 1.07 in 1992). The ratios are high for landlocked countries. Malawi, for example, had the highest ratio, at 1.667.

The combined effect of domestic and international transportation costs on the price of a good can be large. Transportation costs can double the price of a good, but typically account for 10 to 20 per cent of the value of exports (Amjadi and Yeats, 1995; Byerlee and Morris, 1993, p. 807; Maddison, 1983; Morisset, 1998; OECD, 1992a, p. 79). Rousslang and To (1993) showed that, for the United States in 1987, tariffs accounted for 4 percentage points, international freight for 5.2 percentage points, domestic freight for 3 percentage points and wholesale margins for 9.7 percentage points of the average nominal protection rates. And this even understates the true importance because the authors assumed that the wholesale margins on imports were the same as for domestic shipments while they are likely to be larger owing to higher inventories and additional costs associated with differences in languages, currencies and laws.

Transportation costs differ notably between countries. Amjadi and Yeats (1995), for example, showed that transportation costs are substantially higher for sub-Saharan Africa than for other exporters of the same goods as a result of low volume and small economies of scale, market power and poor infrastructure. If transportation costs are high for exports, they are also likely to be high for imports. Because of the existence of economies of scale in transportation, the total volume of imports is included as an independent variable in the regression analysis in Chapters 10 and 11.

Only recently has research begun to investigate explicitly the role of transportation costs in the failure of the law of one price to hold. Engel and Rogers (1995, p. 21), for example, argued that the variability of relative price indices for different locations (cities within North America and countries in Europe and Asia) should be small if the law of one price holds and found evidence that the law of one price fails partly because of geographical distances and that policy-induced trade barriers only play a weak role (see also O'Connell and Wei, 1997; Parsley and Wei, 1996).

In sum, transportation, insurance, processing and distribution costs are reinforcing price differences across countries, although perhaps less so for homogeneous, primary commodities (tradables II). The producer will pass more of these costs on to consumers when it has more market power, which exists even for primary commodities but might be smaller (see section 7.1). In addition, geographical distances and transportation costs create market power (see section 5.2).

7.4 OTHER BARRIERS

There have been a number of studies on the determinants of international trade and purchasing power parities over time that argued that borders are an important obstacle to trade and goods arbitrage, in addition to variables such as distance and tariffs. One can think of an array of factors associated with borders, such as asymmetric information, exchange rate uncertainty, rules, regulation, legal barriers, cultural differences and language barriers. These factors enhance the market power of the domestic firms compared to foreign firms.

Domestic firms, for example, are likely to have information advantages. The investment needed to acquire knowledge about local conditions can be relatively high for a foreign firm compared with the size of the market. A foreign investor that operates behind these barriers has significant market power, particularly in small markets. The existence of one foreign producer might discourage other firms from entering the market because of the relatively high set-up costs.

There is some evidence in support of these factors. For instance, McCallum (1995) found that trade between Canadian provinces was much larger than trade between a Canadian province and a state in the United States, even when accounting for distance and GDP per capita. He concluded that borders matter (see also Helliwell, 1997; Wei, 1996). Similarly, for price differences over time, Engel and Rogers (1994, p. 24) calculated that "crossing the border is equivalent to adding ... 7182 miles between cities." McCallum (1995) and Engel and Rogers (1994) just added border dummies to the regression equations and found them to be significant. Wei and Parsley (1995) attempted to explain partly why these dummies are important. They argued that a common language would facilitate goods arbitrage. However, a dummy variable that takes the value of one if the trade partners share a common language was not significantly different from zero. Wolf (1997) also found a bias towards intrastate trade as opposed to interstate trade within the United States, casting some doubts on the importance of borders as they signify language, cultural or institutional differences. Two factors remain to explain this pattern, according to Wolf: industrial policies of states and the effect of formal and informal trade barriers in combination with spatial nonlinear transaction costs.

As this field of inquiry is relatively young, many questions remain unanswered, yet the empirical significance of the results so far is interesting and these kinds of barriers – yet to be clarified – are also likely to affect price levels across countries.

NOTES

1. Hazledine (1990) assumed three values for the weight γ: 0.55 (Canadian School, pricing-to-market model and mainstream industrial organization), 0.05 (monopolistic competition) and zero (economist's model). The zero value for the economist's model, which he described as being close to a perfect competition model ("markets work" and elasticities are large), is odd. A value of one would be more appropriate.

2. Norman (1996, p. 519) argued that the substitutability for intermediate imports is higher than for final goods. This is probably the case as intermediate goods are likely to be less differentiated. One could ask, however, why domestic producers competing with intermediate imports do not expand production when tariffs increase. This is ignored by Norman (1996). The answer might be that the expansion of production in sectors producing intermediate inputs is constrained by supply and not by demand, as agriculture and mining account for a large share of intermediate inputs.

PART II

Empirical Evidence

8. From model to data to testing

In this chapter we will examine the price level data that we are trying to explain and discuss how we are going to test the theory we have developed in the previous chapters. The price level data are presented and explored in section 8.1. The second section discusses how the data on price levels can be used to test our model. This section specifies a generic regression equation that is used in various incarnations in the next three chapters to test different aspects of our model.

8.1 THE PRICE LEVEL DATA

The most comprehensive source for the international comparison of prices is the United Nations International Comparison Programme (ICP), formerly the United Nations International Comparison Project. The ICP uses the expenditure approach for the measurement of purchasing power parities (PPPs) and publishes PPPs for expenditure components of GDP. In contrast, the International Comparison of Output and Productivity (ICOP) project of the University of Groningen, led by Professor Angus Maddison, has calculated PPPs by industry of origin. PPPs covering all sectors for a limited number of countries have recently become available (Pilat, 1994). (Appendix 1 discusses the methodological differences between the industry-of-origin approach and the expenditure approach.) This book uses data from the ICP and the ICOP.

The PPPs from these two data sets are divided by exchange rates to yield price levels, which can be directly compared across sectors and countries. On the basis of price level data, one can, for example, conclude that in 1985 bread and cereals were cheaper in France than in the United States but fuel and power were more expensive, or that meat was twice as expensive in Japan than in the United States. Or one can infer that the price level for investment in machinery and equipment was 121 for Nigeria in 1985, which means that investment goods were 21 per cent more expensive in Nigeria than in the United States. But this price level was 73 in Thailand and investment goods were thus cheaper in Thailand than in the United States. Comparisons within countries are also possible. The price level of clothing and footwear was 70 in Nigeria and 49 in Thailand in 1985, implying that these items were cheaper than in the United States but also that, compared to clothing and footwear, investment goods were more expensive in Nigeria than in Thailand (United Nations and EUROSTAT, 1994).

How reliable are these data? Apart from the index-number problem, which is discussed in Appendix 1, the quality of the data depends to a large extent on the matching of goods and services across countries and the pricing of the equivalent outputs. Much effort and care has been put into this exercise (Appendix 1; Maddison and Van Ark, 1987; United Nations, 1992a; Van Ark, 1992), yet it remains, admittedly, less than perfect. This is particularly true for certain services, the so-called "comparison-resistant services." These are services where the output unit is hard to define. This is the case for education, health care and many government services. These services are also often paid for through government budgets and are not transacted through the market, and our pricing model is therefore not applicable anyway. Yet for the goods and services that are not comparison-resistant, the ICP and ICOP data are the best available and certainly satisfactory despite their imperfections.

Table 8.1 Price levels of GDP components of selected countries

	Agriculture 1975	Manufacturing 1975	1985	GDP 1985	C 1985	I 1985	G 1985
Argentina	38	106	108	54	53	84	40
Brazil	90	96	79	42	40	53	34
Egypt				38	47	159	14
India	94	106	97	40	43	68	17
Kenya				35	35	71	20
R. of Korea	143	81	65	59	60	72	37
Mexico	104	110	99	44	41	61	30
Nigeria				85	92	105	46
France	130	143	97 [a]	83	87	83	75
Germany	135	137	101 [a]	88	89	85	85
Japan	227	83	68	102	103	120	77
Netherlands	120	118	88 [a]	79	79	86	71
United Kingdom	110	103	101 [a]	75	78	85	63
United States	100	100	100	100	100	100	100

Notes: C = consumption; I = investment; and G = government.
[a] 1984.
Sources: First three columns: Maddison (1990); other columns: Summers and Heston (1991), data diskette.

Exchange rates usually deviate from PPPs and are therefore misleading when used in international comparisons of incomes. PPP-converted GDP of a low-income country can be two or three times as high as exchange-rate-converted GDP. "In general, the use of exchange rates as conversion ratios will overstate the GNP of high-income countries and understate that of low-income countries, with the degree of overstatement increasing as income levels rise" (Balassa, 1964, p. 596).

For certain components of GDP these deviations are much higher. As a result, price levels, defined as the ratio of the purchasing power parity to the actual exchange rate, are very different from country to country. Table 8.1 shows some selected price levels. With the exception of agriculture in Argentina and Japan in 1975, price levels for goods-producing sectors were within 50 per cent of the price levels in the United States. Price levels for expenditure components were usually lower. For almost all developing countries, expenditure price levels were less than 50 per cent of US price levels. Price levels were the lowest for government expenditures and the highest for investment.

Low price levels for developing countries are usually attributed to the low prices of nontradables. This is illustrated in Table 8.2, where the expenditure shares in international prices (I$) and in national prices (NC) are compared for 1980 (NC as a percentage of I$). It shows that tradables, such as food and investment goods, were generally cheaper than total GDP in developed countries (NC as a percentage of I$ is decreasing when GDP per capita rises). Nontradables (construction and services) were cheaper than GDP in developing countries (NC as a percentage of I$ is increasing when GDP per capita rises). But prices of construction were relatively high in developing countries in contrast to prices of services. Investment (investment goods and construction) was relatively expensive compared to other GDP components in poorer countries (see also Nuxoll, 1994). Some have suggested that the reason for this might be that investment goods are imported at high prices because of tariffs (Summers and Heston, 1991, p. 337; United Nations and EUROSTAT, 1987, p. 16; Yeats, 1990a). This question will be further explored in Chapter 11. In interpreting the data, one has to keep in mind that tradables contain nontradable components, such as transportation and trade margins. For these reasons, a model that explicitly incorporates intermediate inputs and imports can shed some light on these issues.

Table 8.3 gives a more detailed breakdown of the price levels of the expenditure components for three different regions in 1985. For almost all categories, the average price level for developing countries was lower than the average price level for developed countries and the average price levels for service categories for developing countries were among the lowest. Thus, not only were nontradables cheaper in developing countries, but nearly all goods

Table 8.2   Expenditure shares of GDP in national and international prices, 1980

GDP per capita (% of US)		Country Income Groups					
		< 10	10–20	20–35	35–60	60–75	> 75
Number of countries		12	14	10	10	8	6
Food	NC	36.2	29.3	23.7	18.7	11.7	9.8
	I$	34.0	27.8	22.4	18.3	12.2	10.8
NC as % of I$		106	105	106	102	96	91
Domestic	NC	20.6	25.5	28.1	25.1	24.6	23.5
investment	I$	13.3	17.5	25.0	26.4	26.4	25.1
NC as % of I$		155	146	112	95	93	94
Investment	NC	8.5	10.0	6.4	8.6	9.0	8.6
goods	I$	5.7	5.8	4.9	7.5	10.7	10.2
NC as % of I$		149	172	131	115	84	84
Construction	NC	10.2	13.9	14.7	15.1	14.1	13.7
	I$	6.0	10.3	15.0	17.4	14.2	13.7
NC as % of I$		170	135	98	87	99	100
Services	NC	31.5	29.9	29.9	35.7	40.7	41.6
	I$	43.4	37.9	34.1	34.3	39.0	36.9
NC as % of I$		73	79	88	104	104	113
Nontradables	NC	41.7	43.8	44.6	50.7	54.8	55.3
	I$	49.3	48.2	49.1	51.7	53.2	50.6
NC as % of I$		85	91	91	98	103	109

Notes: NC = national currencies; I$ = international prices.
Source: Summers and Heston (1991, p. 338).

and services were. The exceptions were some investment categories, in particular construction, reaffirming the conclusion drawn from Tables 8.1 and 8.2 that the price levels of investment goods and construction in developing countries were relatively high. The variation of investment price levels was rather high as well in developing countries. Moreover, the categories with the highest standard deviations in the developed countries were tobacco and alcoholic beverages, probably the effect of taxes.

Table 8.3 Summary statistics of price levels in 1985 by country grouping (US = 100)

Country groupings	European Union			Developed countries			Developing countries		
Number of countries	10			21			32		
	AV	SD	MM	AV	SD	MM	AV	SD	MM
Private consumption	77	10	41	81	17	67	35	17	82
Food, beverages, tobacco	81	13	49	90	24	80	53	28	122
Food	80	9	38	88	22	71	57	30	138
Meat	105	15	60	114	40	145	110	75	397
Beverages	64	18	55	87	40	135	40	28	105
Alcoholic beverages	65	20	60	91	46	165	39	32	95
Tobacco	109	44	125	111	41	144	48	43	242
Clothing and footwear	85	10	29	92	16	59	32	18	68
Gross rents, fuel, power	61	13	40	63	21	87	22	16	77
Fuel and power	109	14	49	96	24	99	48	17	62
Household equipment and operation	89	7	28	90	13	59	49	28	139
Medical care	51	10	34	54	16	75	23	11	61
Transport and communication	114	23	82	115	25	98	50	21	86
Transport equipment	99	23	69	104	25	80	82	111	653
Operation of equipment	183	21	68	175	40	153	107	51	225
Transport services	64	20	67	68	22	84	22	13	61
Communication	66	29	93	70	28	109	36	11	58
Recreation, education	81	14	51	82	21	85	23	17	88

Table 8.3 (continued)

Country groupings	European Union 10			Developed countries 21			Developing countries 32		
Number of countries	AV	SD	MM	AV	SD	MM	AV	SD	MM
Books, newspapers, magazines	112	26	83	116	46	231	52	22	99
Education	72	16	48	73	23	84	19	17	74
Miscellaneous goods and services	89	11	42	92	19	89	46	26	137
Restaurants, cafés, etc.	101	15	59	107	30	121	59	29	141
Government consumption	66	9	29	69	18	84	37	21	87
Gross fixed capital formation	81	7	23	86	13	57	73	30	145
Construction	81	10	34	84	17	79	93	73	415
Residential buildings	98	18	57	103	27	125	108	72	385
Non-residential buildings	78	9	31	83	17	72	46	28	165
Other construction	61	8	34	65	15	61	138	126	705
Machinery and equipment	83	7	27	90	12	50	70	28	148
Transport equipment	81	19	71	93	21	90	84	76	301
Nonelectrical machinery	92	5	16	95	10	36	80	26	91
Electrical machinery	63	6	20	72	14	47	75	37	125
Gross domestic product	76	9	37	79	16	62	38	17	79

Notes: AV = average; SD = standard deviation; MM = maximum value minus minimum value.
Source: Author's calculation, based on United Nations and EUROSTAT (1994).

Another interesting aspect of these data is the high price levels and the high variance of several food categories in developing countries. Food was even relatively more expensive in developing countries in 1980 than in richer countries (Table 8.2). Meat, for example, was, with construction, among the most expensive in developing countries (Table 8.3). Several factors might play a role, including low productivity in agriculture, protection and tax rates. As mentioned in Chapter 2, food prices have recently attracted some attention from researchers, confirming some of these expectations (Clague, 1992; 1993a; 1993b; Lipsey and Swedenborg, 1993).

One can look at even more disaggregate price levels than those of Table 8.3. However, we have not presented these data but performed a different kind of exercise. It has been argued that the law of one price is most likely to hold for primary commodities (tradables II). If prices of tradables II are more equal across countries, they should be highly correlated. We therefore calculated the correlation coefficients of the price levels of 11 detailed categories of tradables II for each pair of 57 countries for 1980 with data from the ICP as published by the World Bank (1993a). The 11 categories are rice, beef, pork and veal, fish, milk, coffee, tea, cocoa, sugar, liquid fuels and fuel and lubricants. The pattern that emerges confirms that the law of one price is violated even for these commodities. There are some very high correlation coefficients (higher than 0.9) but this does not necessarily reflect integration. High correlation coefficients are found in Africa (a poorly integrated region) as well as in Europe (a highly integrated region). There are also some countries that have only a handful of correlation coefficients higher than 0.4 (Bolivia, Canada, Hong Kong, Indonesia, Japan, Niger, Philippines, Venezuela).

New estimates of PPPs by industry of origin for Japan and the Republic of Korea have recently been published (Pilat, 1994). Table 8.4 shows price levels for all sectors of these two economies in 1985. Price levels were generally lowest in the Republic of Korea, although there are some important exceptions. Mining, for example, was more expensive than in either Japan or the United States and total manufacturing was more expensive than in Japan. Most services were cheaper in Japan and the Republic of Korea than in the United States and cheapest in the Republic of Korea (except for finance), compared with both Japan and the United States. Moreover, the differences between Japanese and Korean price levels of mining and manufacturing, two goods-producing sectors, were the smallest of all sectors although the difference with the United States was larger than for some services. It is also interesting to note that agriculture had a relatively high price level in both countries. The data also confirm that real estate was expensive in Japan (before the asset bubble burst in the 1990s), contributing to the advice "never [to] buy a Japanese camera in Japan" as it makes retail space expensive (see, for example, Knetter, 1994; Marris, 1984, p. 45).

Table 8.4   *Price levels across sectors for Japan and the Republic of Korea, 1985 (US = 100)*

Sector	Japan	Republic of Korea
Agriculture	312	208
Mining	112	114
Manufacturing	73	81
Construction	126	60
Public utilities	172	147
Wholesale & retail trade	107	84
Transport, storage	125	71
Communication	97	35
Finance	99	114
Insurance	73	40
Real estate	226	57
Education	46	17
Health	47	
Other services	98	40
Government	73	38
Total economy	101	66

Source: Pilat (1994, pp. 233, 256).

The evidence on price levels discredits the absolute version of the purchasing power parity theory of exchange rate determination. The absolute version of this theory states that exchange rates will be equal to purchasing power parities, while the relative version claims that changes in exchange rates will be equal to changes in purchasing power parities. The tables show that exchange rates deviate considerably from purchasing power parities. The relative version can more easily be tested by assuming changes in the purchasing power parities to be equal to changes in a ratio of price indices. It can be argued that the empirical relevance of the relative version is larger if transportation costs and tariffs are unchanged. The evidence on the relative version is mixed, however.[1] The relative version has however no relevance for the matter under discussion because it refers to movements over time and is mostly interested in exchange rate determination rather than price determination.

In conclusion, price levels were generally lower in developing countries in the 1980s. This can often (but not always) be attributed to lower prices of some services. The data also highlight that a focus only on tradables versus nontradables is too narrow and that investment goods were relatively expensive in developing countries compared to other GDP components.

8.2 FROM MODEL TO TEST

At this point we have to take the model presented in Chapter 3 and adapt it so that it can be tested. This adaptation is partly based on Kravis *et al.* (1983). Following the price equation (3.2), two price equations can be defined, one for country r ("rich") and one for country p ("poor"):

$$\mathbf{p}^p = (\mathbf{I} - \mathbf{ts}^p\, \mu^p\, \mathbf{A}^{p\prime})^{-1}\, \mathbf{ts}^p\, \mu^p\, l^p\, \mathbf{w}^p + \mathbf{ts}^p\, \mu^p\, \mathbf{m}^p \tag{8.1}$$

and

$$\mathbf{p}^r = (\mathbf{I} - \mathbf{ts}^r\, \mu^r\, \mathbf{A}^{r\prime})^{-1}\, \mathbf{ts}^r \mu^r\, l^r\, \mathbf{w}^r + \mathbf{ts}^r\, \mu^r\, \mathbf{m}^r \tag{8.2}$$

where $\mathbf{p}^r$ and $\mathbf{p}^p$ are vectors as in Chapter 3. If the rich country is the numéraire country, the United States, $\mathbf{p}^r$ is in US dollars. Prices $\mathbf{p}^p$ can be converted at exchange rates (XR) with the United States:

$$\mathbf{P}^p = \frac{\mathbf{p}^p}{\mathrm{XR}},\ \mathbf{W}^p = \frac{\mathbf{w}^p}{\mathrm{XR}}\ ,\ \text{and}\ \mathbf{M}^p = \frac{\mathbf{m}^p}{\mathrm{XR}}\ . \tag{8.3}$$

Substitution of (8.3) into (8.1) gives

$$\mathbf{P}^p = [(\mathbf{I} - \mathbf{ts}^p\, \mu^p\, \mathbf{A}^{p\prime})^{-1}\, \mathbf{ts}^p\, \mu^p\, l^p\, \mathbf{W}^p\, \mathrm{XR} + \mathbf{ts}^p\, \mu^p\, \mathbf{M}^p\, \mathrm{XR}]\,/\,\mathrm{XR}$$

$$= (\mathbf{I} - \mathbf{ts}^p\, \mu^p\, \mathbf{A}^{p\prime})^{-1}\, \mathbf{ts}^p\, \mu^p\, l^p\, \mathbf{W}^p + \mathbf{ts}^p\, \mu^p\, \mathbf{M}^p. \tag{8.4}$$

The ratio of the price vectors, indicating the relative prices between countries, is equal to

$$\frac{\mathbf{P}^p}{\mathbf{p}^r} = \frac{(\mathbf{I} - \mathbf{ts}^p\, \mu^p\, \mathbf{A}^{p\prime})^{-1}\, \mathbf{ts}^p\, \mu^p\, l^p\, \mathbf{W}^p + \mathbf{ts}^p\, \mu^p\, \mathbf{M}^p}{(\mathbf{I} - \mathbf{ts}^r\, \mu^r\, \mathbf{A}^{r\prime})^{-1}\, \mathbf{ts}^r\, \mu^r\, l^r\, \mathbf{w}^r + \mathbf{ts}^r\, \mu^r\, \mathbf{m}^r}\ . \tag{8.5}$$

As described in more detail in Appendix 1, the ICP calculates these ratios across countries. At the most disaggregate level, the result is, for example, five francs per dollar for a loaf of 500 grams of white bread that is water-based, made of wheat flour and not wrapped or sliced. At a more aggregate level, it is possible to compare the prices of bread and cereals, food or consumption in France with the United States. The ratio $\mathbf{P}_i^p\,/\,\mathbf{p}_i^r$ is equal to the price level of expenditure category *i* of country *p* compared to country *r* and is unitless, and $\mathbf{p}_i^p / \mathbf{p}_i^r$ is equal to the purchasing power parity of *i* of country *p* compared to country *r*. Purchasing power parities are expressed as national currencies per international dollars; that is, the price of bread in France relative to the world average price of bread. The world average prices are normalized in such a way that the GDP of the United States in dollars is the same as the GDP in international prices, hence international dollars (see Appendix 1). Thus if, for a certain category in country *p*, the ratio $\mathbf{P}_i^p / \mathbf{p}_i^r$ is larger (smaller) than one, it means that prices of *i* are high (low) relative to those of the United States.

In our model, the ratio of prices has five components: intermediate inputs, the markups, taxes minus subsidies, the labor inputs per unit of output and the wage rates. We showed in Chapter 5 that the markup μ is a behavioral function of three factors. Thus

$$\mu = f(K, MP, LP)$$ (8.6)
$$+ \quad + \quad -$$

where

K = the need to finance investment;
MP = market power; and
LP = labor union power.
LP is also a determinant of the wage rate. In order to operationalize and give empirical content to this function – and thus to the price equation – these three factors are replaced by determinants or proxies that can be measured. Thus $\mu = f(K, MP, LP)$ can be replaced by a function $\mu = g(.)$ with the factors that directly determine K, MP and LP and indirectly determine μ. Function $g(.)$ can be substituted into price equation (3.2), yielding a behavioral equation that can be estimated. At least one proxy for each factor will be included in the regression and the effects of economies of scale and trade barriers on these components are also considered.

Because the price equation is a linear system, equation (8.5) can be estimated in the following form:

$$PL_{it}^p = \alpha + \beta_1 X_{1it}^p + \ldots + \beta_m X_{m\,it}^p + \varepsilon$$ (8.7)

where all terms are relative to the United States, and where PL_{it}^p is the price level for year *ts* in sector *i* and country *p* and where X_{it}^p are independent variables for sector *i*, year *t* and country *p*.

This equation will be used to test our model by means of regression analysis in three different ways, as presented in Table 8.5. The first one analyzes price levels for major economic sectors in Japan and the Republic of Korea, with the United States as the country of comparison. Thus *i* comprises 22 major sectors of Japan and 17 of Korea, ranging from agriculture to community and social services. This test uses data from Pilat (1994), which have never been used before in this kind of study. The second test focuses on the price level of GDP; i refers to total GDP and t to 1980 and 1985; p comprises 57 countries for 1980 and 53 countries for 1985. The third test concentrates on one component of GDP, viz. investment goods. Thus i refers to investment in machinery and equipment and t to 1980 and 1985; p also comprises 57 countries for 1980 and 53 countries for 1985. The second and third test employ data from Phases IV and V of the United Nations International Comparisons Programme (United Nations and EUROSTAT (1986; 1987; 1994); see Appendix 1). Phases IV and V included 60 and 56 countries, respectively, from most regions of the world, although Latin America and the Caribbean did not participate in Phase V (see Table A.1.2). Phases IV and V also covered Hungary, Poland and Yugoslavia, but these three countries were omitted from our sample because our model is not applicable to their economic system.

Table 8.5 Overview of tests

Test	Dependent variable	Sectors i	Years t	Countries p	Data source	Chapter
1	PL_{it}^{p}	22 sectors	1985	Japan	Pilat	9
		17 sectors	1985	R. of Korea	(1994)	
2	PL_{it}^{p}	total	1980	57	ICP	10
		GDP	1985	53		
3	PL_{it}^{p}	investment	1980	57	ICP	11
		goods	1985	53		

In each test, proxies for productivity, market power, wages, economies of scale and trade barriers are included as independent variables. But some variables are either not available at the aggregate level or not available at the disaggregate level. Certain aspects of our model thus cannot be tested at all levels of aggregation. At the aggregate level, the sectoral variation of independent variables (such as intermediate inputs) is lost. On the other hand, aggregate regressions allow the inclusion of some variables that are not available at a sectoral level, for example proxies for external economies of scale, such as degree of urbanization and population density, and proxies for transportation costs, such as geographical distances, c.i.f.–f.o.b. ratios and road densities.

The cross-sector test is particularly suited to addressing the effect of market power and accounts for intermediate inputs by using the marked-up direct and indirect labor requirements. In addition, sectoral economies of scale, interindustry wage differences and the variation of tariffs across sectors are included.

The third test is interesting because it is applied to investment goods, which are tradable and are indeed mostly traded. In the traditional model, the variation of price levels of investment goods across countries can thus only be explained by the nontradable component, trade barriers and transportation costs. A number of variables suggested by our model will be included in the regression.

NOTE

1. Dornbusch (1987a, p. 1080) argued that "evidence on deviations from PPP leaves little doubt that they have been large and persistent." Others argued that there is some evidence that the relative PPP holds in the long run and that it holds somewhat better for effective exchange rates than for bilateral rates and for export and wholesale prices than for consumer prices (Argy, 1981, p. 253; McKinnon, 1979, ch. 6). De Gregorio *et al.* (1994) argued that there is some empirical evidence in support of the relative version for the original six members of the European Monetary System. They found, however, the same bilateral pattern of correlations for tradable inflation as for nontradable inflation. Froot and Rogoff (1994) surveyed the more recent literature and concluded that "there seems to be long-run convergence to PPP ... though most convincing evidence ... comes from data sets that employ some fixed-rate data." This convergence takes a very long time, however, and is only tested for countries that have been continuously wealthy. If developed and developing countries are included, convergence fails as the relative movement of nontradable prices becomes important (see also O'Connell, 1998; Rogoff, 1996; Williamson, 1994, p. 3).

9. Evidence on price levels by sector in Japan and the Republic of Korea

Japan and the Republic of Korea are two countries where the model of Chapter 3 is particularly valid, as oligopolistic conditions are widespread in these economies (Amsden, 1989; Singh, 1998). Both countries have also pursued rather active industrial, trade and competition policies (Amsden, 1989; Matsushita, 1997; Pack and Westphal, 1986; Singh, 1995b; 1998; World Bank, 1993b). These characteristics reveal themselves in the size of the independent variables that will be used in the regression analysis, such as those measuring market power and protection. There are, however, other aspects of these two economies that might be harder to capture in the independent variables. For example, Japan and the Republic of Korea have relied more than other countries on loans for investment finance, as retained earnings might have been insufficient to finance the fast growth of corporations (Singh, 1998). Moreover, the consensual and harmonious culture in these two countries might affect the impact of trade unions on wages (Aoki, 1984; Nakane, 1973; World Bank, 1993b). It will thus be interesting to see to what extent our model will find empirical support in these two countries.

This chapter will test the model of Chapter 3 on sectoral price levels of Japan and the Republic of Korea, using a new data set and allowing the use of the adapted HRR sectoral productivity measures developed in Chapter 4. Before the regressions are discussed, a decomposition of the price equation (3.2) will be presented in order to elucidate the relative weight of the different factors that play a role in the formation of prices.

9.1 COST COMPONENTS

The different parts that make up the price equation (3.2) can be viewed as the outcome of some behavioral equations that, for example, determine the markup and the wage rate. A decomposition of the price equation can show the relative size of the different costs components for each sector. Theory then needs to explain how the behavior of firms can generate these sectoral cost components.

All the variables on the right-hand side of the price equation (3.2) can be quantified by using national accounts data and input–output tables. If the markup is calculated as the ratio of the value of gross output to the sum of the wage bill and the intermediate inputs, following Sylos-Labini (1979), then the equation becomes an identity. This can be shown in the following way. Multiplying equation (3.1) by $\mathbf{Q}$ as gross output gives

$$\mathbf{p\,Q} = (\,\mathbf{ts}\,\mu\mathbf{A'p\,Q} + \mathbf{ts}\,\mu\,l\,\mathbf{w\,Q} + \mathbf{ts}\,\mu\,\mathbf{m\,Q}\,). \qquad (9.1)$$

Manipulation yields

$$\mu = \frac{\mathbf{p\,Q}/\mathbf{ts}}{\mathbf{A'p\,Q} + l\,\mathbf{w\,Q} + \mathbf{m\,Q}}, \qquad (9.2)$$

which can be quantified. Equation (3.2) can thus be decomposed, not unlike growth accounting. The components are ($\mathbf{I} - \mathbf{ts}\,\mu\,\mathbf{A'}$)$^{-1}$ (the indirect inputs, including the markup and taxes and subsidies), $\mu\,l\,w$ (labor costs, that is direct labor requirements multiplied by the wage rate and the markup), $\mu\,\mathbf{m}$ (imported intermediate inputs multiplied by the markup) and $\mathbf{ts}$ (taxes and subsidies).

The results for the Republic of Korea are shown in Table 9.1, from which the following can be concluded. First, on average only 41.5 per cent of the costs were direct labor and imported intermediaries ($\mathbf{ts}\,\mu\,l\,\mathbf{w} + \mathbf{ts}\,\mu\,\mathbf{m}$) and 58.5 per cent domestically produced intermediate inputs (($\mathbf{I} - \mathbf{ts}\,\mu\mathbf{A'}$)$^{-1}$). Direct labor costs accounted only for 19.4 per cent on average but varied between nearly 50 per cent in mining and public administration and 5 per cent in food and beverages and primary metal manufacturing. This illustrates the deficiency of the traditional explanations for price levels that focus on direct labor productivity and wages alone.

Second, the markup varied considerably. The markup can be compared to the expectations about its size as summarized in Table 5.1. Contrary to expectations, the markup was high – indeed the highest – in the agricultural sector. The price level in this sector also happened to be high in 1980: 216 per cent of the US level (see Table 9.1). This partly reflects the fact that a large part of the income in this sector appears as operating surplus in the national accounts; that is, the income/profit, rather than wages, accruing to the farmer who is also the owner. Protection might also play a role. Markups in manufacturing were among the lowest, which is contrary to expectations, although in developing countries, such as the Republic of Korea in 1980, the scope for product differentiation is still rather limited, depressing the markup. It never reached more than 1.17 in manufacturing, while the other sectors (excluding public administration) range from 1.13 to 2.48. Markups were, however, generally higher in manufacturing sectors with high capital–output ratios (for example, nonmetal minerals) or in those producing more complicated products (for example, machinery and miscellaneous

Table 9.1 Cost components of prices by sector in the Republic of Korea in 1980 (percentages, except markup, which is a multiplication factor)

Sector	Price level	Markup μ	Labor		Import		Taxes ts	Total
			lw	μlw	m	μm		
Agriculture	216	2.48	9.7	24.1	2.2	5.5	0.3	29.9
Mining	74	1.38	49.7	68.8	0.6	0.8	-7.6	62.0
Food & beverage	189	1.05	5.0	5.3	10.2	10.7	2.5	18.5
Textiles & leather	101	1.10	12.5	13.7	15.0	16.4	0.6	30.7
Lumber & wood products	86	1.00	12.8	12.8	53.2	53.1	1.9	67.7
Paper, print & publishing	113	1.11	15.7	17.4	16.5	18.2	0.7	36.4
Chemicals	214	1.11	6.3	7.0	42.2	46.7	3.2	56.9
Nonmetal mineral prdcts	114	1.17	13.7	16.0	5.7	6.7	0.6	23.3
Primary metals	161	1.09	4.8	5.2	20.2	22.0	0.1	27.4
Metal products & mach.	90	1.12	14.0	15.6	21.1	23.5	1.8	40.9
Misc. manufacturing	141	1.16	14.9	17.4	9.4	10.9	1.1	29.4
Construction	76	1.13	24.3	27.4	3.8	4.3	2.0	33.7
Electricity, gas & water	327	1.41	11.4	16.1	5.2	7.3	0.7	24.1
Wholesale & retail trade	121	2.15	17.9	38.5	2.3	5.0	-2.7	40.8
Transport, wrhs & comm	128	1.29	24.7	31.9	16.5	21.3	2.6	55.8
Finance, ins & real est	75	1.96	20.6	40.5	0.7	1.3	5.9	47.8
Public admin & defense	44	1.01	49.3	49.9	16.3	16.5	0.0	66.4
Restrnt & hotel, others	32	1.24	41.6	51.6	1.7	2.1	2.2	55.8
Unweighted average	128	1.31	19.4	25.5	13.5	15.1	0.9	41.5

Notes: $\mu = 1 +$ markup rate; $l =$ direct labor requirements per unit of output; $w =$ wage rate; $m =$ imported intermediate inputs; $ts =$ taxes minus subsidies.
Sources: Author's calculation based on data from Bank of Korea (1983), Republic of Korea (1981), Pilat (1991b), Szirmai and Pilat (1990).

manufacturing), which increases the possibilities for product differentiation and confirms our expectations. Markups in producer services, such as wholesale and retail trade and finance, insurance and real estate, were among the highest, which also confirms our expectations, as expressed in Chapter 5.

Third, the import component of costs varies dramatically, from nearly zero in mining and finance, insurance and real estate to about 50 per cent in chemicals and lumber and wood products. Taxes minus subsidies were generally small. However, net taxes reached almost 6 per cent in finance, insurance and real estate, while mining was subsidized on a net basis in the order of 7.5 per cent.

9.2 REGRESSION ANALYSIS

In this section, the price levels of 39 sectors in Japan and the Republic of Korea are regressed on a number of independent variables. The price levels used in this regression are from Pilat (1994), estimated with the industry-of-origin approach (see Appendix 1). Regressing disaggregate price levels by industry of origin is more complicated than regressing aggregate expenditure price levels for countries because in the cross-country regression the numéraire country (the United States) has only one data point for each variable and hence each independent variable does not have to be divided by the value for that variable in the United States (because the regression is unaffected when a variable is divided by a scalar); but when regressed across sectors, the numéraire country has as many data points as sectors for each independent variable and each data point (as opposed to each variable in the case of cross-country regression) thus has to be divided by the corresponding sectoral value for the United States.

The regressions for sectoral price levels can reveal the importance of factors that are not included in the regressions for the price level of aggregate GDP. Testing at the sectoral level is particularly interesting for the pricing model presented in Chapter 3 and the determinants of prices discussed in Chapters 5, 6 and 7 because the different cost components and markup determinants show distinct patterns across sectors. The disaggregate regressions will include sectoral factors such as advertising expenditures, labor inputs, imported intermediate inputs, final demand imports, wages and unionization. Cross-sector analysis also calls for the use of the HRR measures of productivity developed in Chapter 4. The sources and the methods followed to construct the independent variables are described in Appendix 2. Table A.2.1 of the Appendix shows the data.

Table 9.2 provides an overview of the sign expectations of the variables used, which are mostly self-explanatory. There are three variables with ambiguous signs. The discussion in Chapter 7 made clear that the price effect of a tariff on final demand imports is different from a tariff on an imported intermediate input. Data on tariffs differentiated by end-use are not available. Instead, final demand imports and intermediate imports as a percentage of GDP are used as proxies. This, however, introduces some ambiguity as more intermediate imports (IMP_I) can indicate that costs of intermediate inputs are higher, which could be a result of foreign market power, or that foreign producers are cheaper than domestic producers (see section 7.2). The ambiguity of the sign expectation of IMP_D follows from the discussion in Chapter 7: domestic firms are likely to expand production if tariffs on final demand imports increase and imports decline, although an increase of prices cannot be excluded. IMP_D can also reflect market power of foreign companies, as IMP_D could be a proxy for the market share of foreign producers, or imply that domestic firms have less power because the concentration decreases. Foreign market power might lead to higher prices of domestic producers if the foreign supplier is a price leader.[1]

Concentration ratios are perhaps the best measures of market power, but they are not available for all sectors for the three countries. Instead we used the average employment of establishments (AS and AS/Y). There are some problems with these measures, however. There are the usual problems of where to delineate a market with regard to geography and products (see Chapter 5). Exports, for example, are not excluded. The average size of firms would have been better, as one firm can own a number of establishments, but data are not available. Measuring the size of establishments by employment tends to underestimate the true concentration because the largest establishments tend to be owned by multi-establishment firms and because the largest firms tend to have a higher capital–labor ratio (Lee, 1984, p. 69). The signs of AS and AS/Y are ambiguous because they might indicate market power but also economies of scale. A larger firm might have more market power and a larger markup but still have lower prices as a result of economies of scale. A similar effect might also operate for K/Y, which can reflect finance requirements as well as economies of scale (see Chapter 5).

Four dummies are used in the regression. Looking at the price level data (Tables 8.4, 9.1 and A.2.2), it is clear that the price levels for agriculture in Japan and the Republic of Korea and for real estate in Japan are exceptionally high. Dummies are used to account for the possibility that these levels cannot be explained by using the independent variables. The dummy for real estate, for example, can reflect demand pressures on land (see Chapter 3) or the speculation that fueled the real estate prices in Japan in the 1980s (United Nations, 1996, pp. 99–100). The high price level for agriculture might be easier to explain by using the independent variables. It is often argued that high agricultural prices are caused by protective policies. Indeed, the data in Table A.2.2 show that nontariff barriers in Japan and the Republic of Korea and tariffs

Table 9.2　Variable definitions and sign expectations

Variable	Sign expectation PL	Markup	Definition	Explanation for sign expectation
Productivity				
HRR	+	–	marked-up direct and indirect labor requirements	productivity
L	+	–	direct labor requirements	productivity
Labor costs				
UNION	+	–	union members as % of employed	labor union power
WAGE	+	–	average wage	labor costs
Markup				
MARKUP	+		markup	market power
AS, AS/Y	+/–	+	average size of establishment	market power/ economies of scale
ESTABLS/Y				
ESTABLS	–	–	number of establishments	market power
K/Y	+	+	capital–output ratio	finance requirements
I_GR	+	+	growth rate investment	finance requirements
R&D	+	+	R&D expenditures	product differentiation
ADVERTS	+	+	advertising expenditures	product differentiation
Economies of scale				
GDP	–	+	GDP of the sector	internal economies of scale
International trade				
TARIFF	+	+	tariffs	taxes, international competition
NTB	+	+	nontariff barrier	international competition
IMP_D	+/–	+/–	final demand imports	foreign market power/ international competition
IMP_I	+/–	–	imports of intermediate inputs	costs, foreign market power/international competition

Variable	Sign expectation PL Markup		Definition	Explanation for sign expectation
Other				
D_Japan	+	+	dummy = 1 for Japan	unexplained variance
D_AGR_J	+	+	dummy = 1 for agriculture in Japan	unexplained variance
D_AGR_K	+	+	dummy = 1 for agriculture in Republic of Korea	unexplained variance
D_RE	+	+	dummy = 1 for real estate in Japan	unexplained variance

Sources: See Appendix 2 (also gives exact definition and methodology of variables).

in Japan for agriculture are higher than in any other sector. Moreover, labor productivity is rather low, as the high values for HRR and L in Table A.2.2 reveal. A dummy is also used for all observations for Japan in case there are specific factors associated with Japan. The expectation is that the dummy for Japan will be positive, as almost all price levels for comparable sectors are higher in Japan than in the Republic of Korea.

Table 9.3 presents the regression results. All equations are estimated with OLS with a heteroskedasticity-consistent covariance matrix (White method). Regression equation (1) of Table 9.3 includes all independent variables. The results are mixed: 94 per cent of the variance of the price level is explained but other tests, that is, the Jarque-Bera and RESET statistics, indicate that this equation might be misspecified. HRR, L, WAGE and ADVERTS have the expected sign (positive) and are significant. The fact that HRR is significant in addition to L supports our postulate that intermediate inputs have an important effect on prices. AS is significant but its sign is negative, which indicates that the economies-of-scale effect of larger establishments might be larger than the market power effect. AS/Y, which perhaps gives a better indication of the effect of market power, because it relates the size of the establishment to the size of the economy, has a positive sign (as expected) but is not significant. R&D also has a positive sign as expected, but is also insignificant. IMP_D and IMP_I have positive signs, indicating that the foreign market power factor (or cost factor in the case of IMP_I) dominates, but are insignificant. Two of the four dummies have signs as expected and are significant. Two dummies, D_AGR_J and D_AGR_K, have signs contrary to expectations, but this is probably a result of the large values of L in the agricultural sector.[2] Thus, if L has the same effect on the price level of agriculture as in the other sectors, the fitted price level would be higher than the actual price level and the negative dummies correct for this. ESTABLS, ESTABLS/Y, GDP and TARIFF all have signs as expected but are insignificant.

Table 9.3   Regression results for sectoral price level and markup

Dependent variable:	PL	PL	MARKUP	PL
Independent		Regression number		
variable	(1)	(2)	(3)[a]	(4)
MARKUP				62.04 ***
				(4.13)
HRR	6.89 ***	3.85 **	2.87 ***	6.44 **
	(3.54)	(2.56)	(6.39)	(2.48)
L	16.94 ***		1.39 ***	
	(3.69)		(7.18)	
UNION	−0.63		1.93 ***	
	(1.02)		(5.13)	
WAGE	124.03 ***		−20.60 **	80.26 **
	(4.55)		(2.39)	(2.22)
AS	−24.59 **		−8.62 ***	
	(2.21)		(3.19)	
AS/Y	0.52		0.46***	
	(0.73)		(3.61)	
ESTABLS	−3.93			
	(0.76)			
ESTABLS/Y	−0.73		−0.52 ***	
	(1.34)		(6.39)	
K/Y	−0.17	−6.93 ***	3.21 ***	
	(0.05)	(3.17)	(5.77)	
I_GR	−0.01			
	(0.28)			
R&D	0.45			
	(0.04)			
ADVERTS	7.53 ***	10.01 ***	1.18 **	
	(4.12)	(5.46)	(2.25)	
GDP	−11.47			−67.06 *
	(0.31)			(1.95)
LGDP	8.94	−14.01 ***		
	(0.63)	(3.54)		
TARIFF	0.85		−1.12**	1.10
	(0.41)		(2.85)	(0.73)
NTB	−5.17			−8.74
	(0.63)			(1.17)
IMP_D	0.00		−0.01 ***	−0.01
	(0.03)		(3.95)	(0.46)

Dependent variable: PL Independent variable	PL	PL	MARKUP	PL
			Regression number	
	(1)	(2)	(3)[a]	(4)
IMP_I	1.11		−0.97 ***	1.08
	(0.98)		(5.41)	(1.10)
D_Japan	34.18 *	59.66 ***	15.36 ***	69.19 **
	(2.17)	(5.17)	(5.04)	(2.63)
D_AGR_J	−12.79	191.07***	−17.60***	171.10 ***
	(0.18)	(19.82)	(4.27)	(6.93)
D_AGR_K	−324.68 **	94.88 ***		75.14 **
	(2.43)	(5.67)		(2.65)
D_RE	41.76 **	117.61 ***	78.07***	
	(2.61)	(15.31)	(13.19)	
Adjusted R²	0.933	0.891	0.958	0.800
F-statistic	22.63***	37.92 ***	50.59 ***	14.07 ***
Jarque-Bera stat.	1.332	10.594	0.704	1.492
RESET(n) stat.	1.252(3)	0.003(1) **	0.59(2)	0.095(2) *
White statistic	–	0.217 ***	0.696	5.441
Number of observations	35	37	34	37

Notes: Absolute value t-statistics are in parentheses; constant is not shown; L as first letter of variable name refers to logarithmic transformation.
*significant at the 10 per cent level.
** significant at the 5 per cent level.
*** significant at the 1 per cent level.
[a] Estimated coefficients of equation (3) are multiplied by 100; one observation is deleted from equation (3).

On the other hand, I_GR, K/Y, LGDP, NTB and UNION have signs contrary to expectations and are also insignificant. The insignificance of I_GR and K/Y might be a result of the fact that Japan and the Republic of Korea have relied less on retained earnings for the finance of investment (Singh, 1998). The effect of UNION might reflect the more consensual and harmonious nature of unions in these two countries (Aoki, 1984; Nakane, 1973; World Bank, 1993b) or the poor quality of the data (see Appendix 2). The result for LGDP is likely the effect of multicollinearity, as GDP and LGDP have a simple correlation coefficient of 0.872 and LGDP is also correlated (r > 0.5) with AS/Y, ESTABLS, ESTABLS/Y, IMP_I, TARIFF and D_Japan. Moreover, when GDP and LGDP are included separately, they both have negative – yet still insignificant – signs (see also equation (2) in Table 9.3). The results for TARIFF and NTB might also be caused by multicollinearity as NTB is correlated with

D_AGR_K (r = 0.591), HRR (r = 0.520) and L (r = 0.679) and TARIFF with, for example, D_AGR_J (r = 0.475) and HRR (r = 0.544). Indeed, high trade barriers might have caused high values of HRR and L (low labor productivity) in agriculture, as neoclassical theory argues. Additional regressions confirm that TARIFF and NTB are both significant when regressed on HRR but only NTB is significant when TARIFF and NTB are regressed on L. If, however, the same regressions are run without agriculture only TARIFF is significant in the case of HRR (which could also be a result of higher tariffs on intermediate imported inputs). Thus combining the results for the dummies, HRR, L, TARIFF and NTB, it can be concluded that the high agricultural price levels are particularly associated with low labor productivity in agriculture (that is, high L) rather than trade barriers, yet low productivity might be a result of trade barriers.

In fact, the results of the dummies are disappointing. One would expect, at least in equation (1) of Table 9.3 where all independent variables are included, that the dummies for Japan and for the agricultural sectors would be insignificant.[3] Even the high tariffs and high incidence of NTBs cannot explain the high price level of agriculture. Indeed, TARIFF and NTB alone explain together only 15 per cent of the variance of PL and only NTB is significant (at the 5 per cent level). Thus there are still factors, beyond the variables included, that are associated with the dummies. As discussed in Chapter 3, the dummies for agriculture might, for example, reflect demand pressure on prices of primary commodities, because they are more sensitive to it.[4]

In equation (2) of Table 9.3, some variables with t-statistics below one are eliminated from equation (1). This criterion has been used because elimination of a variable with a t-statistic smaller than one would not bias the regression results (Kennedy, 1992, p. 70). Different sequences of elimination have been followed to allow for the fact that multicollinearity changes the t-statistics when the list of independent variables is altered (Johnston, 1972, p. 160; Kennedy, 1992, ch. 11). Indeed, multicollinearity is rather high between several independent variables, and some arbitrariness remains. ADVERTS, AS, IMP_D, IMP_I, I_GR, K/Y, R&D and TARIFF are the only variables that do not have a simple correlation coefficient of 0.6 or higher with at least one other independent variable. Variables such as ESTABLS, ESTABLS/Y, IMP_D, IMP_I, K/Y, NTB, TARIFF, UNION and WAGE change signs at least once when the sample or the list of independent variables is changed. Often, however, the sign of IMP_D is negative and the sign of IMP_I positive, while both are mostly insignificant (see, for example, equation (4) of Table 9.3). The positive sign of IMP_I is in accordance with expectations, as expressed in Chapter 7, that prices will increase as costs rise for all producers. IMP_I also often has a t-statistic larger than one. The negative sign of IMP_D implies that final demand imports are more likely to reduce the power of the domestic firms and lead to lower prices.

Four variables are most robustly estimated; that is, their sign and level of significance is rather constant independent of the sample and regardless of which other independent variables are included. These four variables are HRR, L, ADVERTS and LGDP (or GDP). HRR and L are rather robust but HRR in particular is in some cases insignificant, although in almost all cases positive, because HRR and L have a simple correlation coefficient of 0.604 and HRR in particular is correlated with a number of other independent variables, such as D_Japan, (r = –0.716), ESTABLS/Y (r = 0.691), LGDP (r = –0.701) and WAGE (r = –0.670).

Advertising expenditures as a percentage of GDP (ADVERTS) is one of the (if not *the*) most robustly estimated variable. This supports the hypothesis that the markup is positively influenced by the extent of product differentiation as proxied by ADVERTS. ADVERTS performs more consistently in the cross-sector analysis than in the cross-country analysis of Chapter 10, where R&D is more robust. This might be a result of the measurements problems, which are larger for R&D in the cross-sector analysis but larger for ADVERTS in the cross-country analysis (see Appendix A.2.4 and Chapter 10).

Either LGDP or GDP is in most equations also significant and negative as expected, indicating that economies of scale have an important effect. That multicollinearity might be the cause of the insignificance of LGDP and GDP in equation (1) of Table 9.3 is highlighted in equation (2) of Table 9.3 where GDP is dropped and the sign of LGDP becomes negative and significant. K/Y is in equation (2) also significant but with a negative sign (as in equation (1)), which might indicate that economies of scale or demand play a role. The four dummies all have signs according to expectations and are significant.

The adjusted R^2 of equation (2) of Table 9.3 is, at 0.89, only slightly lower than in equation (1) despite fewer variables, although they cannot strictly be compared because the sample is different. The White statistic (no cross-terms) indicates that heteroskedasticity can be rejected and the RESET statistic shows that misspecification (regarding functional form and omitted variables) can be rejected. However, the Jarque-Bera statistic indicates that a normal distribution for the residuals should be rejected.

The importance of the determinants of the markup, as discussed in Chapter 5, can also be tested with these data. The markup is calculated as described in the previous section (9.1). In equation (3) of Table 9.3, the markup is regressed on a number of independent variables. As higher costs could lead to a lower markup and higher prices, the sign expectation of some variables is now different (see Table 9.2). ADVERTS, ESTABLS/Y, IMP_D, IMP_I, K/Y and WAGE have the expected signs and are significant. The positive effect of K/Y on the markup is in contrast with the negative effect on prices in equation (2). This might be a result of the dual nature of K/Y. It might reflect the need to finance investment – hence the positive effect on the markup – but it might also have a negative effect on prices because it can also be a proxy for economies of scale or demand pressure. The negative signs of WAGE and IMP_I indicate that the markup is reduced when firms are faced with costs increases, as discussed in Chapter 3, while the total effect of WAGE and IMP_I on price levels is positive, although only significant in the case of WAGE (see equation (1) of Table 9.3). The negative signs of IMP_D and ESTABLS/Y indicate that more competition, either from foreign imports or from domestic firms, is associated with lower markups.

Yet tariffs also reduce markups, which is contrary to expectations, although other authors have found similar results. Willmore (1989) argued and confirmed that higher tariffs allow more room for domestic producers and lower concentration. UNION has a positive effect on the markup, which is contrary to expectations. This could reflect the fact that unions in Japan and the Republic of Korea are concentrated in the large companies where productivity, wages and profits are generally higher (Aoki, 1984). HRR and L both have a positive effect on the markup, indicating that lower labor productivity is associated with higher markups. It is not immediately clear why this is the case. One possible explanation is that lower labor productivity is translated into lower wages and hence higher markups.

There are two variables (AS and AS/Y) that in the price equation can either have a positive sign if it is a proxy for market power or a negative sign if it is a proxy for economies of scale. In the markup equation (equation (3) of Table 9.3), a positive sign in the case of economies of scale is more likely.[5] The results are ambiguous because AS/Y has a significant positive sign, but AS has a significant negative sign.

Finally, having explained the markup separately, we can also regress the price level on the markup and a number of other factors that could affect the price level directly (that is, not through the markup), which are productivity, wages, economies of scale and trade barriers. This regression is shown in equation (4) of Table 9.3 and provides rather strong support for our model. HRR, GDP, MARKUP, WAGE and the dummies have the expected signs and are significant. On the other hand, none of the four variables associated with international trade (TARIFF, NTB, IMP_D and IMP_I) is significant. All variables together explain 80 per cent of the price level variance. Moreover, the RESET test statistic shows that misspecification (regarding functional form and omitted variables) can be rejected. The White statistic (no cross-terms) indicates, however, that heteroskedasticity cannot be rejected and the Jarque-Bera statistic indicates that a normal distribution for the residuals should be rejected.

In sum, there is support for the post-Keynesian pricing model. In particular, productivity, product differentiation, intermediate inputs and economies of scale are important determinants of price levels. The conclusion about the importance of the marked-up direct and indirect labor requirements is somewhat tentative because the specification is plagued by multicollinearity. Moreover, the high price levels of agriculture are associated with low productivity and not with high trade barriers, although high trade barriers could have caused low productivity in agriculture. There is also evidence that higher costs of wages and intermediate imported inputs lead to lower markups, but only in the case of wages to higher prices. The evidence further suggests that trade-related variables do not affect prices, which is closer to our model than to the neoclassical theory. More domestic competition or more imports lower the markup as our model predicts and higher tariffs (paradoxically) also reduce the markup. Yet tariffs, other protective measures and imports do not have a significant effect on prices. Finally, two variables (UNION and K/Y) show ambiguous results, which might reflect the specific characteristics of the Japanese and Korean economies.

NOTES

1. It should be pointed out that the sectoral price levels used in this section are estimated according to the industry-of-origin approach and exclude final demand imports. Final demand imports can thus only have an effect on the pricing of domestic firms if they affect the market structure, for example because the foreign supplier is a price leader or reduces the power of the domestic firm. In the expenditure approach of Chapters 10 and 11, foreign market power can lead directly to higher price levels because final demand imports are included.

2. The simple correlation coefficient between D_AGR_K and L is 0.836 and between D_AGR_J and L is 0.453. Indeed, D_AGR_K and D_AGR_J have positive, significant signs in equation (2) of Table 9.3 where L is dropped.

3. The four dummies alone explain together 72 per cent of the variance for this sample, but this high R^2 is of course largely a result of the fact that these dummies are precisely introduced to explain outliers. (The variance of the price levels without the two agricultural sectors and real estate in Japan is half the variance of the complete sample.) For a sample excluding the agricultural sectors of Japan and the Republic of Korea and the real estate sector of Japan, all variables of equation (1) explain 78 per cent of the variance of the sectoral price level.

4. Thus one could argue that mining also needs a dummy. In equations (1), (3) and (4) of Table 9.3, however, mining is excluded because of missing data (see Table A.2.2). A dummy for mining in equation (2) of Table 9.3 is not significant.

5. A negative effect of economies of scale on the markup is unlikely unless economies are producing beyond normal capacity on the upward-sloping part of the average cost curve (see Figure 3.1). If an economy is growing and a firm knows it can benefit from this through economies of scale, it will take that into account when firms determine their normal level of production. Thus one can argue that economies of scale as such do not have any effect on the markup, assuming they are all at normal production. Larger firms in bigger economies usually have larger markups because the capital–output ratio is bigger. (Prices can still be lower in the larger economy as average total costs can be lower.)

10. Evidence on price levels of GDP

The second test of the theoretical model entails regressing the price levels for GDP in 1980 and 1985 for a large number of countries on a number of independent variables. This is relatively easy because sectoral factors are ignored and only economy-wide observations are needed. This test is particularly useful for assessing the importance of variables that are not available at the sector level, such as the degree of urbanization, population density and geographical distances.

Table 10.1 shows the definitions, abbreviations and the sources of the variables used in the regression analysis in this chapter. The sign expectations are listed in Table 10.2 (see p. 137). Most sign expectations are self-explanatory and specific references to the theoretical discussions in the preceding chapters can be found in the last column. A number of variables, however, have ambiguous sign expectations. One of them is urbanization. As discussed in sections 5.2 and 6.2, urbanization is associated with lower market power and externalities, leading to lower prices. On the other hand, land is limited in quantity in urban areas and cannot be reproduced (Kurz, 1978). Hence higher degrees of urbanization lead to higher demand, which can drive up the price of land and of the goods and services produced and sold on it. This might particularly affect services because many need to be close to the consumer, while manufacturers can move to other areas, although this also adds transportation costs. Indeed, if services are relatively expensive in developed countries, the aggregate price level is likely to be higher in urban areas than in rural areas because there are more service providers in cities and thus the share of higher priced services will be higher in urban areas. Furthermore, food needs to be transported to cities, adding transportation costs and wholesale and retail services. In general, the service component in goods sold in cities is likely to be larger than in goods sold in rural areas. Indeed, several writers have argued that the share of services in GDP increases with urbanization (Fuchs, 1968; Gemmell, 1985; Oberai, 1981; Sabolo, 1975; Thompson and Stollar, 1983; Udall, 1976; UNIDO, 1985b).

Another variable with ambiguous sign expectation is the ratio of output to value added (Y/VAM). On the one hand, more intermediate inputs might mean higher costs, although they probably also mean a smaller direct labor input (see Chapter 4). On the other hand, outsourcing might be cheaper when the economy grows, as production outside the firm might benefit from economies of scale

Table 10.1 Variable abbreviations, definitions and sources

Variable	Definition	Source
PL	price level of GDP (US = 100)	ICP [a]
Productivity		
GDPC	GDP per capita (in thousands)	PWT 5.6a
Labor costs		
UNION	union members as % of labor force	Kurian (1984) and ILO (1989)
WAGE	average wage in manufacturing goods (converted with PPP of consumption)	United Nations, Industrial Statistics data base
Markup		
AS	average size of establishment in manufacturing by employment	Nugent and Nabli (1989) [b]
ASM	average size of establishment in manufacturing by number of engaged (most) or employed (some)	United Nations, Industrial Statistics data base
ASM/Y	average size as a ratio of GDP	
I/Y	Gross Domestic Investment as percentage of GDP at current local prices	World Bank (WT)
FI/Y	Gross Domestic Fixed Investment as percentage of GDP at current local prices	World Bank (WT)
K/Y	capital–output ratio (total capital, including non-residential and other construction, at 1985 international prices)	PWT 5.6a
I_GR	growth rate of Gross Domestic Investment (at local, constant prices)	World Bank (WT)
R_LOAN	real lending interest rate	IFS, line 60p
R&D	research and development expenditures as % of GDP	R&D: UNESCO (1995); GDP: World Bank (CD-ROM) and IFS
ADVERTS	advertising expenditures [c] as % of GDP	Hutton (1998); Kurian (1984); Appendix 2; GDP: World Bank (CD-ROM) and IFS

Table 10.1 (continued)

Variable	Definition	Source
COMP_LAW	dummy = 1 if country has competition law	UNCTAD (1997, p. 290)
Intermediate inputs		
Y/VAM	ratio of output to value added in manufacturing	United Nations, Industrial Statistics data base
Taxes		
YM/YF	ratio of GDP at market prices and GDP at factor prices	World Bank (WT) and United Nations
TARIFF	import-weighted average tariff on imports of intermediate and capital goods	Jong-Wha Lee (1992)
Economies of scale		
(L)GDP	GDP (= GDPC * POP)	
(L)POP	population (in thousands)	PWT 5.6a
URB	percentage of population in urban areas	World Bank (SID)
POPURB	population in urban areas (= POP * (URB/100))	
POPDEN	population per square km	World Bank (SID)
GDPDEN	GDP per km^2 (= GDP/(POP/ POPDEN)) (in thousands)	
AGR	agricultural land as percentage of total land area	World Bank (SID)
POPDENAGR	population per km^2 of agricultural land	World Bank (SID)
Transportation costs		
CAR	population per passenger car	World Bank (CD-ROM)
ROADDEN	road length in km per km^2 of total land area	World Bank (1994b)
INDIST	hinterland distances in nautical miles	Linnemann (1966)
LDISTANCE	import-weighted international distance in 1000 km^d between capital cities	Jong-Wha Lee (1992)
CIF/FOB	ratio of c.i.f. and f.o.b.	IMF (1990b)
(L)IMP	imports of goods and nonfactor services (in current thousand dollars)	World Bank (WT)

Variable	Definition	Source
Foreign competition		
IMP/Y	IMP/GDP (at current dollars) (converted by exchange rates, except Argentina and Bolivia) [e]	World Bank (WT)
OPEN	exports and imports as percentage of GDP at current international prices	PWT 5.6a
OPENLee	import share at free trade level (determined by land area and import-weighted distance[f])	Jong-Wha Lee (1992)
FDI	stock of foreign direct investment as percentage of GDP	UNCTAD (1993); World Bank (WT)
ARREARS	external debt service arrears (principal and interest) as % of exports of goods and services	World Bank, World Debt Tables
TDS/EXP	debt service payments as % of exports of goods and services	World Bank, World Debt Tables
Other		
ERPREM	log (1 + BLACK), BLACK is the average black market exchange rate premium	Fischer (1993) from World Bank, Website
ER8580	ratio exchange rate (currency/$) of 1985 to 1980	IFS
DDC	dummy = 1 if developing country	
DAfrica	dummy = 1 if in Africa	
ODA	Official Development Assistance	World Bank (WT)

Notes: L as first letter of variable name refers to logarithmic transformation; IFS = IMF, *International Financial Statistics*, tape; PWT = Penn World Table (http://www.nber.org/); World Bank (SID) = World Bank, *Social Indicators of Development*, data diskette (some variables for former F.R. Germany and former Yugoslavia are from the United Nations or national sources); World Bank (WT) = World Bank, *World Tables*, data diskette.
[a] Kindly provided by Magdolna Csizmadia of the United Nations Statistics Division.
[b] Kindly provided by authors.
[c] Data from Hutton (1998) are for 1986 rather than 1985. Data for Japan and the Republic of Korea for 1985 are from Appendix 2.
[d] Calculated by substituting land area (millions km^2) into equation for OPENLee.
[e] Converted by so-called "Additional Conversion Factor" from World Bank (WT).
[f] Jong-Wha Lee (1992) regressed the ratio of imports to GDP on structural factors (land area and import-weighted distance) and policy factors (tariff and black market exchange rate premium). The free trade import share is defined as the value of the imports-to-GDP ratio generated from the regression equation when zeros are substituted for the two policy variables.

(see Chapter 6). This ambiguity is similar to the one associated with IMP_I discussed in Chapter 9.

The ambiguity about the import variable IMP/Y reflects the discussion in Chapter 7, where it is argued that a distinction needs to be made between final demand imports and imports of intermediate inputs. The variable IMP/Y, however, does not make this distinction. Moreover, if IMP/Y reflects intermediate inputs, the same ambiguity that applies to IMP_I is operative here as well and if IMP/Y reflects final demand, the ambiguity that applies to IMP_D is operative (see Chapter 9). The only difference is that, here, we are dealing with price levels of expenditures and imports of final demand are included. Foreign market power can thus have a direct positive effect on prices (see Chapter 9, note 1). Generally, the sign of IMP/Y is ambiguous because a larger IMP/Y can reflect either more competition and lower markups, higher intermediate costs or a higher market share of foreign producers and thus foreign market power.

Domestic market structure is a factor for which no direct measurement exists for a sufficient number of countries. A sales concentration ratio would be preferred, but this is only available for a few countries. As an alternative, we have used the average size of establishments in manufacturing by numbers engaged or employed (AS, ASM and ASM/Y). The ambiguity of the sign expectation for AS, ASM and ASM/Y is discussed in Chapter 9.

Two dummies have been included as well, one for developing countries and one for Africa. This might shed some light on one particular problem mentioned (but not solved) in the literature, namely that in many regressions – using a wide variety of independent variables – a dummy variable for Africa is often significant. This indicates that there are some "omitted variables." Factors that might explain the special status of Africa are the poor state of the infrastructure (which drives up costs), the foreign exchange scarcity (which makes imports expensive and curtails import competition) and the limited possibilities of reaping economies of scale owing to the small size of many African economies.

Finally, a number of other variables are added without any reference to the preceding theoretical discussion. Because the price level is calculated by dividing the purchasing power parity by the exchange rate, the exchange rate determines in part the price level. Thus, if an exchange rate is overvalued vis-à-vis the dollar (that is, a low price in national currencies for one US dollar), the price level will be too high. In 1985, the dollar exchange rate was considered overvalued. Thus other exchange rates were undervalued vis-à-vis the dollar and their price levels were too low. If the extent of overvaluation was the same for all the countries in our sample, the regression results for 1985 alone would be unbiased. However, when 1980 and 1985 are pooled, there might be a bias when all price levels in 1985 were too low compared to 1980. To correct for this possibility, we have included the ratio of the exchange rate (national currency

Table 10.2 Sign expectation when dependent variable is price level

Independent variable	Sign expectation	Explanation for sign expectation	Reference in text
Productivity			
GDPC	+	relative low labor productivity in nontradables in high-income country	2.1
Labor costs			
UNION	+	labor union power	5.3
WAGE	+	labor costs	5.3
Markup			
AS, ASM, ASM/Y	+/−	market power/economies of scale	5.2
K/Y, FI/Y, I/Y, I_GR	+	finance requirement of investment	5.1, 4.2
R_LOAN	+	finance costs	5.1
R&D, ADVERTS	+	product differentiation	5.2
COMP_LAW	−	curbs market power	5.2
Intermediate inputs			
Y/VAM	−/+	economies of scale/intermediate inputs	6 / 4
Taxes			
YM/YF	+	taxes	3.1
TARIFF	+	taxes	7.2
Economies of scale			
POPURB, POPDEN	−	economies of scale	6
POP, GDPDEN, GDP	−	economies of scale	6
URB, POPDEN, GDPDEN	−/+	spatial monopoly, economies of scale/ scarce resource, more services (retail trade, transport costs of food)	5.2 6.2
AGR	−	natural resource scarcity	3.1
POPDENAGR	+	natural resource scarcity	3.1
Transportation costs			
CAR	+	domestic transportation costs	5.2, 6
ROADDEN	−	domestic transportation costs	5.2, 6
INDIST	+	domestic transportation costs	5.2, 6
DISTANCE	+	international transportation costs	7.3

Table 10.2 (continued)

Independent variable	Sign expectation	Explanation for sign expectation	Reference in text
CIF/FOB	+	international transportation costs	7.3
LIMP	–	economies of scale in importing	7.3
Foreign competition			
IMP/Y	–/+	international competition / costs, foreign market power	7
OPEN, OPENLee	–	international competition	7
FDI	+	market power TNCs	5.2, 7.3
ARREARS,TDS/EXP	+	foreign exchange shortage	7, 3.1
Other			
ERPREM	+	exchange rate overvaluation	
ER8580	–	dollar appreciation between 1980 and 1985	
DDC or DAfrica	+/–	unexplained factors	

per US dollar) of 1985 to 1980 (ER8580). Another measure for exchange rate overvaluation is the black market exchange rate premium (ERPREM), which is especially relevant for developing countries where the official exchange rate was pegged at an unrealistic level.

Many different regressions were run, ranging from an equation with as many variables as possible for as large a sample as possible (n = 110) to an equation with only a few variables for a relatively small sample. Different elimination sequences, as in Chapter 9, were followed to assess the robustness of the estimates. All equations are estimated with OLS with a heteroskedasticity-consistent covariance matrix (White method). Table 10.3 presents three regressions. Each regression is for a different sample and includes different independent variables. The picture that emerges is mixed. Adjusted R^2 is rather high, reaching 0.98 in equation (2) where the sample is relatively small. The hypothesis that all coefficients combined are equal to zero can be rejected at the 1 per cent level as indicated by the high F-statistics in each equation. The RESET statistics of equation (1) and (2) indicate that the specification can be accepted and the Jarque-Bera statistic accepts a normal distribution for the residuals for equation (1). On the other hand, the Jarque-Bera statistics reject a normal distribution for the residuals for the other equations and the White statistics (no cross-terms) indicate that the presence of heteroskedasticity cannot be rejected in equations (1) and (3).

The most robust variable is WAGE, which in nearly all cases has a positive and significant sign. A number of other variables are significant and add

Table 10.3 Regression results with price levels of GDP as dependent variable

Independent variable	Regression number		
	(1)	(2)	(3)
GDPC		− 0.006 *** (8.09)	− 0.001 (1.38)
WAGE	0.005 *** (9.03)	0.003 *** (5.08)	0.005 *** (8.31)
UNION		0.194 *** (4.01)	
ASM/Y	− 0.142 ** (2.18)	9.754 *** (4.06)	
(F)I/Y [a]	0.462 (1.40)	1.070 ** (2.32)	
K/Y			59.673 ** (2.12)
R_LOAN		0.237 (1.51)	− 0.973 *** (2.92)
R&D		5.256 ** (2.89)	4.373 (1.51)
Y/VAM		4.557 (1.50)	
GDP	−1.1 E-8 *** (3.60)		−1.2 E-8 *** (3.20)
LPOP		− 56.648 *** (13.06)	
POPDEN	0.005 *** (2.69)	0.111 *** (4.58)	
POPDENAGR		− 0.021 *** (5.73)	
AGR	0.163 * (1.73)	0.199 ** (2.28)	
CAR	− 0.004 *** (3.06)	0.125 *** (9.92)	
LDISTANCE		39.059 *** (9.65)	9.166 ** (2.37)
LIMP	2.453 (1.29)	49.210 *** (11.28)	
IMP/Y	− 0.198 * (1.95)	−1.471 *** (10.02)	

Table 10.3 (continued)

Independent variable	Regression number		
	(1)	(2)	(3)
AREARS	− 0.365 **		
	(2.36)		
TDS/EXP	0.266 *	−1.77 ***	
	(1.82)	(6.27)	
ERPREM	8.092	210.943 ***	
	(1.19)	(4.23)	
ER8580	− 8.054 ***		
	(4.81)		
DAfrica	15.028 ***	− 85.006 **	
	(2.74)	(2.92)	
Adjusted R^2	0.824	0.979	0.867
F-statistic	28.85 ***	76.08 ***	42.96 ***
Jarque-Bera stat.	0.142 **	15.379	1.188
RESET(n) stat.	0.001(1) **	0.148(3) *	0.119(2)
White statistic	1.240	−	0.657
Number of observations	84	32	46

Notes: See Table 9.3.
[a] FI/Y in equation (1) and I/Y in equation (2).

explanatory power to the equation, but which variables are significant is partly dependent on the sample and the specification. This is probably the result of multicollinearity.

Many of the collinear variables are part of the same cluster of factors, and when their definitions are examined, collinearity is often indeed what one would expect. First, several proxies for economies of scale such as GDPDEN, POPDEN and POPDENAGR are highly correlated with a simple correlation coefficient higher than 0.8 (see Table 10.4). Second, the determinants of the markup are correlated. For example, the simple correlation coefficient between R&D and K/Y is 0.649 and between R&D and ADVERTS is 0.609. Third, some proxies for foreign competition are correlated. The simple correlation coefficients between OPENLee and OPEN or IMP/Y are between 0.672 and 0.700 and between OPEN and IMP/Y 0.943. Finally, proxies for transportation costs are correlated as well. LDISTANCE is highly collinear with OPENLee (r = −0.965) but also with ROADDEN (r = −0.602).

Because of the multicollinearity between proxies for the same factor,

Table 10.4 *Simple correlations between some proxies for economies of scale*
(if larger than |0.4|; 110 number of observations)

	LPOP	POP	POPURB	POPDEN	POPDENAG	GDPDEN	GDP	LGDP
LPOP	1							
POP	0.64	1						
POPURB	0.72	0.85	1					
POPDEN				1				
POPDENAG				0.99	1			
GDPDEN				0.99	0.97	1		
GDP	0.52	0.45	0.83				1	
LGDP	0.80	0.47	0.70				0.63	1

equation (3) in Table 10.3 only contains one proxy for economies of scale (GDP) and one for transportation costs (LDISTANCE). Of course, problems arise partly because multicollinearity not only exists between proxies for the same factor but also between proxies for different factors. Thus eliminating one of the two multicollinear variables that are proxies for the same factor will not suffice. Moreover, the number of observations for most variables differs and dropping a variable also changes the sample, a notorious problem when multicollinearity is present (Johnston, 1972; Kennedy, 1992).

GDP per capita might be one of the victims of multicollinearity as this variable is correlated with several other independent variables belonging to different clusters of determinants of prices. GDPC is collinear with WAGE ($r =$ 0.781), K/Y ($r =$ 0.562), CIF/FOB ($r =$ –0.575), LDISTANCE ($r =$ –0.558), LIMP ($r =$ 0.791), R&D ($r =$ 0.738), ADVERTS ($r =$ 0.755) and TDS/EXP ($r =$ –0.664). Multicollinearity probably causes GDPC often to have a negative sign, contrary to expectations, and it is also often insignificant.

A number of variables are often significant with a sign according to expectations – even if the sample or the list of independent variables change. They are UNION, (F)I/Y and R&D, all factors influencing the markup, and ERPREM and ER8580. The positive sign of UNION in equation (2) indicates that labor power translates directly into higher prices and is not entirely compensated by a lower markup. The effect of the investment and capital ratios is more robust than in Chapter 9: both I/Y and K/Y have almost always a positive sign but I/Y is more frequently significant than K/Y, which is not as we expected (see section 5.1). Yet I/Y is not always insignificant (see equation (1)). On the other hand, the growth rate of investment (I_GR) nearly always has a sign contrary to expectations and is also mostly insignificant, often with a t-

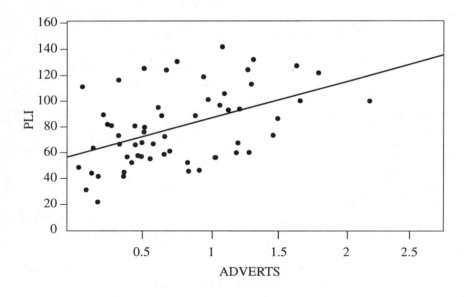

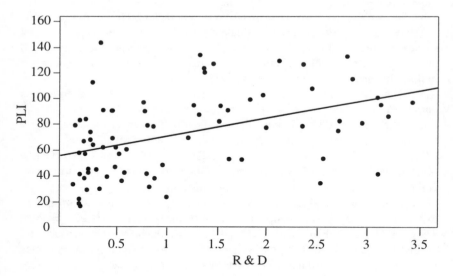

Figure 10.1 Price levels and proxies for product differentiation

statistic smaller than one and is dropped from the regressions. R&D has a sign as expected in equations (2) and (3) but is only significant in equation (2). ADVERTS also often has a positive, yet not always significant, effect on prices, but this variable has only 11 observations for 1985, and in combination with other variables with missing observations, the regression quickly exhausted the degrees of freedom and is therefore not shown in Table 10.3. Yet R&D and ADVERTS, two proxies for product differentiation, show a clear positive correlation with price levels, which is illustrated in Figure 10.1.

In almost all equations there is at least one proxy for economies of scale significant and with a sign according to expectations. In equations (1) and (3) of Table 10.3 that proxy is GDP and in equation (2) LPOP. Other proxies for economies of scale, such as POPDEN, POPDENAGR and AGR, have signs contrary to expectations and are also significant, which might be caused by multicollinearity. POPDEN, for example, gets a negative sign in equation (2) when POPDENAGR (r = 0.985) and IMP/Y (r = 0.433) are both dropped. URB often has a negative sign (indicating the importance of economies of scale and more competition, rather than resource scarcity or the high share of services in urban areas) but this is frequently insignificant, and hence does not appear in Table 10.3.

There are a number of variables that are not robustly estimated. ASM/Y, CAR, COMP_LAW, POP, R_LOAN, Y/VAM and DAfrica, for example, switch signs regularly when the sample or the list of independent variables change, even if significant (see also Table 10.3). COMP_LAW and Y/VAM frequently have negative signs (although Y/VAM not in Table 10.3), yet these are mostly insignificant. The negative sign for COMP_LAW suggests that prices are lower in countries that adopted a competition law but COMP_LAW is nearly always insignificant with a t-statistic smaller than one and is therefore dropped from the equation. The negative sign for Y/VAM indicates that economies of scale in the production of intermediate inputs might have a depressing effect on prices. ASM/Y is positive and significant in equation (2) but negative and significant in equation (1). ASM/Y probably suffers from problems similar to those discussed in Chapter 9 for AS/Y. In contrast to Chapter 9, however, the market power interpretation (a positive sign) seems a little stronger than the economies of scale interpretation (a negative sign). R_LOAN is negative and significant in equation (3) while one would expect a positive sign because a higher lending rate would increase external borrowing costs and thus raise the need for internal financing. DAfrica sometimes also switches signs, although it often has a positive sign, indicating that the variables introduced in this study, such as economies of scale and transportation costs, also appear not to be able to explain the special conditions in Africa.

The proxies for transportation costs do not always have a sign according to expectations even in cases when they are significant. In Table 10.3, only the signs of CAR in equation (2) and LDISTANCE are as expected but, CAR in particular is not very robustly estimated. INDIST and ROADDEN often have a sign according to expectations, but are mostly insignificant and are therefore eliminated from the equations in Table 10.3. CIF/FOB and LIMP have at times signs contrary to expectations, even if significant. CIF/FOB is, however, mostly insignificant and is dropped from the equations. Thus LDISTANCE is the most robustly estimated proxy for transportation costs with a sign that is mostly positive, as expected, and is also often significant.

IMP/Y, a proxy for foreign competition, usually has a negative sign and is also often significant. This indicates that imports as a percentage of GDP have a negative effect on prices and that the effect of international competition might dominate the effect of foreign market power or costs. OPEN often also has a negative, significant effect on prices, but is highly collinear with IMP/Y. IMP/Y and OPEN are therefore not used together in one equation. OPENLee often has a positive sign, contrary to expectations, but is highly collinear with a number of other variables, often insignificant and omitted. FDI usually has a negative sign, contrary to expectations, but is not always significant and is therefore not included in Table 10.3. The proxies for foreign exchange scarcity, ARREARS and TDS/EXP, generally have a negative sign, which is contrary to expectations, even when they are significant, although TDS/EXP has a positive sign in equation (1) and is also significant.

Finally, as already indicated, there are a number of variables (for example, CIF/FOB, COMP_LAW, DDC, FDI, I_GR, URB, YM/YF) that are insignificant with a t-statistic lower than one, indicating that elimination from the equation would not bias the regression results (Kennedy, 1992, p. 70). Perhaps the most important variable in this group, TARIFF, has not been discussed yet. TARIFF often has a positive sign as expected, but is frequently insignificant. Again, this might be partly explained by multicollinearity as TARIFF is correlated with such variables as GDPC ($r = -0.544$), LDISTANCE ($r = 0.458$) and OPENLee ($r = -0.470$).

In conclusion, there is some evidence that the factors we have identified in the theoretical chapters are indeed empirically important for the explanation of price levels across countries. In particular, the finance requirement of investment, proxied by the investment ratio or capital–output ratio, product differentiation as proxied by R&D expenditures, labor power as proxied by unionization and economies of scale as proxied by GDP or population size are often statistically significant with the expected sign. Geographical distances, although less robust, are also often significant with a sign as expected.

11. Evidence on price levels of investment

This chapter will focus on the third test of our model and will focus on evidence for one component of GDP, viz. investment in machinery and equipment, for a cross-section of countries. Price levels of components of GDP, such as food, have only recently gained some attention (Clague, 1992; 1993a; Lipsey and Swedenborg, 1993). Price levels of investment have not been the subject of any investigation as far as we are aware. This is surprising because investment goods are expensive in developing countries compared to other GDP components and their prices display a large variation across countries despite the fact that they are tradable. Investment goods are more expensive than other components of GDP in developing countries, while they need more of it in order to raise living standards. This is an issue too important to be left ignored. Lee (1995) showed, for example, that economic growth increases if developing countries raise the share of imports in investment because imports from developed countries are presumably cheaper. However, he did not explore why these imports are cheaper. This requires more research.

This chapter will explore the factors that determine the differences in prices of investment goods across countries. First, the price level of investment across countries will be explored. Then investment volumes are compared with volumes of imports of investment goods. This reveals to what extent the price level is influenced by imports. The next step will show that the traditional explanation for the failure to equalize prices of tradables across countries, that is tariffs and transportation costs, cannot explain many of the facts with regard to the prices of investment goods. In the final section, regression analysis will be used to determine empirically the significance of the factors discussed in Part I. In addition to the variables included in the regressions of the GDP price levels in Chapter 10, there are some factors that will be taken into account in the regression analysis of price levels of investment: foreign market power, tying of aid and the share of investment goods that are imported.

11.1 THE DATA ON PRICE LEVELS OF INVESTMENT

It has been recognized for some time that investment goods are relatively expensive in developing countries. Summers and Heston (1991, p. 337) for example stated that

[t]he average share in national currencies (NC) [for the poorest countries] is 20.6 percent while the average share in international prices (I$) is only 13.3 percent. This is because investment goods are relatively expensive in low-income countries, by a factor of 1.55, compared with all countries, rich and poor. The decline in the percentage entries across the columns [of Table 8.2 above] shows this dramatically. The major explanation for this price pattern undoubtedly lies in the area of public policy. (See also Lee, 1995; Nuxoll, 1994.)

This statement has to be qualified, however. Investment as a percentage of GDP depends not only on prices of investment but also on prices of other GDP components. A closer look at the data reveals that investment goods are expensive in developing countries relative to other GDP components (more expensive by at least 50 per cent in the poorest countries; see Table 8.2) but not necessarily in comparison with other countries. Data on price levels of investment are given in Table 8.3. They show that total investment actually is on average cheaper in developing countries. Only residential and other construction and electrical machinery are more expensive in developing countries. Table 8.3 also shows that investment compared to GDP (last line) is relatively expensive in developing countries, supporting the same conclusion for 1985 as Table 8.2 for 1980.

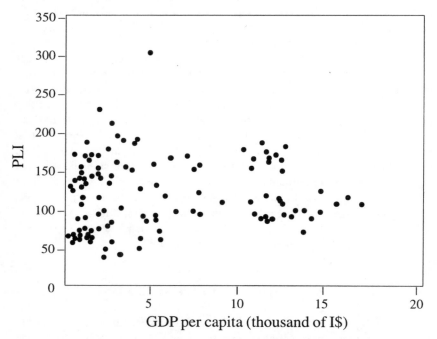

Figure 11.1 Price levels of investment goods and GDP per capita

Another interesting aspect revealed in Table 8.3 and illustrated in Figure 11.1 is the large variation in the investment price levels across developing countries and among investment components. Standard deviations for investment are about the same as for GDP in developed countries, but in developing countries the standard deviation is much higher for investment than it is for GDP. Actually, the standard deviations of investment price levels across developing countries are among the highest of the 50 GDP categories for which ICP reports PPPs. Following the traditional reasoning, one would have expected that the variation would be rather small, as investment goods are tradable and are indeed often traded.

11.2   EXPLAINING PRICE LEVELS OF INVESTMENT GOODS

In this section we will try to explain the variation in price levels of investment goods. First the percentage of investment goods that are imported is calculated; then price levels are regressed on natural and policy-induced trade barriers, the two factors emphasized by the traditional explanation for differences in price levels. In the last section a more extensive number of variables, following the discussion in Part I, are included in the regression equation.

Share of Imported Capital Goods

We first determine to what extent investment goods are produced domestically and to what extent they are imported. This can be done by comparing imports of investment goods with domestic investment or by comparing exports with domestic production of investment goods. There are a number of problems with the matching of the different classification systems (see Table 11.1). First, there is no perfect match between production data and trade data. For example, imports of machinery and transport equipment, as codified by the Standard International Trade Classification (SITC 7), are not distinguished by the different uses: investment, intermediate consumption, inventories or final consumption. This is particularly a problem in a number of divisions, such as transport equipment (passenger cars) and office machines (computers). To partly solve this we have subtracted from SITC 7 imports the SITC items that most likely are dominated by consumption categories: domestic appliances (SITC 719.4 and 725), televisions (724.1), radios (724.2), passenger cars (732.1), motorcycles (732.9), bicycles (733.1), invalid carriages (733.4) and warships (735.1).[1]

Second, some countries include re-exports in their imports and do not report them separately. For nearly all countries that do report re-exports separately, re-exports are rather small – a few per cent of imports. Hong Kong is the only country where re-exports account for more than 6 per cent of total imports, amounting to 25 per cent of total imports of SITC 7 in 1980. We have excluded re-exports from imports for those countries that distinguish between imports and re-exports, which most likely include all countries where re-exports are substantial. Third, investment in the SNA is estimated at purchasers' values, while imports of investment goods include international transport costs (c.i.f. – costs, insurance, freight) but not domestic transport costs, trade margins, subsidies and tariffs. No attempt was made to correct for this.

Table 11.1 Matching of classification systems

	ICP	SNA[a]	SITC	ISIC
Gross fixed capital formation	4	2.7		
Construction	4.2	2.7		5
Residential buildings	4.2.1	2.7/1		
Non-residential buildings	4.2.2	2.7/2		
Other construction	4.2.3	2.7/3		
Producers' durable goods	4.1	2.7/5	7	
Transport equipment	4.1.3	2.7/5A	73	384
Machinery & nonelectr. eq.	4.1.1	2.7/5B	71	382
Electrical equipment	4.1.2	2.7/5B	72	383, 385

Notes: ICP = United Nations International Comparison Programme; SNA = System of National Accounts, 1968; SITC = Standard International Trade Classification, Revision 1; ISIC = International Standard Industrial Classification of all Economic Activities, Revision 2.
[a] Refers to table number / item number. Table 2.7 is in current prices and 2.8 in constant prices.
Sources: United Nations (1961; 1968, pp. 114–15; 1990c; 1992a).

We have calculated the share of the imported investment goods as a percentage of domestic investment. Generally, as expected, larger, more closed countries import a smaller share of their investment. India, Japan and the United States, for example, import less than 20 per cent of their producers' durables. On the other hand, this percentage is about 90 in Ireland and Tanzania. Table 11.2 gives the averages and standard deviations only for 1980, but the results are similar for 1985.

It is striking that developing countries import on average a smaller percentage of their producers' durables, and the standard deviation is smaller as well. This is contrary to expectations and is perhaps partly caused by measurement errors because developed countries might, for example, import relatively more machinery and equipment that is in fact used as an intermediate or consumption good. A regression of the imported investment goods as a percentage of domestic investment for 1980 and 1985 on GDP per capita, tariffs and the size of the domestic capital goods industry shows that GDP per capita is not significant but that the other two variables are significant (at the 5 and 1 per cent level, respectively) and enter with a negative sign. The variables used, as defined in Tables 10.1 and 11.5, are IMPINV2, GDPC, TARIFF and IQ, respectively. The adjusted R^2 of the equation is 0.23. This confirms our expectations: higher tariffs and a larger domestic capital goods industry discourage imports of investment goods, perhaps because domestically produced investment goods are cheaper as a result of economies of scale.

Table 11.2   Imported investment goods as percentage of domestic investment, 1980

| | Developed Countries | | Developing Countries | |
	Average[a]	SD	Average[a]	SD
Gross fixed capital formation	26.3	13.2	28.9	11.9
Producers' durable goods	66.1	38.1	59.7	24.7
Transport equipment	75.3	65.1	52.0	23.7
Machinery & equipment	63.6	32.1	62.4	29.9

Notes: SD = standard deviation.
[a] Unweighted average.
Source: Author's calculation, based on data from United Nations, COMTRADE.

Barriers to Trade

Traditional explanations usually quickly abstract from barriers to trade and assume that tariffs and transportation costs are zero. As a corollary, these factors are easily blamed when prices of tradables are not equalized across countries (and if it is ignored that investment goods also have a nontradable component). Can trade barriers indeed explain price differences of tradables like investment goods?

Table 11.3 shows the incidence of policy-determined trade barriers for a number of developing countries in our sample. The data are from UNCTAD (1994) which only covers developing countries. Given the large variability in the incidence of these measures across countries, one would suspect this to be an important variable in explaining price levels of investment goods, but high trade barriers cannot easily be matched with high price levels. India, for example, protected its investment goods industry to a considerable extent in the 1980s, but its price level of machinery and equipment was only 98.6 in 1985. Hong Kong had a very low level of protection but its price level was only 12 points lower than India's. Nigeria had among the highest price levels in 1985, 121, but relatively low protection. The poor matching of policy-induced trade

Table 11.3   Tariff and nontariff incidence in developing countries (percentages)

	1980–83 Mean tariff rate[a]				1984–87 Mean total charges[ab]				1984–87 NTM incidence[a]				1984–87 QR incidence[a]			
	1	2	3	4	1	2	3	4	1	2	3	4	1	2	3	4
Bangladesh	84	67	112	86	65	59	99	46	35	25	33	50	35	25	33	50
Côte d'Iv.	25	22	29	26	21	16	25	23	13	5	8	28	13	5	8	28
Cyprus	16	11	25	17												
Egypt					41	31	52	46	31	10	20	66	31	10	20	66
Ethiopia	20	16	23	22												
Hong Kong					7	0	0	21	1	0	3	0	1	0	3	0
India	67	55	88	67	136	137	143	129	88	88	84	92	88	88	84	92
Indonesia	27	19	35	32												
Iran					64	34	88	83	100	100	100	100	100	100	100	100
Kenya	37	27	46	44	37	32	46	36	74	60	81	87	74	60	81	87
R. of Korea					24	22	26	27	22	12	13	42	22	12	13	42
Madagascar					35	29	43	38	67	94	33	58	67	94	33	58
Malawi					21	21	26	17	100	100	100	100	100	100	100	100
Malaysia	14	7	17	20												
Mexico	33	16	22	61												
Morocco	40	34	49	42	34	32	39	34	20	18	8	31	20	18	8	31
Nigeria	22	17	37	17	20	15	24	24	11	3	1	29	11	3	1	29
Pakistan	60	48	78	63	69	59	90	69	80	77	67	95	64	77	53	55
Paraguay	8	5	13	10												
Sierra Leone					23	22	25	24	100	100	100	100	100	100	100	100
Singapore	3	0	0	8												
Sri Lanka	21	18	27	21	26	22	29	29	15	5	3	37	15	5	3	37
Tanzania	17	15	15	20	44	16	115	25	50	83	54	5	0	0	0	0
Thailand	26	15	27	39	40	30	43	50	23	9	20	44	23	9	20	44
Tunisia	22	14	27	28	28	20	33	36	67	60	53	87	67	60	53	87
Turkey					51	39	42	71	100	100	100	100	22	12	19	39
Zimbabwe	7	3	12	7	18	15	19	20	0	0	0	0	0	0	0	0

Notes: NTM incidence = percentage of tariff lines affected by nontariff measures; QR incidence = percentage of tariff lines affected by quantitative restrictions; 1 = machinery and equipment; 2 = nonelectrical machinery; 3 = electrical machinery; 4 = transport equipment.

[a]   Import-weighted average.

[b]   Includes tariffs and paratariffs, such as customs surcharges and import license fees.

Source: UNCTAD (1994).

barriers and price levels might be explained by exemptions or by mismeasurement of certain trade barriers. Yet the highest price level in 1985 was found in Iran and protection was also relatively high.

Let us examine more systematically whether the variation in the price levels can be explained by the variation in trade barriers. The logarithms of the price levels of transport equipment, nonelectrical machinery and electrical machinery of the developing countries for 1985 are pooled and regressed on trade barriers. All equations have been estimated with OLS with a heteroskedasticity-consistent covariance matrix (White method). The regression results are shown in Table 11.4. (For African countries no separate price levels for nonelectrical and electrical machinery are available and the aggregate price level for machinery and equipment and the corresponding trade barriers were used instead. Taking the absolute values of the price levels as the dependent variable – instead of the logarithmic values – yields results that are worse with regard to adjusted R^2 and nearly all t-statistics are lower as well.)

The three trade barriers of Table 11.3 explain only 10 per cent of the variation in the price levels of the three investment goods (see equation (1) of Table 11.4). Only TARIFFME is significant, NTM does not have the expected sign and the RESET statistic indicates that there might be a specification error.

Can transportation costs explain more? Three proxies are used: CIF/FOB, LDISTANCE and INDIST, the same variables as in Chapter 10. CIF/FOB is the c.i.f. to f.o.b. ratio, indicating transport, insurance and finance charges. LDISTANCE is the logarithm of the import-weighted geographical international distance. Transport is the ultimate example of a sector where increasing returns to scale are prevalent because of the area–volume relationship (Eatwell, 1987). Weighing distances by imports is therefore important. INDIST refers to hinterland geographical distances. These three variables improve the explained variance only marginally, but the F-statistic is no longer significant. (Strictly speaking, the adjusted R^2 of equations (1) and (2) cannot be compared because the number of observations is different. The adjusted R^2 is 0.085 for regression (1) for the same sample as equation (2).) Of the three added variables in equation (2), only CIF/FOB is significant but has a sign contrary to expectations. NTM and QR are now significant – rather than TARIFFME in equation (1) – but only QR has the expected sign. The RESET statistic still indicates a specification error.

Two more proxies for transportation costs are tested, road density (ROADDEN) and car density (CAR) (see Table 10.1). The adjusted R^2 deteriorates and the F-statistic is again insignificant. ROADDEN is significant but has a sign contrary to expectations. TARIFFME, NTM, CIF/FOB and INDIST also have signs that are not expected but only CIF/FOB is significant. On the other hand, LDISTANCE and QR are significant with the expected sign.

Table 11.4   Regression results for developing countries

Dependent variable: log of price level of investment of 1985

Independent variable	Regression Number		
	(1)	(2)	(3)
TARIFFME	0.006 **	0.001	− 0.001
	(2.62)	(0.27)	(0.14)
NTM	− 0.008	− 0.009 **	− 0.007
	(1.68)	(2.10)	(1.37)
QR	0.007	0.013 **	0.012 **
	(1.49)	(2.38)	(2.05)
LDISTANCE		0.100	0.481 **
		(0.46)	(2.05)
CIF/FOB		− 1.774 **	− 1.778 **
		(2.45)	(2.43)
INDIST		0.0001	− 0.0004
		(0.20)	(0.55)
ROADDEN			0.588 **
			(2.25)
CAR			4.1 E-5
			(0.54)
Adjusted R^2	0.098	0.101	0.094
F-statistic	2.783 *	1.826	1.548
Jarque-Bera statistic	0.324	0.034 **	0.625
RESET (2) statistic	3.107	0.542	1.659
White statistic	1.152	0.824	0.947
Number of observations	50	45	43

Notes: See Table 9.3.

Running the three regressions for the 43 observations of regression (3) – making the adjusted R^2 comparable – is even more disappointing. The F-statistic is insignificant in all three cases. Regression (2) yields a negligible improvement (0.007 percentage points) in the adjusted R^2 over regression (1) and regression (3) yields a negligible improvement (0.015 percentage points) in the adjusted R^2 over regression (2).

In sum, the variables suggested by the traditional framework explain only 10 per cent of the variance of the price level of investment goods but collectively they are not significantly different from zero in nearly all cases. Individually, they are often insignificant as well, do not have the expected sign or both. None of the variables is robust in sign and significance except CIF/FOB, but with a sign contrary to expectations.

Regression Analysis

In this section, we will see to what extent the alternative model developed in Part I can explain the variation of price levels of investment goods. Some of the variables that were used in Chapter 10 can be used here as well; they are described in Table 10.1 and the sign expectations are in Table 10.2. Additional variables used only in the regressions for the investment price level are described in Table 11.5 and the sign expectations are shown in Table 11.6.

Two variables are particularly interesting because they are proxies for foreign market power. These two variables are COUNT, which measures the total number of partners from which investment goods are imported, and CR4, which measures the concentration of these trade partners. They are imperfect measures of foreign market power as they ignore the number of foreign firms within the exporting country competing in the domestic market. Yeats (1990a) assumed for the iron and steel industry that there is only one firm per country, but this industry is probably more concentrated than the investment goods-producing sector. One argument in favor of these proxies is that collusion is more likely between firms exporting from the same country than between firms exporting from different countries. Regarding domestic market power, the number of establishments (ESTABLS_I) is used in addition to ASI, similar to ESTABLS and AS in Chapter 9.

Some additional comments are in order. TARIFF is the same variable as in Chapter 10 and is not the same variable as TARIFFME in Tables 11.3 and 11.4. TARIFFME is only available for developing countries and TARIFF is taken from Jong-Wha Lee (1992) instead. TARIFF is for "various years in the 1980s" (Jong-Wha Lee, 1992, p. 22) and is used here for 1980 and 1985. We feel reasonably comfortable using this variable because regressing TARIFF on TARIFFME yields significant coefficients that are not significantly different from one for both years. The adjusted R^2 is 0.73 for 1985 and 0.36 for 1980.

Yeats (1990a) suggested that tied aid might perhaps explain why Africa paid higher prices for iron and steel imports from France. The variable ODA/GDP is included to test his hypothesis as comprehensive data on tied aid are not available. If tying is important then one would expect a positive sign on ODA/GDP.

Table 11.5 Variable abbreviations, definitions and sources

Variable	Definition	Source
PLI	price level of investment goods (US = 100)	ICP [a]
GDPC	GDP per capita at 1985 I$	PWT 5.5
PRODTY	labor productivity in manufacturing of investment goods (value added, at PPPs, divided by number of engaged or employed)	United Nations, Industrial Statistics data base
WAGE_I	average wage in manufacturing of investment goods (converted with PPP of consumption)	United Nations, Industrial Statistics data base
(L)ASI	average size of establishment in manufacturing of investment goods (by employment)	United Nations, Industrial Statistics data base
(L)IQ	investment goods gross output (at PPPs)	United Nations, Industrial Statistics data base
(L)AS/Q	ratio of ASI and IQ (multiplied by 1,000,000)	
ESTABLS_I	number of establishments in manufacturing of investment goods	United Nations, Industrial Statistics data base
(L)TIMP_I	total [b] imports of investment goods (in US $)	United Nations, COMTRADE
COUNT	number of countries from which TIMP_I imported	United Nations, COMTRADE
CR4	share of 4 largest exporters in TIMP_I	United Nations, COMTRADE
IMPINV	imported investment goods as percentage of gross domestic investment	World Bank (CD-ROM)
IMPINV2	imported investment goods [b] as percentage of gross domestic investment (see Table 11.2)	United Nations, COMTRADE; National Accounts data base
ODA/GDP	Official Development Assistance (per cent of GDP)	World Bank (WT)
D1980	dummy = 1 for 1980	

Notes: L as first letter of variable name refers to logarithmic transformation; PWT = Penn World Table (http://www.nber.org/); World Bank (SID) = World Bank, *Social Indicators of Development*, data diskette (some variables for Germany and Yugoslavia are from the United Nations or national sources); World Bank (WT) = World Bank, *World Tables*, data diskette.

[a]   Kindly provided by Magdolna Csizmadia of the United Nations Statistics Division.
[b]   Excluding some categories. See text section 11.2.

Table 11.6 Sign expectation when dependent variable is price level of investment goods

Independent variable	Sign expectation	Explanation for sign expectation
PRODTY	−	labor productivity
WAGE_I	+	labor costs
GDPC	+	relative low labor productivity in nontradables in high-income country
ASI, AS/Q	+/−	market power/economies of scale
ESTABLS_I	−	market power
IMPINV	−/+	international competition/costs, foreign market power
COUNT	−	foreign market power
CR4	+	foreign market power
IQ	−	economies of scale
TIMP_I	−	economies of scale in importing
ODA/GDP	+	tying of aid
D1980	−/+	unexplained factors

Many regressions were run and different elimination sequences were followed, similar to those in Chapters 9 and 10, to assess the robustness of the estimates. The selected equations are presented in Table 11.7. The results are somewhat mixed. The equations are estimated with OLS with a heteroskedasticity-consistent covariance matrix (White method). More than 70 per cent of the variance is explained and the hypothesis that all coefficients are jointly equal to zero could be rejected for both equations. The White tests for heteroskedasticity (with no cross-terms) reveal that homoskedasticity is accepted for equation (1) but rejected for equation (2). Moreover, the RESET statistics indicate that the equations might be misspecified (regarding functional form and omitted variables) and the Jarque-Bera statistics reject a normal distribution for the residuals.

The most fundamental variables, PRODTY and WAGE, have the most robustly estimated coefficients. Their signs are as expected, negative for PRODTY and positive for WAGE, and they are significant. These two variables plus the two dummies explain 62 per cent of the variance for a sample of 88 observations. Other variables are however less robust, which is perhaps partly the result of multicollinearity, as already indicated in Chapter 10, where most variables have also been used.

*Table 11.7   Regression results with price levels of investment goods as
dependent variable*

Independent variable	Regression number			
	(1)		(2)	
PRODTY	− 0.002	(5.16) ***	− 0.002	(4.66) ***
WAGE_I	0.005	(4.26) ***	0.005	(3.61) ***
GDPC	0.02	(4.36) ***		
GDPC²	− 1.1 E-6	(3.93) ***		
R&D			11.64	(2.14) **
LAS/Q	11.62	(3.81) ***	− 3.44	(1.22)
ESTABLS_I	− 0.0003	(1.29)		
(F)I/Y [a]	0.51	(0.95)	1.60	(2.27) **
COMP_LAW	− 15.58	(1.63)		
TARIFF	− 11.10	(0.29)		
IMPINV	1.03	(4.49) ***	0.41	(1.77) *
CR4	− 0.71	(2.51) **		
OPENLee	− 1066.36	(2.62) **	1389.86	(6.18) ***
FDI	− 0.91	(3.92) ***		
LASI	− 16.91	(2.95) ***		
POP	9.5 E-5	(1.56)		
POPDEN	− 0.01	(2.73) **	− 0.17	(4.94) ***
ROADDEN	33.37	(3.93) ***		
LDISTANCE	− 84.73	(1.90) *	168.71	(6.61) ***
ERPREM	− 21.98	(1.92) *	18.89	(1.72) *
D1980	75.98	(7.13) ***		
DDC	33.32	(2.20) **		
Adjusted R^2	0.879		0.702	
F-statistic	19.338 ***		12.066 ***	
Jarque-Bera statistic	1.295		2.766	
RESET (n) statistic	1.447(2)		1.299(5)	
White statistic	0.418 **		1.182	
Number of observations	54		48	

Notes: See Table 9.3.
[a]   FI/Y in equation (1) and I/Y in equation (2).

GDP per capita (GDPC) and $GDPC^2$ are significant in equation (1). ($GDPC^2$ is included because the graph of GDP per capita and PLI shows a parabola; see Figure 11.1. Other functional forms, using the logarithm of GDPC, were also tested but rejected because the coefficient is insignificant or because adjusted R^2 is lower (or both).) The significance of GDPC and $GDPC^2$, however, raises a problem. Most empirical studies of price levels included GDP per capita because a better measure of labor productivity was lacking. Hence one would not expect GDP per capita to have additional explanatory power with the inclusion of PRODTY. It is possible, however, that GDP per capita is a proxy for the relative low productivity of nontradable inputs in the production of investment goods in high-income countries. As Kravis and Lipsey (1983, p. 23) stated, "if there were pure tradable goods and if trade equalized their prices in different countries, no correlation at all would be expected between their prices and income levels, and the [observed influence of real income per capita on the price levels of tradables] would have to be thought of as reflecting the nontradable element in all tradable-goods prices." GDP per capita might also be a proxy for omitted variables associated with the level of development, but with the inclusion of several other variables it is not clear what GDP per capita is a proxy for. Yet GDPC and $GDPC^2$ are insignificant in equation (2), with a t-statistic smaller than one and dropped.

There are a number of variables that are proxies for market power in the domestic market. The first and most robust is R&D. R&D is nearly always positive and often significant, as in equation (2). (R&D is not included in equation (1) because it has only 69 observations and reduces the degrees of freedom. ADVERTS is not included as advertising is not as important in the capital goods industry as in the consumption goods industry and separate data on advertising in the investment goods industry are not available.) The next two are LAS/Q and ESTABLS_I. LAS/Q is highly correlated with LIQ ($r = -0.943$), with LGDP ($r = -0.812$) and with LTIMP_I ($r = -0.870$). (LIQ and LASI combined are perfectly collinear to LAS/Q and cannot be included together in the regression; see Table 11.5.) Consequently, levels of significance of LAS/Q are better when these variables are excluded from the regression, but LAS/Q still lacks robustness. LAS/Q has a positive sign and is significant in equation (1), indicating that market power is probably important, but the sign becomes negative and insignificant in equation (2) when some of the variables that are correlated with LAS/Q (ESTABLS_I, ROADDEN, GDPC) are dropped. ESTABLS_I enters equation (1) with a negative sign, which confirms expectations, but is often insignificant and is dropped from equation (2). ESTABLS_I, however, becomes positive when ROADDEN is dropped from equation (1), perhaps owing to multicollinearity, but remains insignificant. (The simple correlation coefficient between ROADDEN and ESTABLS_I is 0.506.) The negative and significant sign of FDI in equation (1) suggests that multinational corporations do not contribute to higher concentration and, hence, to higher prices, but the sign of FDI is not very robust, nor is it always significant; it is dropped from equation (2). Another indicator of market power is (F)I/Y, as argued in Chapter 5. (K/Y could not be used as not enough data on capital stocks for the investment producing sector are available.) (F)I/Y is less robust than R&D but is nearly always positive and is often significant. I_GR has a sign contrary to expectations and is also insignificant, as was the case for sectoral and GDP price levels (Chapters 9 and 10), and is dropped from the equations. COMP_LAW has mostly the expected sign, but is nearly always insignificant, as was the case in Chapter 10; it is eliminated from equation (2).

Regarding foreign market power, two variables are particularly crucial: COUNT, measuring the total number of trade partners, and CR4, measuring the concentration of trade partners. (CR3 was also calculated but performed more poorly in the regressions than CR4.) However, COUNT and CR4 nearly always have signs contrary to expectations and CR4 is often significant. COUNT generally has a t-statistic smaller than one and was therefore dropped from the equations. IMPINV^2 is significant with a positive sign, indicating that the price level is higher when the share of imported investment goods in domestic investment is higher. This suggests that there might be foreign market power beyond what is presumably captured by COUNT and CR4. A positive sign for IMPINV might, however, also indicate that imported investment goods are used as inputs in the production of investment goods and drive up costs, or that imported investment goods are of higher quality that is not adequately recognized in the measurement of PPPs.

TARIFF enters equation (1) with a negative sign, contrary to expectations, and is not significant. TARIFF is collinear with POP ($r = 0.729$) and a positive sign appears if POP is omitted or if the logarithm is taken of POP (LPOP; but then LPOP becomes insignificant). In both cases, TARIFF becomes significant but this is an aberration as TARIFF is insignificant in nearly all other regressions we ran and is therefore eliminated from equation (2). A negative sign is contrary to our expectations, but other authors gave some explanation for this finding. Willmore (1989) found that tariffs have a negative effect on concentration and argued that higher protection levels allow more room for domestic producers and more domestic competition. If this is the case, tariffs have a negative effect on price levels. Others have argued that protection, in the presence of imperfect competition and economies of scale, might yield dynamic benefits (Dornbusch, 1992; Pack and Westphal, 1986; Rodrik, 1992a; 1992b; 1995). These dynamic changes could translate into lower prices but not necessarily contemporaneously. It is indeed interesting to note that TARIFF becomes negative when POP, a proxy for economies of scale, is included.

None of the proxies for transportation costs is robust. The signs and coefficients of these variables are rather unstable when the sample or included variables change, probably resulting from multicollinearity. CIF/FOB often has a sign according to expectations but is generally insignificant and is eliminated from the equations. INDIST and CAR have signs contrary to expectations and were not significant; they also were deleted. LDISTANCE and ROADDEN are significant but both have signs contrary to expectations in equation (1). LDISTANCE is particularly correlated with OPENLee, but also with CIF/FOB and ROADDEN. When OPENLee is removed from equation (1), LDISTANCE becomes positive and remains significant. (The sign of OPENLee remains negative and significant when LDISTANCE is removed from equation (1).) LDISTANCE and OPENLee switch signs and become positive in equation (2) and each remains positive (yet becomes insignificant) when the other is removed. The lack of robustness of the transportation variables, as well as of the openness variable OPENLee, prevents a solid conclusion.

Regarding economies of scale, LASI and POPDEN are both significant in equation (1). POPDEN has a sign in accordance with expectations and the sign of LASI indicates that the effect of economies of scale dominates the effect of market power. POP does not have the expected sign and is also insignificant. LIQ, LGDP and URB are insignificant and their signs are rather unstable. These three variables were deleted because they are collinear with LAS/Q, with each other and with other variables and because they serve as proxies for factors that are covered by other variables. POPDEN and URB might also function as proxies for spatial monopoly and the significance of POPDEN indicates that, when population density is higher, there is less scope for spatial monopoly. Total imports might be an indicator for economies of scale in transportation, as Yeats (1978; 1990a) found. LTIMP_I has in some equations a negative sign, confirming expectations, but the sign was not robust and the coefficient was nearly always insignificant. LTIMP_I was therefore omitted.

ODA/GDP is not very robust when the sample or the number of independent variables change but is mostly negative, which is contrary to expectations, and nearly always insignificant with a t-statistic smaller than one; it is therefore eliminated from the equations. The instability of ODA/GDP might be related to the fact that it is somewhat collinear with a number of other variables ($r < 0.7$). A negative sign might be an indication of a foreign-exchange constraint, which ODA alleviates. However, better proxies for foreign-exchange scarcity, such as total debt service payments or total debt arrears, both as a percentage of exports of goods and services, were both insignificant (usually with t-statistics smaller than one) and were not included. YM/YF and Y/VAM are not very robust and generally have t-statistics smaller than one; they also were eliminated. The dummies show that there is some unexplained variance associated with 1980 (D1980) and developing countries (DDC). A dummy for African countries was also tested but insignificant. The signs of ERPREM and ER8580 are not very robust but ERPREM is at times significant.

In conclusion, the variation of price levels of investment goods is much higher for developing countries than for developed countries. As investment goods are considered tradable, the traditional explanation for this variation is limited to trade barriers, such as tariffs and transportation costs. Policy-induced trade barriers and proxies for transportation costs regressed on three categories of investment goods yielded insignificant results. These findings contradict a conjecture aired by Summers and Heston (1991, p. 337) that "this price pattern undoubtedly lies in the area of public policy," if they refer to tariffs, nontariff measures and quantitative restrictions.

This section has explored additional factors, such as market power and economies of scale. Regression analysis shows that the most important determinants of price levels of investment goods across countries are labor productivity and wages. There is evidence that differences in domestic market power and economies of scale across countries are also important and that a larger stock of foreign direct investment does not lead to a higher price level of investment goods. Moreover, there is some tentative indication that foreign market power drives up the costs of investments. On the other hand, the empirical research could not confirm the importance of competition laws, transportation costs, the tying of aid and tariffs.

NOTES

1. SITC Revision 1, the one used here, does not have more detailed subgroups which would, for example, make it possible to separate car parts or pleasure boats. Revision 1 is used because a number of countries do not report data in Revision 2 for 1980.
2. IMPINV is not the same as IMPINV2 which is used to calculate the data in Table 11.2. IMPINV was used because it has more observations. IMPINV regressed on IMPINV2 yields an adjusted R^2 of 0.811 and an estimated coefficient which is not significantly different from one.

12. Conclusions and implications

To recapitulate, a post-Keynesian markup pricing model has been developed to explain price levels across countries. This model incorporates input–output relations and the effects on prices of market power, economies of scale and trade barriers. The empirical support for the model, which is summarized in Table 12.1, is mixed. Let us first discuss the more positive results. Some of the innovative aspects of the model, that is, product differentiation (proxied by research and development and advertising expenditures) and economies of scale, found empirical support. The importance of product differentiation for price levels and the markup is a particularly interesting result, although in some cases research and development expenditures (R&D) and in other cases advertising expenditures (ADVERTS) were more important. Market power as proxied by product differentiation and the markup had a positive effect on prices, but market power was apparently not curtailed by the presence of a competition law (COMP_LAW). Yet more competition, either from foreign imports (IMP_D) or from domestic firms (ESTABLS/Y), is associated with lower sectoral markups (less market power), although not with lower prices. There is also evidence that higher costs associated with wages and intermediate imported inputs (IMP_I) led to lower markups and, in the case of wages, to higher sectoral prices. This confirms (at least partly) our postulate that firms are likely to increase prices and may reduce markups if costs rise, depending on the properties of the cost increase and the power it has in the product market. Moreover, wage and productivity variables (HRR, L, PRODTY) were among the most robustly estimated coefficients in the price equations. The effect of input–output relations is likely to be important, but the conclusions are somewhat tentative as the regression is plagued by multicollinearity. The results also showed that the high price levels of agriculture in Japan and the Republic of Korea were associated with low productivity and not with high trade barriers, although high trade barriers could have caused low productivity.

Other aspects of the model found mixed empirical support. The effect of proxies for transportation costs, concentration, labor power and the need to generate financing for investment was not consistently estimated for the different price levels. The investment ratio or capital–output ratio (proxies for the financing requirements) for example had positive effects (as expected) on the price levels of GDP and investment, but a negative (sometimes significant) effect on the sectoral price levels, although that may be related to the fact that

Japan and the Republic of Korea used relatively few retained earnings for the financing of investment. The growth rate of investment (I_GR) was negative, contrary to expectations, and insignificant in each equation, yet the capital–output ratio did have a positive effect on sectoral markups. These results can thus not exclude a negative effect of economies of scale or demand pressure on price levels as proxied by the capital–output ratio, although a positive effect of the capital–output ratio, indicating higher financing requirements, is more likely. The power of labor unions, proxied by the percentage of the employed (or labor force) who are members of a union, had a positive significant effect on GDP price levels but a negative insignificant effect on sectoral prices. The positive significant relation between unionization and sectoral markups in Japan and the Republic of Korea is not as expected but may reflect the specific position of unions in these countries. The size of the establishment (AS) compared to the size of the economy, which should give an indication of concentration, appeared positive and significant in some equations but negative and significant in others. Another disappointing result was found in the case of price levels of investment goods where the most direct – yet still imperfect – proxies for foreign market power (COUNT and CR4) had signs contrary to expectations, although another possible proxy of foreign market power (IMPINV) showed a positive significant effect on investment price levels. On the other hand, imports (IMP/Y) had a negative effect on GDP price levels. Slightly more encouraging was the result for the number of establishments (ESTABLS) which, as a proxy for market power, often had a negative sign (as expected), yet was mostly insignificant. No or very little evidence could be found for a positive effect of tied aid (ODA/GDP), market power of transnational corporations (FDI) or foreign exchange shortage on prices. In fact FDI had a negative effect on prices of investment goods. The dummy for Africa was not very robust, indicating that variables introduced in this study, such as economies of scale and transportation costs, were also unable to explain fully the price levels in Africa. Furthermore, the signs of several proxies for transportation costs (for example, DISTANCE and CIF/FOB) were not very robust. This instability may be caused by multicollinearity. Further investigation is needed to determine more exactly the influence of transportation costs.

Finally, tariffs and non-tariff barriers were mostly insignificant and appeared with positive as well as negative signs. Moreover, the variation of the price levels of investment goods could not be explained by policy-induced trade barriers and proxies for domestic and international transportation costs. These results challenge the conventional emphasis on policy-induced trade barriers as an explanation for high price levels and its corollary trade liberalization as the solution to high price levels. The analysis here has shown that this effect is only one possible determinant of price levels and is likely to be small or negligible.

In sum, wages, productivity, product differentiation and economies of scale are the most important variables for the explanation of price levels across countries. These are the most robust results. On the other hand, little evidence could be found for the importance of policy-induced trade barriers or competition policy. As with all empirical research, the results are not entirely unambiguous and even for some of the more positive results we would have liked a higher degree of robustness. The lack of stability is probably a result of multicollinearity, which is partly related to the small samples. This problem may be alleviated when new phases of the ICP become available and the samples can be extended.

The effect of policies is smaller than is often assumed by mainstream economists. They have argued that increasing competition, either through trade liberalization or by introducing or tightening competition policies, reduces price levels. The analysis presented above showed that these policies have their limitations. The adoption of a competition law, for example, has no discernible effect on prices. Moreover, policies can reduce transportation costs, which is an important determinant of market power, only up to a certain point: a landlocked country cannot change its geographical position. And the extent to which a country can benefit from economies of scale only changes slowly as the economy grows. Yet there are endless possibilities for product differentiation and there are no public policy tools that can limit these – unless deceptive advertising or false claims about a product are used.

Abandoning the dichotomy between tradables and nontradables and taking into account input–output relations has important consequences for structural adjustment programs in developing countries, which try to change relative prices in favor of tradables in order to stimulate export. If exportables use many intermediate inputs that are nontradable or imported, a focus only on the prices of exportables will yield disappointing or counterproductive results (see also Ajakaiye and Ojowu, 1994; Delgado, 1992; Kyle, 1992).

The analysis also casts doubts on the use of PPPs to indicate whether exchange rates are under- or overvalued, which has been popularized by the Big Mac index of *The Economist*. The idea is that exchange rate movements and arbitrage would equalize the prices of McDonald's Big Mac hamburgers across the world. However, prices of Big Macs are not equal across the world, and this information is used to indicate exchange rate misalignments. This is, however, problematic. In theory one can only use the purchasing power parity of a perfectly tradable good to determine whether a currency is overvalued or not and the Big Mac is not a tradable. Some components, such as beef, are traded globally, but most components (restaurant space, labor) and the final product are not tradable at all. Moreover, McDonald's has local market power, based on image, product differentiation and on nontradability, and uses it to set the price in each market differently (see also Rogoff, 1996). Thus a high price for a Big

Table 12.1 Selected regression results

Variables	PL sign expectation	Sectoral PL	GDP PL	Investment PL	MARKUP sign expectation	Sectoral MARKUP
Positive results						
HRR, L	+	+			−	+
PRODTY	−			−	−	−
WAGE(_I)	+	+	+	+	+	+
R&D, ADVERTS	+	(+)+	+(+)	+	+	+
ESTABLS(_I), ESTABLS/Y	−	(−)		(−)	−	−
MARKUP	+	+				
Economies of scale	−	−	−	−		
IMP_I	+/−	(+)	−	−	−	−
COMP_LAW	−		+			
Ambiguous results						
GDPC	+	(−)	(+)−(−)	+(+)		+
UNION	+	(−)−	+	(+)+	−	+
(F)I/Y, K/Y	+	(−)	+(+)	(−)	+	+
I_GR	+	(−)	−+	+−(−)	+	
AS(I), AS/Y, AS/Q	+/−	−(+)	−+	+−(−) (+)	+	+−
COUNT	−			−		
CR4	+			−		
DISTANCE	+		+	+		

164

Variables	PL sign expectation	Sectoral PL	GDP PL	Investment PL	MARKUP sign expectation	Sectoral MARKUP
CIF/FOB	+		(−)	(+)		
TARIFF, NTB	+	(+)(−)	(+)(+)	(−)		−
FDI	+		(−)	−	+	
IMP_D, IMP/Y, IMPINV	−/+	(+)(−)	−	+	+/−	−
Foreign exchange shortage	+		−+	(+)(−)		
ODA/GDP	+			(−)		
DAfrica	+		+−	(+)(−)		

Notes: + = positive significant coefficient; (+) = positive insignificant coefficient; − = negative significant coefficient; (−) = negative insignificant coefficient.

Mac might reflect market power and nontradable inputs rather than an overvalued exchange rate.

PPPs for total GDP are often used to provide evidence on exchange rate under- or overvaluation but they are as useless as PPPs of Big Macs because these PPPs also include large nontradable components and are also affected by market power. This is even the case for PPPs of tradables alone. The rejection of the law of one price, even for homogeneous tradables, makes any PPP as a measure for exchange rate under- or overvaluation very dubious. Whether exchange rates are under- or overvalued can instead be determined by assessing the sustainability of the balance of payments, taking into account factors like capital inflows, terms of trade, trade policy, foreign exchange reserves and the level of development (Williamson, 1994; Yotopoulos, 1996).

Price levels (of tradables) have also been used to indicate the trade orientation of a country. The most widely used index is the one Dollar (1992) devised. He regressed price levels on GDP per capita (GDP per capita)^2 and two dummies for Africa and Latin America and defined the real exchange rate distortion index as the ten-year average of the actual price level divided by the price level that this equation predicted. He argued that the predicted price level is the price level adjusted for differences in nontradable prices across countries. He defined the outward orientation index as a weighted average of the real exchange rate distortion index plus its coefficient of variation. This method is flawed, however, as it equates differences in (tradables') price levels with exchange rate distortions and exchange rate distortions with trade orientation. Rodrik (1994) pointed out that increasing trade restrictions can move the outward orientation index based on the price levels of tradables in either direction. An import tariff will raise the domestic price of tradables and the export tax will reduce it. Yet Rodrik (1994) argued that an import tariff and an export tax have identical consequences for resource allocation (owing to the Lerner symmetry theorem) and for openness which should be based on the comparison of the domestic ratio of prices of importables to exportables with the international ratio. An index of outward orientation based on the price levels of tradables has thus no direct connection with the appropriate measure of openness.

Moreover, Pritchett (1996) found that two trade intervention indices and tariffs had a perverse relation with price distortions as measured by price levels, indicating that more intervention or higher tariffs are associated with lower price distortions. (The trade intervention indices were based on deviations of the actual trade values from the values predicted by endowments, distances and the trade balance.) Harrison (1996) also found that two measures of price distortions did not show a consistent or general significant relationship with other measures of openness. She used as measures of price distortions the index of Dollar (1992) and an index which compares changes in the relative price of tradables from its national accounts with the relative price of consumption goods in Summers and Heston (1988). The analysis and evidence presented here give additional arguments against the use of a price-based measure as an indicator for trade orientation because they show that market power and economies of scale might be more important in determining "price distortions" than tariffs (see also Harrison, 1996, p. 425).

The importance of investment good price levels for economic growth has been pointed out in recent articles by Barro (1991) and Lee (1995). However, price levels of investment goods may have less to do with "distortions of market prices" owing to "interferences" (Barro, 1991, p. 433) if they refer to trade barriers. Instead they may be related to productivity, wages, market power and economies of scale in the domestic investment-producing sector and foreign market power. Lee (1995) argued that developed countries have lower prices for investment goods (which could be the result of economies of scale, although that was not discussed). Imports of capital goods from developed countries would thus be cheaper than production at home for developing countries, but only if transportation costs and foreign market power are ignored, as in Lee (1995). In fact, investment goods are generally cheaper in developing countries and imports might be rather expensive as they include a markup accruing to exporting countries. Yet the positive effect of the share of imports in investment on growth of GDP that Lee (1995) found could be explained by technology spillovers.

Appendix 1 The methods of the International Comparison Programme

The prime reason for calculating PPPs is to compare output across countries. Comparing output across countries is basically the same as comparing output over time (Hill, 1986, pp. 134–5; Marris, 1984, pp. 40–41; United Nations, 1992a, pp. 28–9). In both cases values are deflated by a price index. Most estimates of real product (PPP-converted) are based on calculating quantity ratios between countries by dividing expenditure ratios by price ratios. This is the method used by the United Nations International Comparison Programme (ICP), formerly known as the International Comparison Project, and will be more fully described (see also Kravis, 1984; 1986; Kravis *et al.*, 1982; United Nations, 1992a). See Table A.1.1 for the different phases of the ICP.

The ICP divides GDP into about 150 (for some regions up to 250) expenditure categories (approximately 110 consumption, 35 investment and 5 government). Within these categories, items of equal quantity and quality which are commonly consumed and widely available are matched across countries and priced (including taxes and subsidies). Items are considered identical when size, physical and functional properties (such as thread count in fabrics), outlet type, delivery conditions (for example, packaging, warranty and transportation costs) and other factors that might affect prices are the same. This stage is very crucial for the quality of the price and output comparisons and accordingly receives careful attention. Next, the prices of the items are expressed as ratios of the corresponding prices in the numéraire country, the United States (for example, five francs per dollar for a loaf of 500 grams of white bread that is water-based, made of wheat flour and not wrapped or sliced). The Country Product Dummy Method is used to fill in the prices for products not produced or provided. This method infers a price from the regressed relation found in other countries between missing price and prices of other items. The price ratios for the different items are averaged, yielding purchasing power parities for each detailed category (also referred to as "basic heading"). A geometric mean is used. The price ratios are in most cases not weighted because weights at such a detailed level are not available.

The following step is an aggregation procedure that yields prices and quantities for GDP and approximately 50 components. An average world price for each basic heading, also referred to as the international price, is used to value the quantities of the expenditure categories the same across countries. An international price (instead of the prices of the numéraire country) is used to make the international comparison base country invariant; that is, to make the comparison invariant to which numéraire country is chosen. This average world price, however, cannot be calculated without knowing the PPPs because the price ratios at the basic heading level are in national currencies and therefore cannot be added. But PPPs cannot be calculated without the average world prices. Therefore these two variables are solved simultaneously by using a method first devised by Robert Geary and elaborated by S.H. Khamis. The equations, slightly modified to accommodate the requirements of the ICP, are as follows.

$$IP_i = \sum_i \frac{p_{ij}}{PPP_j} \ [\frac{q_{ij}}{\Sigma q_{ij}}] \quad i=1,\dots,m$$

$$PPP_j = \frac{\sum p_{ij} q_{ij}}{\sum IP_i q_{ij}} \quad j=1,\dots,n$$

where ps are prices, qs are quantities and IP_i is the average international price of good i. There are m detailed expenditure categories and n countries. The p_{ij} is the purchasing power parity at the basic heading. The second equation gives the definition of PPP as the ratio of GDP in national currencies to GDP where the quantities are valued at international prices.

This method yields some desirable properties for multilateral comparisons such as transitivity, base country invariance and matrix consistency. Transitivity (or circularity) means that the price or quantity relationship between any two of three countries is the same whether derived from an original-country comparison between them or from a comparison of each country with a third country. Matrix consistency means that in a matrix, with countries as rows and with GDP and its components as columns, comparisons can be made across both rows and columns. There are also other methods but the Geary–Khamis method is the one most widely used (Kravis *et al.*, 1982, pp. 89–98; World Bank, 1993a, pp. 11–12, 72–9).

For reasons of convenience, the resulting world prices are normalized in such a way that the GDP of the United States in dollars is the same as the GDP in international prices, hence called international dollars. This normalization resulted previously in a purchasing power parity of the United States (of the dollar compared to the international dollar) of one only for total GDP. Subsequently, in Kravis *et al.* (1982, pp. 172–5) and from Phase V of the ICP on, the PPPs and the price levels are all 1.0 at the disaggregate level for every category, which means that international dollars are equal to US dollars. This is a result of the different ways in which the Geary–Khamis formula can be calculated (United Nations, 1992a, p. 74; World Bank, 1993a, p. 15).

Countries are weighted according to their importance in the world economy. A group of countries is assigned to a representative country (a benchmark country) whose price and quantity structures are similar. This group is called a supercountry. To allow for omitted countries, all the countries in the world are assigned to one of the benchmark countries. The aggregate (exchange rate-converted) GDP of the supercountry is used as a weight.

The ICP uses the expenditure approach as opposed to the industry-of-origin or production approach to estimate PPPs. The first method focuses on prices and quantities of categories of final demand and the second method on gross output or value added in production sectors. Thus the expenditure approach measures prices at the retail level and includes trade and transport margins, taxes and subsidies. The industry-of-origin approach values physical output of individual commodities by a common set of prices. This method is followed by Maddison and his collaborators (Maddison, 1990; Maddison and Van Ark, 1989; Pilat, 1994). The industry-of-origin approach compares, at least initially, countries bilaterally and thus avoids the more complicated multilateral comparisons.

The expenditure approach and the industry-of-origin approach would give the same result only if complete information on prices and quantities, trade and transport margins, taxes and subsidies were available, allowing, for example, double-deflation for all sectors, and if the weights used in the two approaches were the same. These conditions are not met (Maddison and Van Ark, 1987, pp. 2–3; Szirmai and Pilat, 1990, p. 1; Van Ark, 1992, pp. 26–7). Another difference is that the expenditure approach excludes exports, while imports are included. In contrast, the industry-of-origin approach includes imports only as far as they enter into the production of other goods and services, but includes all exports. Imports are excluded if they are directly consumed by households or the government.

In the expenditure approach, intermediate services such as transportation and trade are included in the prices of goods. The amount of these intermediate services is, however, smaller in developing countries than in developed countries, but this is only partly taken into account. The ICP has for some purposes adopted the "potato-is-a-potato" principle, based on the argument that "the utility derived from consuming a potato is the same whether it is purchased from a roadside stall or supermarket. ... This principle seems to make sense for many commodities, but it certainly is not acceptable for services, so that ... the outlet has always been an essential part of the ICP specification" (United Nations, 1992a, p. 34).

This can be related to the discussion on product differentiation in Chapter 5.

Variations in the quality and ancillary services are used to differentiate products. To some extent this is accounted for in the ICP as it tries to compare identical products, for example keeping constant outlet type and quality. ICP, however, might fail to capture all quality differences and hence underestimate PPP in poor countries where quality is likely to be lower. Moreover, ICP does not correct for all product differentiation, nor does it correct for market power resulting from quality variations. The potato-is-a-potato principle and the fact that richer countries consume a higher share of goods that are bought in urban specialty stores and contain more intermediate services and customer amenities lead to higher prices in richer countries (Ahmad, 1994, pp. 61–4; Kravis *et al.*, 1982, p. 30; Maddison, 1983; United Nations, 1992a, pp. 33–9; see also Fuchs, 1968, ch. 5). As a result, prices for "potatoes" will be lower in developing countries even if the good component of the "potato" is the same. Similarly, prices for goods are likely to be higher in developed countries. Hence, the credo, "never buy a Japanese camera in Japan" (United Nations, 1992a, p. 34). The international price of "potatoes," which is influenced by the larger weights in developed countries, will be overestimated. The higher the international price compared with the price in the national currencies, the smaller is the PPP and the higher the PPP-converted GDP. Hence the PPP-converted GDP of developing countries might be overestimated. The extent of this overestimation is unclear, although it is unlikely that the systematic gap between PPPs and exchange rates is bridged (Maddison, 1983).

The European Union and other European countries have pressed to maintain the comparisons of real output among their member countries fixed in world comparisons ("fixity rule"). This, coupled with the fact that the involvement of the United Nations Statistics Division in the ICP was reduced after Phase III, led to regionalization (Kravis, 1984, pp. 35–7). Austria, EUROSTAT (the statistics office of the EU), the OECD and the regional commissions of the United Nations are involved in the regional comparisons. Regionalization, however, has advantages and disadvantages (Kravis, 1984, pp. 16–17). Comparing countries that are more similar with regard to their price and quantity structure increases what has been called "characteristicity." But the fixity rule improves the intragroup comparisons at the expense of the comparisons between countries in different regions. Characteristicity of the Germany/France comparison, for example, has increased but it has decreased for the Germany/Japan comparison. The latter comparison is affected by the prices of all European countries and all Asian countries, while the former is only affected by European prices. As a result, the Germany/Japan comparison uses a different set of prices (a different measuring rod) than the Germany/France comparison. Furthermore, matrix consistency is not achieved in the regional comparisons. Within the ICP, the World Bank links the regions to form global comparisons. Summers and Heston (1991) use the detailed data from the regional comparisons to create their Penn World Table (PWT) without using the fixity rule. The PWT contains the most extensive real output estimates available.

Table A.1.1   United Nations International Comparison Programme: coverage and references

	Benchmark		Reference
	Countries	Year	
Phase I	10	1970	Kravis, Kenessey, Heston and Summers (1975)
Phase II	16	1970	Kravis, Heston and Summers (1978)
Phase III	34	1975	Kravis, Heston and Summers (1982)
Phase IV	60	1980	United Nations and EUROSTAT (1986;1987)
Phase V	56	1985	United Nations and EUROSTAT (1994), OECD (1988), EUROSTAT (1989), UNECE (1988)
Phase VI	35	1990	United Nations Statistical Commission and Economic Commission for Europe (1994)

Source: Summers and Heston (1991).

Table A.1.2 Countries in ICP Phases IV (1980) and V (1985)

Developed countries		Socialist economies	Developing countries	
ICP Phase IV				
Austria		Hungary	Argentina	Korea, R. of
Belgium		Poland	Bolivia	Madagascar
Canada		Yugoslavia	Botswana	Malawi
Denmark			Brazil	Mali
Finland			Cameroon	Morocco
France			Chile	Nigeria
Germany			Colombia	Pakistan
Greece			Costa Rica	Panama
Ireland			Côte d'Ivoire	Paraguay
Israel			Dominican R.	Peru
Italy			Ecuador	Philippines
Japan			El Salvador	Senegal
Luxembourg			Ethiopia	Sri Lanka
Netherlands			Guatemala	Tanzania
Norway			Honduras	Tunisia
Portugal			Hong Kong	Uruguay
Spain			India	Venezuela
United Kingdom			Indonesia	Zambia
United States			Kenya	Zimbabwe
ICP Phase V				
Australia	Luxembourg	Hungary	Bangladesh	Mauritius
Austria	Netherlands	Poland	Benin	Morocco
Belgium	New Zealand	Yugoslavia	Botswana	Nigeria
Canada	Norway		Cameroon	Pakistan
Denmark	Portugal		Congo	Philippines
Finland	Spain		Côte d'Ivoire	Rwanda
France	Sweden		Egypt	Senegal
Germany	United Kingdom		Ethiopia	Sierra Leone
Greece	United States		Hong Kong	Sri Lanka
Ireland			India	Swaziland
Italy			Iran	Tanzania
Japan			Kenya	Thailand
			Korea, R. of	Tunisia
			Madagascar	Turkey
			Malawi	Zambia
			Mali	Zimbabwe

Sources: United Nations and EUROSTAT (1986; 1994).

Appendix 2 Data methodology and sources for cross-sector analysis of Chapter 9

This appendix describes how the dependent and independent variables were constructed for the cross-sector tests conducted in Chapter 9. As the dependent variable is expressed as a ratio of the United States (US = 100), the independent variables are also expressed as ratios of the US values. For the cross-country regression analysis this was not needed because this would involve dividing all observations of each variable by the same (US) number, which would leave the regression analysis unaffected (Pindyck and Rubinfeld, 1981, p. 18). For the cross-sector analysis, it involves dividing every observation of each variable by a different, corresponding US value.

A laborious effort was made to match the different sectors as closely as possible, but if it was impossible to match the sectors of the independent variables and the dependent variable, then the sectors of the United States were as closely matched as possible to the sectors of Japan and the Republic of Korea, respectively, so it is hoped that errors were canceled out when the ratios were calculated. Table A.2.1 gives an overview of the mismatches and Table A.2.2 presents the data as used in the regression analysis of Chapter 9 (except for the fact that the data here are shown as percentages instead of ratios).

A.2.1 PRICE LEVELS (PL)

PPPs for industrial sectors are from Pilat (1994, pp. 154–5, 157, 233, 242, 256, 265). These PPPs are geometric averages of the PPPs based on US weights and PPPs based on Japanese or Korean weights. PPPs for some subsectors are aggregated to match independent variables. Aggregations of PPPs are weighted by GDP from Pilat (1994), a method followed by Pilat as well (Szirmai and Pilat, 1990, pp. 41–2). In contrast to the PPPs from ICP, PPPs are at factor costs and therefore exclude subsidies and taxes (see Appendix 1) (Szirmai and Pilat, 1990, pp. 74, 83).

PPPs for manufacturing subsectors in Pilat (1994) are for 1987 and are extrapolated to 1985 by using implicit GDP deflators. The method is described in Szirmai and Pilat (1990, p. 50). For Japan, for instance, the method is as follows: PPP for 1985 = PPP for 1987 divided by the ratio of the increase in the price index in Japan to the increase in the price index in the United States. Implicit GDP deflators for Japan, the Republic of Korea and the United States are from OECD (1995b). PPPs are converted into price levels by using the average annual exchange rates from the IMF, *International Financial Statistics*, data tapes.

Pilat (1994) deviated in a few categories from the International Standard Industrial Classification of all Economic Activities (ISIC), Rev. 2 (Szirmai and Pilat, 1990, p. 99). He lumped fabricated metals (ISIC 381) together with basic metals (ISIC 37) and professional instruments (ISIC 385) with other manufacturing (ISIC 39). His classifications are followed as far as possible.

Pilat (1994) did not discuss where restaurants and hotels are classified but his values for GDP and employment suggest that for the Republic of Korea they are included in wholesale and retail trade, but for Japan in other services (Pilat, 1994, pp. 231, 254). Pilat (1991a; 1991b), which were the bases for the Japan and the Korea comparisons, respectively, in Pilat (1994), confirmed this explicitly. In the calculation of PPPs, however, restaurants and hotels are not considered by Pilat (1994).

A larger problem emerged for business services. Pilat (1991a, pp. 3, 10; 1994, p. 117) included business services in other services for Japan. However, GDP for finance, insurance and real estate in Pilat (1994, p. 231) is exactly the same as GDP for finance, insurance, real estate and business services in United Nations (1994) and GDP for finance, insurance and real estate in Economic Planning Agency (1995). Shuichi Watanabe of the Management and Coordination Office, in a personal communication, stated that business services, as well as sanitation, are part of community, social and personal services.

For the Republic of Korea, business services were lumped with real estate in Pilat (1991b, p. 9) but seemed (comparing GDP values with other sources) to be included in other services in Pilat (1994, p. 254). In the calculation of PPPs, however, business services are not considered by Pilat (1994).

Table A.2.1 Summary of mismatches of sectors for some variables

Section	A.2.1 Price level	A.2.2 Product-tivity (HRR)	A.2.3 Capital–output ratio	A.2.5 GDP (economies of scale)	A.2.6 Markup, Wages, IMP_D	A.2.5 Establish-ments	A.2.7 Imp_I
Comparison of Japan with USA							
Restaurants & hotels	Other services	=	Other services/ Mixed	=	=	=	=
Business services	Other services	Real estate	=	=	=	=	Real estate
Sanitation	Other services	=	Other services/ Utilities	Other services/ Utilities	=	Other services/ Utilities	=
Education & health	Other services	Mixed[a]	Other services/ Mixed	Other services/ Mixed	Mixed[a]	Other services/ Mixed	Mixed[a]
Comparison of Republic of Korea with USA							
Restaurants & hotels	Wholesale & retail trade	=	=	=	=	=	=
Business services	Other services	Real estate	Real estate	Real estate	=	=	Real estate
Sanitation	Other services	=	Other services[b]/ Utilities	Other services[b]/ Utilities	=	Other services[b]/ Utilities	=
Education & health	Other services	=	Other services/ Mixed	Other services/ Mixed	=	Other services/ Mixed	=

Notes: A "=" in a cell indicates that the variable follows the same classification as the price level. A slash "/" in a cell indicates that the data for Japan or the Republic of Korea could not be matched to data for the USA. The sector above or left of the "/" indicates the sector for the Japanese or Korean data and below or right of the "/" the sector for the US data.

[a] For Japan's input–output table, public education and health institutions are included in government (OECD, 1995a, p. 13).

[b] Sanitation is assumed to be included in other services (ISIC 9). For the USA sanitation is part of utilities.

Table A.2.2 Data for cross-sector regression analysis

	PL	MARKUP	HRR	L	WAGES	UNION	AS	ESTABLS	R&D	ADVERTS	K/Y	I_GR	GDP	IMP_D	IMP_I	TARIFF	NTB
Japan as a percentage of USA																	
Agriculture	313	132	898	1 738	17	832	101	186	100	35	162	−207	15	423	35	918	205
Mining	112	60	329	443	45	282	67	16	100	28	40	56	3	7 218	108	216	152
Food etc.	98	107	661	203	44	144	24	369	122	74	85	669	45	120	396	91	153
Textiles etc.	70	103	255	131	47	144	14	564	100	37	105	−2 166	64	38	143	124	39
Wood etc.	182	99	477	254	42	131	27	197	100	26			14	89	503	100	0
Paper etc.	83	98	240	130	57	144	36	135	100	141	122	161	36	68	131	124	0
Chemicals	86	100	254	101	56	144	77	73	108	177	72	291	49	112	245	90	10
Petrol etc.	78	117	327	75	53	144	63	58	106	101	557	295	15	93	325	90	10
Plastic etc.	47	114	225	66	43	144	28	283	144	62			126	24	103	90	10
Nonmet. minrls.	77	106	246	110	46	131	44	219	146	10	130	−18 096	76	30	166	62	10
Iron & steel	75	103	239	91	48	131	24	277	207	11	157	667	73	78	169	103	0
Nonelct. mach.	55	107	226	79	45	131	33	177	29	27	112	192	81	20	38	43	10
Elect. mach.	71	109	216	98	47	131	34	283	71	64	90	171	110	15	53	43	0
Other manuf.	70	106	234	93	37	131	52	64	35	35	255	114	66	51	130	63	0
Utilities	172	107	299	240	67	181	66	57	100	668	60	128	22	1	421	130	0
Construction	126	98	274	247	64	88	88	121	100	106	114	−151	46	100	44	100	100
Trade	107	88	189	166	62	129	49	148	100	32	110	63	35	73	420	100	100
Transportation	125	89	259	257	79	159	117	91	100	41	30	−8 531	41	770	476	100	100
Communication	97	94	199	206	59	154	51	95	100	68	89	3 036	22	58 908	63	100	100
Finance & ins.	93	120	150	112	80	1 700	114	33	100	94	36	44	36	399	222	100	100

Table A.2.2 (continued)

	PL	MARKUP	HRR	L	WAGES	UNION	AS	ESTABLS	R&D	ADVERTS	K/Y	I_GR	GDP	IMP_D	IMP_I	TARIFF	NTB
Real estate	226	197	306	419	109	1 700	47	129	100	18	17	151	14	100	224	100	100
Other services	86	97	199	117	61	276	48	118	100	37	52	491	28	3 133	113	100	100
Republic of Korea as a percentage of USA																	
Agriculture	208	167	1 770	2 910	14	0	130	80	100	11	45	–458	7	252	38	299	360
Mining	114	61	1 116	2 117	23	217	137	7	100	4	60	505	1	2 788	48		61
Food etc.	104	107	1 825	309	28	75	10	186	114	105	179	597	3	104	515	354	196
Textiles etc.	76	104	826	288	25	75	22	219	100	35	322	–8 192	12	40	391	245	1
Wood etc.	130	96	1 321	416	18	68	24	36	100	89	308	–2 216	1	126	2 500	684	0
Paper etc.	78	99	769	308	29	75	36	21	100	78	185	284	2	440	554	1 057	23
Chemicals	107	104	945	346	24	75	54	33	15	155	93	752	4	222	625	414	75
Nonmet. minrls.	55	108	743	176	28	68	52	44	41	18	295	–56 239	10	120	532	472	205
Primary metals	70	103	808	87	26	68	26	48	60	2	163	1 720	5	412	683	425	4
Machinery	69	108	768	286	23	68	51	23	37	45	275	372	3	230	422	623	219
Other manuf.	103	104	1 034	742	10	68	25	79	113	37	154	236	1	34	344	372	64
Utilities	147	129	894	346	64	119	79	5	100	33	89	290	2	3	196	100	100
Construction	60	104	627	243	45	0	272	5	100	215	218	–505	6	100	128	100	100
Trade	84	148	752	542	8	0	19	53	100	13	119	157	2	156	405	100	100
Transportation	56	103	749	277	31	80	96	12	100	20	127	1 348	5	1 527	1 176	100	100
FIRE[a]	67	106	548	235	49	733	62	13	100	3	100	169	2	1 434	587	100	100
Other services	30	91	250	103	53	7	34	20	4	22	256	629	6	1 713	62	100	100

Notes: Data used in regressions are ratios. For presentational purposes, the data are shown here as percentages. [a] Finance, insurance and real estate.

A.2.2   MARKED-UP DIRECT AND INDIRECT LABOR REQUIREMENTS (HRR)

All input–output (I–O) tables are at producer prices. The l in $v^* = l(I - \mu A)^{-1}$ is converted to US dollars by using sectoral PPPs. Pilat (1994) did not give enough disaggregation for PPPs for Japan to match all I–O sectors. Hence the PPP for chemicals is used for drugs and medicine, the PPP for electrical machinery is used for radio, TV and communication equipment, the PPP for machinery and transport equipment is used for five subsectors and the PPP for basic metals and fabricated metal products is used for three subsectors. Pilat (1994) did not treat restaurants and hotels separately and the PPP is from United Nations and EUROSTAT (1994).

The marked-up direct and indirect labor requirements are aggregated, weighted by GDP from the I–O tables, to match the price level and the numéraire country as closely as possible. Sectoral markups have been calculated as indicated in Chapter 9.

Japan

Input–output table (36 by 36) is from OECD (1995a). The number of engaged is for nonmanufacturing sectors from Government of Japan (1990) and for manufacturing from OECD (1995b).

The Republic of Korea

Input–output table (20 by 20) is from Bank of Korea (1988). Data on the number of engaged are from Pilat (1994, pp. 254, 266, 298). Manufacturing employment data are not from the same OECD source as for Japan and the United States because employment is underestimated; see the discussion in Pilat (1994, pp. 147–8, 163). Pilat (1994) estimated employment for manufacturing subsectors only for 1987 and these data are extrapolated back to 1985 by using the number of engaged in total manufacturing for 1985, using the same distribution among subsectors. Because restaurants and hotels are included in wholesale and retail trade in Pilat (1994), employment data for the separate categories are derived by using the proportions reported in the 1986 census (Republic of Korea, 1991, p. 231). Similarly, Pilat (1994) did not report separate employment data for fabricated metals, which are lumped with basic metals. Employment data for the separate categories are derived by using the proportions reported in ILO (1993).

United States

Input–output table (36 by 36) is from OECD (1995a). This source does not give the cost components of value added (that is, compensation of employees, operating surplus and taxes minus subsidies). The compensation of employees is instead taken from US Department of Commerce (1992). Because value added from this source is different from value added in OECD (1995a), the share of compensation of employees in GDP (from US Department of Commerce, 1993b), which is consistent with the compensation of employees' data) is calculated and applied to the GDP as given in OECD (1995a). The compensation of employees in education who are employed by state and local governments was reclassified as a service (community, social and personal services) to match the classification for Japan and the Republic of Korea. The value added produced by these employees, which is not available separately, was deducted from GDP of government in proportion to their share in employment and added to community, social and personal services.

The number of engaged for nonmanufacturing is from Pilat (1994, p. 231) and for manufacturing from OECD (1995b). The number of employees for hotels and business services was reclassified from services to restaurants and hotels and real estate, respectively, and is from US Department of Commerce (1992). Pilat (1994) seems to have included restaurants in retail trade, as becomes clear when his data are compared to Elfring (1988, p. 223). The number of engaged in restaurants was reclassified from retail trade to restaurants and hotels in proportion to the number of employees reported in the US Department of Commerce (1987).

A.2.3 CAPITAL–OUTPUT RATIOS (K/Y) AND INVESTMENT GROWTH RATE (I_GR)

The capital–output ratio is calculated as the ratio of the gross fixed tangible nonresidential capital stock to GDP at factor costs. The growth rate of investment was calculated as the percentage increase of the gross fixed tangible nonresidential capital stock in 1985 at constant prices.

Japan

The private capital stock data (at 1990 prices) are from Economic Planning Agency (EPA), kindly provided by Shigeru Hirota of EPA through Hiroshi Kawamura of the United Nations. GDP is from EPA (1995) (which gives the same totals but more decimal points than United Nations, 1994) and OECD (1995b). GDP of 1985 was inflated to 1990 prices with the implicit GDP deflators from the same sources. Disaggregation of GDP of transport and communication was performed by using the proportions reported in OECD (1995a). The capital stock for general government (public administration and government services) is on a net basis and is from United Nations (1994, Table 2.13). NDP for the capital–output ratio for general government is also from EPA (1995).

GDP of 1985 at 1990 factor costs was derived by first calculating GDP of 1985 at 1990 market prices and then subtracting the share of taxes minus subsidies in value added in the 1990 input–output table at current prices (from OECD, 1995a).

The Republic of Korea

Capital stock estimates are from Pyo (1992). I am indebted to Dirk Pilat for a copy of this working paper. The capital stock for government is included in community, social and personal services and is separated in proportion to its GDP. The capital stock for restaurants and hotels is separated from wholesale and retail trade in proportion to their operating surplus, which is from Bank of Korea (1988). GDP at market prices for nonmanufacturing is from United Nations (1994) and for manufacturing from OECD (1995b). GDP at factor costs for government and other services are from Pilat (1994, p. 254). GDP in Pilat (1994) is the same as in other sources but they do not clearly separate public administration from other government institutions such as education and health. OECD (1995b) gives much more detail than either national or UN sources and total manufacturing is the same as in the other sources. GDP for basic and fabricated metals (the category for the price level) was derived by using the share of fabricated metal products in the sector fabricated metal products and machinery and equipment as reported in the 65 by 65 I–O table in Bank of Korea (1988).

GDP at factor costs is calculated by subtracting taxes minus subsidies from GDP at market prices. Data are from United Nations (1994) for sectors that are defined equally. For other sectors the ratio of taxes minus subsidies to value added is calculated from the 65 by 65 I–O table in Bank of Korea (1988).

United States

The capital stock data are from US Department of Commerce (1993a). The capital stock for 1985 is an average of the end of 1984 and end of 1985 numbers. GDP is from US Department of Commerce (1993b) and OECD (1995b).

Restaurants are included in retail trade in the US data and no separate capital stock data for restaurants are available. Hotels are included in other services. GDP of education is included in the government sector and was reclassified as a service as described in section A.2.2. Sanitation is classified in the United States as a utility and therefore could not also be reclassified as a service. On the other hand, business services were transferred from services to real estate to match the classification of the Korean data.

GDP at factor costs is calculated by subtracting the share of taxes minus subsidies in value added from GDP at market prices. This ratio is calculated from United Nations (1992b). The sectors do not always match completely GDP at market prices (for example for fabricated metals and instruments, which Pilat reclassified) but it is assumed that the ratio of taxes minus subsidies to value added is the same. For the comparison with Japan, GDP at factor costs for the petroleum sector was calculated by using the ratio of taxes minus subsidies to value added from the 1982 input–output table (36 by 36) in OECD (1995a).

A.2.4   RESEARCH AND DEVELOPMENT (R&D) AND ADVERTISING EXPENDITURES (ADVERTS)

Research and Development Expenditures (R&D)

Expenditures on research and development (R&D) are as a percentage of GDP at factor costs. GDP data sources are the same as in section A.2.3. For the United States, R&D expenditures are not disaggregated for nonmanufacturing sectors (about 6 per cent of total R&D). For these sectors it is assumed that the shares are the same across countries, that is, the ratio is one.

Japan
Research and development expenditures are from OECD, *ANBERD* and OECD (1991).

The Republic of Korea
Research and development expenditures are from the Republic of Korea (1995), kindly provided and translated by Byung-Ik Woo of the United Nations. R&D expenditures were not separately available for fabricated metals. Expenditures on R&D as a percentage of GDP are therefore calculated only for basic metals.

United States
Research and development expenditures are from OECD, *ANBERD*.

Advertising Expenditures (ADVERTS)

Advertising expenditures are calculated as a percentage of GDP at factor costs.

Japan

Data are from Government of Japan (1990).

The Republic of Korea

Advertising expenditures are from the Bank of Korea (1986), kindly provided by Byung-Ik Woo. Data are for large enterprises only, which probably creates an upward bias. GDP at factor costs are from United Nations (1992b). Expenditures were not separately available for fabricated metals and the percentage of GDP is therefore calculated separately for basic metals and for fabricated metals and machinery. Business services are included in real estate.

United States

Advertising expenditures and GDP are from the 1987 input–output table in US Department of Commerce (1994a).

A.2.5   ECONOMIES OF SCALE/MARKET POWER (GDP, AS, ESTABLS)

One proxy for economies of scale is total GDP at factor costs by sector. Data sources are the same as in section A.2.3. The sectoral PPPs from Pilat (1994) are used to convert domestic currencies to dollars. For the Republic of Korea, business services were reclassified from real estate to other services by using the proportions from the 65 by 65 input–output table from Bank of Korea (1988). For the Japan comparison, GDP of restaurants in the United States was reclassified from retail trade to other services. GDP was assumed to be in proportion to the number of employees reported in US Department of Commerce (1987).

Another proxy for economies of scale or market power is the size of an establishment measured by the average number of employees or engaged per establishment (AS). Data are from Japan Statistics Bureau (1988, Table 4.4), Republic of Korea (1991, p. 231) and from US Department of Commerce (1987). For Japan and the Republic of Korea, the data are from the Establishment Census of 1986 rather than 1985. This is not considered a problem as it is unlikely that the average size of establishments changes much in a year. The three censuses covered all establishments, including all small ones, head offices and branches, with the following exceptions. The Japanese census excluded "individual proprietorship establishments engaged in agriculture, forestry and fisheries and establishments belonging to domestic services, foreign governments and international agencies." The Korean census excluded "farm households, fishery households and establishments which have no fixed office or fixed equipment, etc." The United States census excluded employment in "government, railroad employment jointly covered by Social Security and railroad retirement programs, self-employed persons, domestic service, agricultural production, foreign, and ships at sea."

The Japanese and the Korean censuses included all persons engaged, including proprietors, unpaid family workers, managers and temporary workers. The US census, however, excluded the self-employed and appears to have excluded also unpaid family workers because only wage and salary employees are covered. On the other hand, managers and temporary workers are included.

For Japan, radio and television broadcasting was reclassified to communication. For the United States, the data for administrative and auxiliary establishments were distributed in proportion to the different subcategories.

All three censuses exclude agricultural production and data for the average size and the number of farms for 1985 are derived in the following way. For all three countries, the number of engaged is from the same sources as described in section A.2.2 and this number and the number of farms (or households) is added to the data for agricultural services from the censuses. For Japan, the number of farm households (small farms) and of agricultural establishments (large farms) is taken from Japan Statistics Bureau (1988, Table 5.1). The numbers for the households refer to 1 January. Hence the average of the 1985 and 1986 numbers are taken. For the Republic of Korea, the number of farm households (minus the number of households without cultivated land) is from Republic of Korea (1989, p. 102). For the United States, the number of farms is from US Department of Commerce (1994b, Table 1085).

The number of establishments (ESTABLS) was also used separately as an independent variable indicating the degree of competition. AS and ESTABLS are also used as a ratio of GDP, denoted AS/Y and ESTABLS/Y, to signify the size of the establishments and the number of establishments in relation to GDP.

A.2.6   MARKUPS, WAGES AND FINAL DEMAND IMPORTS (MARKUP, WAGES, IMP_D)

Although the data used for the calculation of markups, wages and final demand imports are the same as used in section A.2.2, it was possible to reclassify business services from the real estate and business services sector to services for all three countries. For the Republic of Korea, the 65 by 65 input–output table from Bank of Korea (1988) was used for this purpose. For Japan and the United States, it was assumed that the share of business services in real estate and business services for the different variables is the same in OECD (1995a) as in Government of Japan (1990) and the US input–output table of 1985 on data diskette, as described in US Department of Commerce (1990). In addition, compensation of employees in business services for the United States is from US Department of Commerce (1992).

Markups (MARKUP)

Markups were calculated using the method described in Chapter 9. The markup as an independent variable is slightly different from the markup in the marked-up direct and indirect labor requirements in A.2.2 because of the reclassification of business services.

Wages (WAGES)

Average wages in the different sectors were calculated by dividing the compensation of employees by the number of engaged or employed, using the same data as in A.2.2. For the United States, the number of engaged is directly divided into compensation of employees as reported in US Department of Commerce (1992) and not into the compensation of employees as calculated to create consistency with the input–output table. Wages for Japan and the Republic of Korea were converted into international dollars by using the PPP for total consumption from United Nations and EUROSTAT (1994).

Final Demand Imports (IMP_D)

Imports are calculated as a percentage of GDP with data from their input–output table. For government, real estate and construction, imports in the United States were zero and for Japan and the Republic of Korea very small. As dividing by zero is impossible, the ratio was set to one for these three sectors.

A.2.7 IMPORTED INTERMEDIATE INPUTS (IMP_I)

Imports are calculated as a percentage of GDP with data from their input–output table. For Japan and the United States, data are from OECD (1995a), kindly provided in electronic form by Evangelos Ioannidis of the OECD. For the Republic of Korea, data are from Bank of Korea (1988).

A.2.8 UNION MEMBERSHIP (UNION)

Percentage of employed who are members of a union.

Japan

Data are from Japan Statistics Bureau (1986). Data are not disaggregated for manufacturing subsectors and the aggregated number is used for manufacturing subcategories as well.

The Republic of Korea

Data are from Republic of Korea (1986), kindly provided and interpreted by Byung-Ik Woo.

United States

Data are from US Bureau of Labor Statistics (1986). Data are not disaggregated for manufacturing subsectors, beyond the durable/nondurable distinction. Hence, for manufacturing and for some other sectors, the aggregated number is used for the subcategories as well.

A.2.9 TARIFFS AND NONTARIFF BARRIERS (TARIFF, NTB)

Data are from OECD (1996b) for Japan and the United States. In OECD (1996b), tariffs are production-weighted average Most-Favored Nation rates (in percentages) and Nontariff Barriers (NTBs) is the frequency ratio. The frequency ratio indicates the percentage of tariff lines affected by NTBs. For the Republic of Korea, data are from UNCTAD (1994), where tariffs are mean rates (in percentages) weighted by total imports of 120 developing countries and NTBs is the incidence ratio. The NTB incidence is the percentage of tariff lines affected by nontariff measures. For Japan, data refer to 1988; for the United States, to 1989; and for the Republic of Korea to 1984–7. For utilities, construction and all service sectors, the ratio of tariffs and NTBs of Japan and Korea to the United States is assumed to be one. Data are not disaggregated for some sectors, such as chemicals in Japan. Hence the aggregated number is used for subcategories as well. On the other hand, for some sectors, such as textiles and footwear in the Republic of Korea, only disaggregated data were available. In this case a simple average was taken to aggregate. No tariff rates for agriculture and mining were available from OECD (1996b). Agricultural tariffs (for 1986–8) were taken from Burniaux *et al.* (1990, p. 298).

References

Abdel-Rahman, Hesham M. and Masahisa Fujita (1990), "Product Variety, Marshallian Externalities and City Sizes", *Journal of Regional Science*, **30** (2), 165–83.

Abuhadba, Mario and Pilar Romaguera (1993), "Inter-Industrial Wage Differentials: Evidence from Latin American Countries", *The Journal of Development Studies*, **30** (1), 190–205.

Ahmad, Sultan (1994), "Improving Inter-Spatial and Inter-Temporal Comparability of National Accounts", *Journal of Development Economics*, **44** (1), 53–75.

Ajakaiye, D. Olu and Ode Ojowu (1994), "Relative Price Effects of Exchange Rate Depreciation in Nigeria Under Fixed and Fixed/Flexible Mark-Up Pricing Regimes", *World Development*, **22** (8), 1175–82.

Akerlof, George A. (1970), "The Market for 'Lemons': Qualitative Uncertainty and the Market Mechanism", *The Quarterly Journal of Economics*, **84** (3), 488–500.

Amadeo, Edward J. (1994), "Bargaining Power, Mark-Up Power and Wage Differentials in Brazil", *Cambridge Journal of Economics*, **18** (3), 313–22.

Amjadi, Azita and Alexander J. Yeats (1995), "Have Transport Costs Contributed to the Relative Decline of Sub-Saharan Africa Exports?", *Policy Research Working Paper*, no. 1559, Washington, DC: The World Bank.

Amsden, Alice H. (1989), *Asia's Next Giant: South Korea and Late Industrialization*, New York: Oxford University Press.

Amsden, Alice H. (1997), "Bringing Production Back in – Understanding Government's Economic Role in Late Industrialization", *World Development*, **25** (4), 469–80.

Amsden, Alice H. and Yoon-Dae Euh (1990), "Republic of Korea's Financial Reform: What are the Lessons?", *UNCTAD Discussion Papers*, no. 30.

Andersen, Torben M. and Niels Lynggard Hansen (1995), "Price Adjustment in Open Economies", *Open Economies Review*, **6** (4), 303–21.

Anderson Schaffer, Julie (1998), "Premiums to Employment in Larger Establishments: Evidence from Peru", *Journal of Development Economics*, **55** (1), 81–113.

Aoki, Masahiko (ed.) (1984), *The Economic Analysis of the Japanese Firm*, Amsterdam: North-Holland.

Arestis, Philip (1986), "Wages and Prices in the UK: The Post Keynesian View", *Journal of Post Keynesian Economics*, **8** (3), 339–58.

Arestis, Philip (1992), *The Post-Keynesian Approach to Economics: An Alternative Analysis of Economic Theory and Policy*, Aldershot, UK and Brookfield, US: Edward Elgar.

Arestis, Philip (1996), "Post–Keynesian Economics: Towards Coherence", *Cambridge Journal of Economics*, **20** (1), 111–35.

Arestis, Philip and William Milberg (1993–4), "Degree of Monopoly, Pricing and Flexible Exchange Rates", *Journal of Post Keynesian Economics*, **16** (2), 167–88.

Argy, Victor (1981), *The Postwar International Money Crisis, An Analysis*, London: George Allen & Unwin.

Arnott, Richard (1987), "Spatial Economics", in John Eatwell, Murray Milgate and Peter Newman (eds), *The New Palgrave: A Dictionary of Economics*, Vol. 4, New York: Stockton Press, pp. 429–31.

Aschauer, David Alan (1989), "Is Public Expenditure Productive?", *Journal of Monetary Economics*, **23** (2), 177–200.

Asea, Patrick K. and Enrique G. Mendoza (1994), "Do Long-Run Productivity Differentials Explain Long-Run Real Exchange Rates?", *IMF Working Paper*, no. WP/94/60, Washington, DC: IMF.

Athey, Michael J. and Prem S. Laumas (1994), "Internal Funds and Corporate Investment", *Journal of Development Economics*, **45** (2), 287–303.

Athukorala, Premachandra and Jayant Menon (1994), "Pricing to Market Behavior and Exchange Rate Pass-through in Japanese Exports", *The Economic Journal*, **104** (423), 271–81.

Aw, Bee Yan (1992), "An Empirical Model of Mark-ups in a Quality-differentiated Export Market", *Journal of International Economics*, **33** (3/4), 327–44.

Baer, Werner and Michel E.A. Hervé (1966), "Employment and Industrialization in Developing Countries", *The Quarterly Journal of Economics*, **80** (1), 88–107.

Bagachwa, M.S.D. (1992), "Choice of Technology in Small and Large Firms: Grain Milling in Tanzania", *World Development*, **20** (1), 97–107.

Bahmani-Oskooee, Mohsen (1992), "A Time-Series Approach to Test the Productivity Bias Hypothesis in Purchasing Power Parity", *Kyklos*, **45** (2), 227–36.

Bahmani-Oskooee, Mohsen and Farhang Niroomand (1996), "A Reexamination of Balassa's Productivity Bias Hypothesis", *Economic Development and Cultural Change*, **45** (1), 195–204.

Balassa, Bela (1964), "The Purchasing-Power Parity Doctrine: A Reappraisal", *Journal of Political Economy*, **72** (6), 584–96.

Balassa, Bela (1973), "Just How Misleading are Official Exchange Rate Conversions? A Comment", *The Economic Journal*, **83** (332), 1258–67.

Balassa, Bela (1974), "The Rule of Four-Ninths: A Rejoinder", *The Economic Journal*, **84** (335), 609–14.

Balassa, Bela (1981), *The Newly Industrializing Countries in the World Economy*, New York: Pergamon Press.

Bank of Korea (1983), *1980 Input–Output Tables of Korea*, Seoul: Bank of Korea.

Bank of Korea (1986), *Financial Statements Analysis, 1986*, Seoul: The Bank of Korea.

Bank of Korea (1988), *1985 Input–Output Tables of Korea*, Seoul: Bank of Korea.

Barker, Terry (1977), "International Trade and Economic Growth: An Alternative to the Neoclassical Approach", *The Cambridge Journal of Economics*, **1** (2), 153–72.

Barro, Robert J. (1991), "Economic Growth in a Cross Section of Countries", *The Quarterly Journal of Economics*, **106** (2), 407–43.

Bartelsman, Eric J., Ricardo J. Caballero and Richard K. Lyons (1991), "Short and Long Run Externalities", *NBER Working Paper*, no. 3810, Cambridge, MA: National Bureau of Economic Research.

Basile, Liliane and Neri Salvadori (1984–5), "Kalecki's Pricing Theory", *Journal of Post Keynesian Economics*, **7** (2), 249–62.

Baumol, William J. (1985), "Productivity Policy and the Service Sector", in Robert P. Inman (ed.), *Managing the Service Economy: Prospects and Problems*, Cambridge: Cambridge University Press, pp. 301–17.

Baumol, William J. (1987), "Indivisibilities", in John Eatwell, Murray Milgate and Peter Newman (eds), *The New Palgrave: A Dictionary of Economics*, Vol. 2, New York: Stockton Press, pp. 793–5.

Baumol, William J. (1992), "Economies of Scale in Financial Activities", in Peter Newman, Murray Milgate and John Eatwell (eds), *The New Palgrave Dictionary of Money and Finance*, Vol. 1, New York: Stockton Press, pp. 726–8.

Baumol, William J. and Alan S. Blinder (1982), *Economics: Principles and Policy*, 2nd edn, New York: Harcourt Brace Jovanovich.

Baumol, William J., Sue Anne Batey Blackman and Edward N. Wolff (1989), *Productivity and American Leadership; The Long View*, Cambridge and London: MIT Press.

Beckerman, Wilfred and Tim Jenkinson (1986), "What Stopped the Inflation? Unemployment or Commodity Prices?", *The Economic Journal*, **96** (381), 39–54.

Bergstrand, Jeffrey H. (1991), "Structural Determinants of Real Exchange Rates and National Price Levels: Some Empirical Evidence", *The American Economic Review*, **81** (1), 325–34.

Bergstrand, Jeffrey H. (1992), "Real Exchange Rates, National Price Levels and the Peace Dividend", *The American Economic Review*, **82** (2), 55–61.

Bettendorf, Leon and Frank Verboven (1997), "How Competitive is the Dutch Coffee Market?", *CPB Report: Quarterly Review of CPB Netherlands Bureau for Economic Policy Analysis*, no. 4, pp. 27–9.

Bhagwati, Jagdish N. (1984), "Why are Services Cheaper in the Poor Countries?", *The Economic Journal*, **94** (374), 279–86.

Bhalla, A.S. (1970), "The Role of Services in Employment Expansion", *International Labour Review*, **101** (5), 519–39.

Bhalla, A.S. (ed.) (1985), *Technology and Employment in Industry: A Case Study Approach*, 3rd edn, Geneva: International Labor Office.

Bhaskar, V., Stephen Machin and Gavin C. Reid. (1993), "Price and Quantity Adjustment Over the Business Cycle: Evidence from Survey Data", *Oxford Economic Papers*, **45** (2), 257–68.

Bilginsoy, Cihan (1994), "Distributional Consequences of Public Enterprises", *Journal of Post Keynesian Economics*, **16** (4), 563–88.

Bilginsoy, Cihan (1997), "A Macroeconomic Analysis of Agricultural Terms of Trade in Turkey, 1952–1990", *The Journal of Development Studies*, **33** (6), 797–819.

Binswanger, Hans P., Klaus Deiniger and Gershon Feder (1995), "Power, Distortions, Revolt and Reform in Agricultural Relations", in Jere Behrman and T.N. Srinivasan (eds), *Handbook of Development Economics*, Vol. 3B, Amsterdam: North-Holland.

Blades, Derek (1987), "Goods and Services in OECD Countries", *OECD Economic Studies*, no. 8, 159–84.

Blades, Derek, Derek D. Johnston and Witold Marczewski (1974), *Service Activities in Developing Countries: An Analysis Based on National Accounts*, Paris: OECD.

Blaug, Mark (1980), *The Methodology of Economics, Or How Economists Explain*, Cambridge: Cambridge University Press.

Blinder, Alan, Elie R.D. Canetti, David E. Lebow and Jeremy B. Rudd (1998), *Asking About Prices: A New Approach to Understanding Price Stickiness*, New York: Russell Sage Foundation.

Blomström, Magnus and Ari Kokko (1997), "How Foreign Investment Affects Host Countries", *Policy Research Working Paper*, no. 1745, Washington, DC: The World Bank.

Bober, Stanley (1992), *Pricing and Growth: A Neo-Ricardian Approach*, Armonk, NY: M.E. Sharpe.

Bohm, Peter (1987), "External Economies", in John Eatwell, Murray Milgate and Peter Newman (eds), *The New Palgrave: A Dictionary of Economics*, Vol. 2, New York: Stockton Press, pp. 261–3.

Brinkman, Henk-Jan (1991), "An Empirical Analysis of Determinants of Social Indicators", mimeo, New York: United Nations.

Brinkman, Henk-Jan and Alberto Gabriele (1992), "Problems in Agricultural Development in Sub-Saharan Africa", *DIESA Working Papers Series*, no. 17, New York: United Nations Department of International Economic and Social Affairs.

Burniaux, Jean-Marc, John P. Martin, François Delorme, Ian Lienert and Dominique van der Mensbrugghe (1990), "Economy-Wide Effects of Agricultural Policies in OECD Countries: A GE Approach Using the WALRAS Model", in Ian Goldin and Odin Knudsen (eds), *Agricultural Trade Liberalization: Implications for Developing Countries*, Paris: OECD and The World Bank, pp. 283–306.

Byerlee, Derek and Michael L. Morris (1993), "Calculating Levels of Protection: Is It Always Appropriate to Use World Reference Prices Based on Current Trading Status?", *World Development*, **21** (5), 805–15.

Caballero, Ricardo J. and Richard K. Lyons (1989), "The Role of External Economies in U.S. Manufacturing", *NBER Working Paper*, no. 3033, Cambridge, MA: National Bureau of Economic Research.

Campa, Jose and Linda S. Goldberg (1995), "Investment in Manufacturing, Exchange Rates and External Exposure", *Journal of International Economics*, **38** (3/4), 297–320.

Canzoneri, Matthew B., Robert E. Cumby and Behzad Diba (1996), "Relative Labor Productivity and the Real Exchange Rate in the Long Run: Evidence for a Panel of OECD Countries", *NBER Working Paper*, no. 5676, Cambridge, MA: National Bureau of Economic Research.

Capozza, Dennis R. and Robert van Order (1987), "Spatial Competition", in John Eatwell, Murray Milgate and Peter Newman (eds), *The New Palgrave: A Dictionary of Economics*, Vol. 4, New York: Stockton Press, pp. 425–9.

Carlton, Dennis W. (1986), "The Rigidity of Prices", *The American Economic Review*, **76** (4), 637–58.

Carpenter, Robert E., Steven M. Fazzari and Bruce C. Petersen (1994), "Inventory Investment, Internal-Finance Fluctuations and the Business Cycle", *Brookings Papers on Economics Activity*, no. 2, pp. 75–138.

Chamberlin, Edward H. (1960), *The Theory of Monopolistic Competition: A Re-orientation of the Theory of Value*, 7th edn, Cambridge, MA: Harvard University Press.

Charmes, Jacques (1990), "A Critical Review of Concepts, Definitions and Studies in the Informal Sector", in David Turnham, Bernard Salomé and Antoine Schwarz (eds), *The Informal Sector Revisited*, Paris: OECD, pp. 10–48.

Chenery, Hollis B. and Moshe Syrquin (1975), *Patterns of Development, 1950–1970*, New York: Oxford University Press.

Chenery, Hollis B., Sherman Robinson and Moshe Syrquin (1986), *Industrialization and Growth: A Comparative Study*, New York: Oxford University Press.

Ciccone, Antonio and Robert E. Hall (1993), "Productivity and Density of Economic Activity", *NBER Working Paper*, no. 4313, Cambridge, MA: National Bureau of Economic Research.

Clague, Christopher K. (1985), "A Model of Real National Price Levels", *Southern Economic Journal*, **51** (4), 998–1017.

Clague, Christopher K. (1986a), "Determinants of the National Price Level: Some Empirical Results", *The Review of Economics and Statistics*, **68** (2), 320–23.

Clague, Christopher K. (1986b), "Tariff, Transfers and the Real Exchange Rate", *Southern Economic Journal*, **53** (1), 155–69.

Clague, Christopher K. (1988a), "Purchasing-Power Parities and Exchange Rates in Latin America", *Economic Development and Cultural Change*, **36** (3), 529–41.

Clague, Christopher K. (1988b), "Explanations of National Price Levels", in J. Salazar-Carrillo and D.S. Prasada Rao (eds), *World Comparison of Incomes, Prices and Product*, Amsterdam: North-Holland, pp. 237–62.

Clague, Christopher K. (1989), "'The National Price Level: Theory and Estimation': A Comment", *Journal of Macroeconomics*, **11** (3), 375–81.

Clague, Christopher K. (1991), "Relative Efficiency, Self-Containment and Comparative Costs of Less Developed Countries", *Economic Development and Cultural Change*, **39** (3), 507–30.

Clague, Christopher K. (1992), "A Cross-Country Study of the Agricultural Price Level", *IRIS Working Paper*, no. 3, College Park, MD: University of Maryland.

Clague, Christopher K. (1993a), "PPP Puzzles: Food Prices, Agricultural Prices and the Cost of Living in America", *IRIS Working Paper*, no. 37, College Park, MD: University of Maryland.

Clague, Christopher K. (1993b), "Why Are Prices so Low in America?", *The World Economy*, **16** (5), 601–10.

Clague, Christopher K. and Vito Tanzi (1972), "Human Capital, Natural Resources and the Purchasing-Power Parity Doctrine: Some Empirical Evidence", *Economia Internazionale*, **25** (1), 3–18

Clifton, Eric V. (1985), "Real Exchange Rates, Import Penetration and Protectionism in Industrial Countries", *IMF Staff Papers*, **32** (3), 513–36.

Cline, William R. (1997), *Trade and Income Distribution*, Washington, DC: Institute for International Economics.

Cobham, David and Ramesh Subramaniam (1998), "Corporate Finance in Developing Countries: New Evidence from India", *World Development*, **26** (6), 1033–47.

Coddington, Alan (1983), *Keynesian Economics: The Search for First Principles*, London: George Allen & Unwin.

Cohen, Wesley M. and Steven Klepper (1996), "A Reprise of Size and R&D", *The Economic Journal*, **106** (437), 925–51.

Conigliani, Claudio, Giovanni Ferri and Andrea Generale (1997), "The Impact of Bank–Firm Relations on the Propagation of Monetary Policy Squeezes: An Empirical Assessment for Italy", *Banca Nazionale del Lavoro Quarterly Review*, **50** (202), 271–99.

Coutts, K.J. (1987), "Average Cost Pricing", in John Eatwell, Murray Milgate and Peter Newman (eds), *The New Palgrave: A Dictionary of Economics*, Vol. 1, New York: Stockton Press, pp. 158–9.

Datta-Chaudhuri, Mrinal (1990), "Market Failure and Government Failure", *The Journal of Economic Perspectives*, **4** (3), 25–39.

David, Paul A. (1972), "Just How Misleading are Official Exchange Rate Conversions?", *The Economic Journal*, **82** (327), 979–90.

Debreu, Gerard (1959), *Theory of Value: An Axiomatic Analysis of Economic Equilibrium*, New Haven, CT: Yale University Press.

Deckle, Robert and Jonathan Eaton (1994), "Agglomeration and the Price of Land: Evidence from the Prefectures", *NBER Working Paper*, no. 4781, Cambridge, MA: National Bureau of Economic Research.

De Gregorio, José and Holger C. Wolf (1994), "Terms of Trade, Productivity and the Real Exchange Rate", *NBER Working Paper*, no. 4807, Cambridge, MA: National Bureau of Economic Research.

De Gregorio, José, Alberto Giovannini and Holger C. Wolf (1994), "International Evidence on Tradables and Nontradables Inflation", *European Economic Review*, **38** (6), 1225–44.

Delgado, Christopher L. (1992), "Why Domestic Food Prices Matter to Growth Strategy in Semi-Open West African Agriculture", *Journal of African Economies*, **1** (3), 446–71.

Denison, Edward F. (1967), *Why Growth Rates Differ: Postwar Experience in Nine Western Countries*, Washington, DC: The Brookings Institution.

Denison, Edward F. (1989), *Estimates of Productivity Change by Industry, An Evaluation and an Alternative*, Washington, DC: The Brookings Institution.

Desai, Bhupat M. and John Mellor (1993), *Institutional Finance for Agricultural Development: An Analytical Survey of Critical Issues*, Food Policy Review 1, Washington, DC: IFPRI.

Desser, Arna (1994), "Real National Price Levels: An Empirical Assessment", *Journal of Macroeconomics*, **16** (2), 313–27.

Diaz-Alejandro, Carlos (1985), "Good–bye Financial Repression, Hello Financial Crash", *Journal of Development Economics*, **19** (1/2), 1–24.

Dickens, William T. and Lawrence Katz (1987), "Inter-Industry Wage Differences and Theories of Wage Determination", *NBER Working Paper*, no. 2271, Cambridge, MA: National Bureau of Economic Research.

Dixit, Avinash K. and Joseph Stiglitz (1977), "Monopolistic Competition and Optimum Product Diversity", *The American Economic Review*, **67** (3), 297–308.

Dollar, David (1992), "Outward-oriented Developing Economies Really Do Grow More Rapidly: Evidence from 95 LDCs, 1976–1985", *Economic Development and Cultural Change*, **40** (3), 523–44.

Dornbusch, Rudiger (1980), *Open Economy Macroeconomics*, New York: Basic Books.

Dornbusch, Rudiger (1987a), "Purchasing Power Parity", in John Eatwell, Murray Milgate and Peter Newman (eds), *The New Palgrave: A Dictionary of Economics*, Vol. 3, New York: Stockton Press, pp. 1075–85.

Dornbusch, Rudiger (1987b), "Exchange Rates and Prices", *The American Economic Review*, **77** (1), 93–106.

Dornbusch, Rudiger (1992), "The Case for Trade Liberalization in Developing Countries", *The Journal of Economic Perspectives*, **6** (1), 69–85.

Eatwell, John (1977), "The Irrelevance of Returns to Scale for Sraffa's Analysis", *The Journal of Economic Literature*, **15** (1), 61–68.

Eatwell, John (1982), *Whatever Happened to Britain: The Economics of Decline*, New York: Oxford University Press.

Eatwell, John (1987), "Returns to Scale", in John Eatwell, Murray Milgate and Peter Newman (eds), *The New Palgrave: A Dictionary of Economics*, Vol. 4, New York: Stockton Press, pp. 165–6.

Eatwell, John (1997), "International Financial Liberalization: The Impact on World Development", *Discussion Paper Series*, no. 12, New York: UNDP, Office of Development Studies.

Economic Planning Agency (1995) *Annual Report on National Accounts, 1995*, Tokyo: Government of Japan.

Economist, The (1992), "World Banking Survey", 2 May.

Economist, The (1997), "Banking in Emerging Markets", 12 April.

Economist, The (1998), "The Trials of Megabanks", 31 October.

Economist, The (1998), "Unfair Protection", 7 November.

Edwards, Brian K. and Ross M. Starr (1987), "A Note on Indivisibilities, Specialization and Economies of Scale", *The American Economic Review*, **77** (1), 192–4.

Eichner, Alfred S. (1973), "A Theory of the Determination of the Mark-Up under Oligopoly", *The Economic Journal*, **83** (332), 1184–1200.

Elfring, Tom (1988), *Service Sector Employment in Advanced Economies, A Comparative Analysis of Its Implications for Economic Growth*, Aldershot, UK: Avebury.

Engel, Charles and John H. Rogers (1994), "How Wide is the Border?", *NBER Working Paper*, no. 4829, Cambridge, MA: National Bureau of Economic Research; also published in *The American Economic Review*, **86** (5), 1112–25.

Engel, Charles and John H. Rogers (1995), "Regional Patterns in the Law of One Price: The Roles of Geography vs. Currencies", *NBER Working Paper*, no. 5395, Cambridge, MA: National Bureau of Economic Research.

EUROSTAT (1989), *Comparison of Price Levels and Economic Aggregates 1985: The Results for 22 African Countries*, Luxembourg: EUROSTAT.

Faini, Riccardo (1984), "Increasing Returns, Non-traded Inputs and Regional Development", *The Economic Journal*, **94** (374), 308–23.

Falvey, Rodney E. and Norman Gemmell (1991), "Explaining Service-Price Differences in International Comparisons", *The American Economic Review*, **81** (5), 1295–1309.

Falvey, Rodney E. and Norman Gemmell (1996), "A Formalisation and Test of the Factor Productivity Explanation of International Differences in Service Prices", *International Economic Review*, **37** (1), 85–102.

Faruqee, Hamid (1995), "Pricing to Market and the Real Exchange Rate", *IMF Staff Papers*, **42** (4), 855–81.

Fazzari, Steven M., R. Glenn Hubbard, Bruce C. Petersen (1988), "Financing Constraints and Corporate Investment", *Brookings Papers on Economic Activity*, no. 1, pp. 141–206.

Feenstra, Robert C. and Jon D. Kendall (1997), "Pass-Through of Exchange Rates and Purchasing Power Parity", *Journal of International Economics*, **43** (1/2), 237–61.

Feenstra, Robert C., Joseph E. Gagnon and Michael Knetter (1996), "Market Share and Exchange Rate Pass-Through in World Automobile Trade", *Journal of International Economics*, **40** (1/2), 187–207.

Feinberg, Robert (1996), "The Impact of Trade Liberalization and Competition Policy on Domestic Pricing", *Challenge*, **39** (4), 40–44.

Feldman, David H. (1991), "Economic Policy and the Relative Price of Services", *World Development*, **19** (10), 1381–89.

Feldman, David H. and Ira N. Gang (1987), "Financial Repression and the Relative Price of Non-Traded Goods", *Economics Letters*, **25**, 31–4.

Feldman, David H. and Ira N. Gang (1990), "Financial Development and the Price of Services", *Economic Development and Cultural Change*, **38** (2), 341–52.

Fischer, Stanley (1993), "The Role of Macroeconomic Factors in Growth", *Journal of Monetary Economics*, **32** (3), 485–512.

Fisher, Allan G.B. (1939), "Production, Primary, Secondary and Tertiary", *The Economic Record*, **15**, 24–38.

Fishlow, Albert (1965), *American Railroads and the Transformation of the Ante-Bellum Economy*, Cambridge, MA: Harvard University Press.

Franciosi, Robert, Praveen Kujal, Roland Michelitsch, Vernon Smith and Gang Deng (1995), "Fairness: Effect on Temporary and Equilibrium Prices in Posted-Offer Markets", *The Economic Journal*, **105** (431), 938–50.

Francois, Joseph F. (1990), "Producer Services, Scale and the Division of Labor", *Oxford Economic Papers*, **42** (4), 715–29.

Frischtak, Claudio, Ulrich Zachau and Bita Hadjimichael (1989), "Competition Policies for Industrializing Countries", mimeo, Washington, DC: The World Bank.

Froot, Kenneth and Kenneth Rogoff (1994),"Perspectives on PPP and Long-Run Real Exchange Rates", *NBER Working Paper*, no. 4952, Cambridge, MA: National Bureau of Economic Research.

Fuchs, Victor R. (1968), *The Service Economy*, New York and London: Columbia University Press.

Galbraith, John Kenneth (1967), *The New Industrial State*, Boston: Houghton Mifflin.

Garegnani, Pierangelo (1970), "Heterogenous Capital, the Production Function and the Theory of Distribution", *Review of Economic Studies*, **37** (3), 407–36.

Gatica, Jaime, Alejandra Mizala and Pilar Romaguera (1995), "Interindustry Wage Differentials in Brazil", *Economic Development and Cultural Change*, **43** (2), 315–50.

Gaynor, Martin (1994), "Issues in the Industrial Organization of the Market for Physician Services", *NBER Working Paper*, no. 4695, Cambridge, MA: National Bureau of Economic Research.

Gemmell, Norman (1985), "The Growth of Employment in Services: Egypt, 1960–75", *The Developing Economies*, **23** (1), 53–68.

Gemmell, Norman and Peter Wardley (1990), "The Contribution of Services to British Economic Growth, 1856–1913", *Explorations in Economic History*, **27** (3), 299–321.

Geroski, P.A. (1991), "Innovation and the Sectoral Sources of UK Productivity Growth", *The Economic Journal*, **101** (409), 1438–51.

Geroski, P.A. (1992), "Price Dynamics in UK Manufacturing: A Microeconomic View", *Economica*, **59** (236), 403–19.

Gershuny, J.I. and I.D. Miles (1983), *The New Service Economy: The Transformation of Employment in Industrial Societies*, New York: Praeger.

Gibbons, Robert and Lawrence Katz (1992), "Does Unmeasured Ability Explain Inter-Industry Wage Differentials?", *Review of Economic Studies*, **59** (3), 515–35.

Gibson, Heather and Euclid Tsakalotos (1994), "The Scope and Limits of Financial Liberalisation in Developing Countries: A Critical Survey", *The Journal of Development Studies*, **30** (3), 578–628.

Gittleman, Maury and Edward N. Wolff (1993), "International Comparisons of Inter-Industry Wage Differentials", *The Review of Income and Wealth*, **39** (3), 295–312.

Goldberg, Pinelopi Koujianou and Michael M. Knetter (1997), "Goods Prices and Exchange Rates: What Have We Learned?", *The Journal of Economic Literature*, **35** (3), 1243–72.

Gordon, Myron J. (1998), "Monopoly Power in the United States Manufacturing Sector, 1899 to 1994", *Journal of Post Keynesian Economics*, **20** (3), 323–35.

Gordon, Robert J. (1981), "Output Fluctuations and Gradual Price Adjustment", *The Journal of Economic Literature*, **19** (2), 493–530.

Gordon, Robert J. (1990), "What is New-Keynesian Economics?", *The Journal of Economic Literature*, **28** (3), 1115–71.

Government of Japan (1990), *1985 Input–Output Tables*, Tokyo: Management and Coordination Agency.

Gowdy, John M. and Jack L. Miller (1990), "Harrod–Robinson–Read Measures of Primary Input Productivity: Theory and Evidence from U.S. Data", *Journal of Post Keynesian Economics*, **12** (4), 591–604.

Graham, Edward M. and J. David Richardson (eds) (1997), *Global Competition Policy*, Washington, DC: Institute for International Economics.

Gramlich, Edward M. (1994), "Infrastructure Investment: A Review Essay", *The Journal of Economic Literature*, **32** (3), 1176–96.

Green, Francis, Stephen Machin and Alan Manning (1996), "The Employer Size–Wage Effect: Can Dynamic Monopsony Provide an Explanation?", *Oxford Economic Papers*, **48** (3), 433–55.

Greenwald, Bruce and Joseph Stiglitz (1993), "New and Old Keynesians", *The Journal of Economic Perspectives*, **7** (1), 23–44.

Griliches, Zvi (1988), "Productivity Puzzles and R&D: Another Nonexplanation", *The Journal of Economic Perspectives*, **2** (4), 9–21.

Griliches, Zvi (1992), "The Search for R&D Spillovers", *Scandinavian Journal of Economics*, **94** (Supplement), 29–47.

Hall, Robert E. (1986), "Market Structure and Macroeconomic Fluctuations", *Brookings Papers on Economic Activity*, no. 2, pp. 285–322.

Hall, R.L. and C.J. Hitch (1939), "Price Theory and Business Behaviour", *Oxford Economic Papers*, no. 2, 12–45.

Hansen, Niles (1990), "Do Producer Services Induce Regional Economic Development?", *Journal of Regional Science*, **30** (4), 465–76.

Harcourt, G.C. and Peter Kenyon (1976), "Pricing and the Investment Decision", Kyklos, **29** (3), 449–77.

Harrison, Ann (1996), "Openness and Growth: A Time-series, Cross-country Analysis for Developing Countries", *Journal of Development Economics*, **48** (2), 419–47.

Harrod, Roy F. (1957), *International Economics*, 4th edn, Chicago: University of Chicago Press.

Haskel, Jonathan, Barbara Kersley and Christopher Martin (1997), "Labour Market Flexibility and Employment Adjustment: Micro Evidence from UK Establishments", *Oxford Economic Papers*, **49** (3), 362–79.

Hayami, Yujiro and Vernon W. Ruttan (1985), *Agricultural Development: An International Perspective*, Baltimore, MD: Johns Hopkins University Press.

Hazledine, Tim (1990), "Why Do the Free Trade Gain Numbers Differ So Much? The Role of Industrial Organization in General Equilibrium", *Canadian Journal of Economics*, **23** (4), 791–806.

Helleiner, G.K. (1979), "World Market Imperfections and the Developing Countries", in William R. Cline (ed.), *Policy Alternatives for a New International Economic Order: An Economic Analysis*, New York: Praeger Publishers, pp. 355–89.

Helliwell, John F. (1997), "National Borders, Trade and Migration", *NBER Working Paper*, no. 6027, Cambridge, MA: National Bureau of Economic Research.

Helpman, Elhanan and Paul Krugman (1989), *Trade Policy and Market Structure*, Cambridge, MA: MIT Press.

Hermes, Niels and Robert Lensink (1998), "Banking Reform and the Financing of Firm Investment: An Empirical Analysis of the Chilean Experience, 1983–92", *The Journal of Development Studies*, **34** (3), 27–43.

Hicks, John (1965), *Capital and Growth*, Oxford: Clarendon Press.

Hicks, John (1982), *Money, Interest and Wages: Collected Essays on Economic Theory*, Cambridge, MA: Harvard University Press.

Hikino, Takashi and Alice H. Amsden (1992), "Staying Behind, Stumbling Back, Sneaking Up, Soaring Ahead: Late Industrialization in Historical Perspective", paper presented at the conference "Historical Perspectives on the International Convergence of Productivity", 23–24 April, New York University.

Hill, Peter (1986), "International Price Levels and Purchasing Power Parities", *OECD Economic Studies*, no. 6, 133–59.

Hirschman, Albert O. (1958), *The Strategy of Economic Development*, New Haven, CT: Yale University Press.

Hirschman, Albert O. (1981), "The Rise and Decline of Development Economics", in Albert O. Hirschman, *Essays in Trespassing*, New York: Cambridge University Press.

Hirschman, Albert O. (1987), "Linkages", in John Eatwell, Murray Milgate and Peter Newman (eds), *The New Palgrave: A Dictionary of Economics*, Vol. 3, New York: Stockton Press, pp. 206–11.

Hoekman, Bernard (1998), "Free Trade and Deep Integration: Antidumping and Antitrust in Regional Agreements", *Policy Research Working Paper*, no. 1950, Washington, DC: The World Bank.

Hoekman, Bernard and Carlos A. Primo Braga (1997), "Protection and Trade in Services: A Survey", *Policy Research Working Paper*, no. 1747, Washington, DC: The World Bank.

Hoff, Karla and Joseph E. Stiglitz (1990), "Introduction: Imperfect Information and Rural Credit Markets – Puzzles and Policy Perspectives", *The World Bank Economic Review*, **4** (3), 235–50.

Holmstrom, Bengt (1985), "The Provision of Services in a Market Economy", in Robert P. Inman (ed.), *Managing the Service Economy: Prospects and Problems*, Cambridge: Cambridge University Press, pp. 183–213.

Hotelling, Harold (1929), "Stability in Competition", *The Economic Journal*, **39** (41), 41–57.

Hubbard, R. Glenn (1998), "Capital-Market Imperfections and Investment", *The Journal of Economic Literature*, **36** (1), 193–225.

Hutton, R. Bruce (1998), "The Role and Potential of Marketing and Advertising on Global Human Development", Background Paper for Human Development Report 1998, New York: United Nations Development Programme.

Inman, Robert P. (ed.) (1985), *Managing the Service Economy: Prospects and Problems*, Cambridge: Cambridge University Press.

International Labor Office (1985), *World Labor Report 2*, Geneva: International Labor Office.

International Labor Office (1989), *World Labor Report 1989*, Geneva: International Labor Office.

International Labor Office (1993), *Yearbook of Labor Statistics, 1993*, Geneva: International Labor Office.

International Monetary Fund (1990a), *Direction of Trade Statistics, 1990*, Washington, DC: International Monetary Fund.

International Monetary Fund (1990b), *International Financial Statistics, 1990*, Washington, DC: International Monetary Fund.

Isard, Peter (1977), "How Far Can We Push the 'Law of One Price'?", *The American Economic Review*, **67** (5), 942–8.

Isenman, Paul (1980), "Inter-Country Comparison of 'Real' (PPP) Incomes: Revised Estimates and Unresolved Questions", *World Development*, **8** (1), 61–72.

Ito, Takatoshi, Peter Isard and Steven Symanski (1997), "Economic Growth and Real Exchange Rate: An overview of the Balassa–Samuelson Hypothesis in Asia", *NBER Working Paper*, no. 5979, Cambridge, MA: National Bureau of Economic Research.

Jacobs, Jane (1969), *The Economy of Cities*, New York: Vintage Books.

Jaffe, Adam B. (1989), "Real Effects of Academic Research", *The American Economic Review*, **79** (5), 957–70.

Jaffe, Adam B., Manuel Tratjenberg and Rebecca Hendorson (1992), "Geographic Localization of Knowledge Spillovers as Evidenced by Patent Citations", *NBER Working Paper*, no. 3993, Cambridge, MA: National Bureau of Economic Research.

Japan Statistics Bureau (1986), *Japan Statistical Yearbook 1986*, Tokyo: Japan Statistics Bureau.

Japan Statistics Bureau (1988), *Japan Statistical Yearbook 1988*, Tokyo: Japan Statistics Bureau.

Jenkins, Carolyn (1998), "Determinants of Private Investment in Zimbabwe", *Journal of African Economies*, **7** (1), 34–61.

Johnston, J. (1972), *Econometric Methods*, 2nd edn, Tokyo: McGraw-Hill.

Justman, Moshe and Morris Teubel (1991), "A Structuralist Perspective on the Role of Technology in Economic Growth and Development", *World Development*, **19** (9), 1167–83.

Kahneman, Daniel, Jack L. Knetsch and Richard Thaler (1986), "Fairness as a Constraint on Profit Seeking: Entitlements in the Market", *The American Economic Review*, **76** (4), 728–41.

Kaldor, Nicholas (1935), "Market Imperfection and Excess Capacity", *Economica*; reprinted in and quoted from *Essays on Value and Distribution*, 2nd edn, New York: Holmes and Meier Publishers, 1980, pp. 62–80.

Kaldor, Nicholas (1949–50), "The Economic Aspects of Advertising", *Review of Economic Studies*; reprinted in and quoted from *Essays on Value and Distribution*, 2nd edn, New York: Holmes and Meier Publishers, 1980, pp. 96–140.

Kaldor, Nicholas (1961), "Capital Accumulation and Economic Growth", in F. Lutz, *The Theory of Capital*, London: Macmillan, 1961; reprinted in and quoted from *Further Essays on Economic Theory*, New York: Holmes and Meier Publishers, 1978, pp. 1–53.

Kaldor, Nicholas (1967), *Strategic Factors in Economic Development*, Ithaca, NY: Cornell University.

Kaldor, Nicholas (1972), "The Irrelevance of Equilibrium Economics", *The Economic Journal*, **82** (328), 1237–55; reprinted in *Further Essays on Economic Theory*, New York: Holmes and Meier Publishers, 1978, pp. 176–201.

Kaldor, Nicholas (1980), "General Introduction", *Essays on Value and Distribution*, 2nd edn, New York: Holmes and Meier Publishers, pp. vii–xxxi.

Kalecki, Michal (1965), *Theory of Economic Dynamics: An Essay on Cyclical and Long-Run Changes in Capitalist Economy*, 2nd edn, London: Unwin University Books.

Kennedy, Peter (1992), *A Guide to Econometrics*, 3rd edn, Cambridge, MA: MIT Press.

Kenyon, Peter (1978), "Pricing", in Alfred S. Eichner (ed.), *A Guide to Post-Keynesian Economics*, White Plains, NY: M.E. Sharpe, pp. 34–45.

Keynes, John Maynard (1936), *The General Theory of Employment, Interest and Money*, New York: Harcourt, Brace and Company.

Khan, Haider Ali (1985), "Technology Choice in the Energy and Textile Sectors in the Republic of Korea", in A.S. Bhalla (ed.), *Technology and Employment in Industry: A Case Study Approach*, 3rd edn, Geneva: International Labor Office, pp. 361–87.

Khan, Shahrukh R. and Cihan Bilginsoy (1994), "Industry Externalities Revisited", *Kyklos*, **47** (1), 67–80.

Killick, T. (1991), "Financial Management and Economic Development: Some Issues", *The South African Journal of Economics*, **59** (3), 287–312.

King, J.E. (1994), "Kurt Rothschild and the Alternative Austrian Economics", *Cambridge Journal of Economics*, **18** (5), 431–45.

Kirkpatrick, C.H. (1984), "Business Behaviour in the Public Sector", in C.H. Kirkpatrick, N. Lee and F.I. Nixson, *Industrial Structure and Policy in Less Developed Countries*, London: George Allen & Unwin, pp. 150–91.

Knetter, Michael M. (1989), "Price Discrimination by U.S. and German Exporters", *The American Economic Review*, **79** (1), 198–210.

Knetter, Michael M. (1992a), "International Comparisons of Price-to-Market Behavior", *NBER Working Paper*, no. 3304, Cambridge, MA: National Bureau of Economic Research.

Knetter, Michael M. (1992b), "Exchange Rates and Corporate Pricing Strategies", *NBER Working Paper*, no. 4151, Cambridge, MA: National Bureau of Economic Research.

Knetter, Michael M. (1994), "Why Are Retail Prices in Japan so High?: Evidence from German Export Prices", *NBER Working Paper*, no. 4894, Cambridge, MA: National Bureau of Economic Research.

Kornai, János (1980), *Economics of Shortage*, Amsterdam: North-Holland.

Kornai, János (1986), *Contradictions and Dilemmas: Studies on the Socialist Economy and Society*, Cambridge, MA: MIT Press.

Kotz, David M. (1987), "Radical Theories of Inflation", in Robert Cherry, Thomas R. Michl, Christine D'Onofrio, Fred Moseley, Cigdem Kurdas and Michele I. Naples (eds), *The Imperiled Economy: Book I: Macroeconomics from a Left Perspective*, New York: The Union for Radical Political Economics, pp. 83–91.

Kravis, Irving B. (1984), "Comparative Studies of National Incomes and Prices", *The Journal of Economic Literature*, **22** (2), 1–39.

Kravis, Irving B. (1986), "The Three Faces of the International Comparison Project", *The World Bank Research Observer*, **1** (1), 3–26.

Kravis, Irving B., Alan W. Heston and Robert Summers (1978), "Real GDP *Per Capita* for More Than One Hundred Countries", *The Economic Journal*, **88** (350), 215–42.

Kravis, Irving B., Alan W. Heston and Robert Summers (1982), *World Product and Income, International Comparisons of Real Gross Product*, Baltimore and London: Johns Hopkins University Press.

Kravis, Irving B., Alan W. Heston and Robert Summers (1983), "The Share of Services in Economic Growth", in F. Gerard Adams and Bert G. Hickman (eds), *Global Econometrics: Essays in Honor of Lawrence R. Klein*, Cambridge, MA and London: MIT Press, pp. 188–219.

Kravis, Irving B., Zoltan Kenessey, Alan W. Heston and Robert Summers (1975), *A System of International Comparisons of Gross Product and Purchasing Power*, Baltimore and London: Johns Hopkins University Press.

Kravis, Irving B. and Robert E. Lipsey (1983), "Toward an Explanation of National Price Levels", *Princeton Studies in International Finance* (52), International Finance Section, Department of Economics, Princeton University, Princeton.

Kravis, Irving B. and Robert E. Lipsey (1988), "National Price Levels and the Prices of Tradables and Nontradables", *NBER Working Paper*, no. 2536, Cambridge, MA: National Bureau of Economic Research.

Krueger, Anne (1997), "Trade Policy and Economic Development: How We Learn", *The American Economic Review*, **87** (1), 1–22.

Krugman, Paul (1991), *Geography and Trade*, Cambridge, MA: MIT Press.

Krugman, Paul (1995), *Development, Geography and Economic Theory*, Cambridge, MA: MIT Press.

Krugman, Paul (1996), "How I Work", in *Koninklijke Vereniging voor de Staathuishoudkunde: Jaarboek 1995/96*, Rotterdam: ESB, pp. 221–31.

Kurian, George Thomas (1984), *The New Book of World Rankings*, New York: Facts on File Publications.

Kurz, Heinz D. (1978), "Rent Theory in a Multisectoral Model", *Oxford Economic Papers*, **30** (1), 16–37.

Kuznets, Simon (1971), *Economic Growth of Nations: Total Output and Production Structure*, Cambridge, MA: Harvard University Press.

Kyle, Steven C. (1992), "Pitfalls in the Measurement of Real Exchange Rate Effects on Agriculture", *World Development*, **20** (7), 1009–19.

Kyle, Steven C. and Johan Swinnen (1994), "The Theory of Contested Markets and the Degree of Tradedness of Agricultural Commodities: An Empirical Test in Zaire", *Journal of African Economies*, **3** (1), 93–113.

Lai, Cheng-Chung (1991), "Market Structure and Income Distribution in the Dependent Economy: Evidence from Taiwan", *Hitotsubashi Journal of Economics*, **32** (1), 39–48.

Lall, Sanjaya (1978), "Transnationals, Domestic Enterprises and Industrial Structure in Host LDCs: A Survey", *Oxford Economic Papers*, **30** (2), 217–48.

Lancaster, K.J. (1987), "Product Differentiation", in John Eatwell, Murray Milgate and Peter Newman (eds), *The New Palgrave: A Dictionary of Economics*, Vol. 3, New York: Stockton Press, pp. 988–90.

Lancieri, Elio (1990), "Purchasing Power Parities and Phase IV of the International Comparison Project: Do They Lead to 'Real' Estimates of GDP and Its Components?", *World Development*, **18** (1), 29–48.

Lavoie, Marc (1995), "The Kaleckian Model of Growth and Distribution and Its Neo-Ricardian and Neo-Marxian Critiques", *Cambridge Journal of Economics*, **19** (6), 789–818.

Leamer, Edward E. (1984), *Sources of International Comparative Advantage*, Cambridge, MA: MIT Press.

Leamer, Edward E. (1992), "Testing Trade Theory", *NBER Working Paper*, no. 3957, Cambridge, MA: National Bureau of Economic Research.

Lee, Chung H. (1992), "The Government, Financial System and Large Private Enterprises in the Economic Development of South Korea", *World Development*, **20** (2), 187–97.

Lee, Fred (1986), "Post Keynesian View of Average Direct Costs: A Critical Evaluation of the Theory and the Empirical Evidence", *Journal of Post Keynesian Economics*, **8** (3), 400–24.

Lee, Jaewoo (1997), "The Response of Exchange Rate Pass-Through into Market Concentration in a Small Economy: The Evidence from Korea", *The Review of Economics and Statistics*, **79** (1), 142–45.

Lee, Jong-Wha (1992), "International Trade, Distortions and Long-Run Economic Growth", *IMF Working Paper*, no. WP/92/90, Washington, DC: International Monetary Fund.

Lee, Jong-Wha (1995), "Capital Goods Imports and Long-Run Growth", *Journal of Development Economics*, **48** (1), 91–110.

Lee, N. (1984), "Business Concentration in LDCs", in C.H. Kirkpatrick, N. Lee and F.I. Nixson, *Industrial Structure and Policy in Less Developed Countries*, London: George Allen & Unwin, pp. 46–85.

Leff, Nathaniel H. (1978), "Industrial Organization and Entrepreneurship in the Developing Countries: The Economic Groups", *Economic Development and Cultural Change*, **26** (4), 661–75.

Leff, Nathaniel H. (1979), "'Monopoly Capitalism' and Public Policy in Developing Countries", *Kyklos*, **32** (4), 718–38.

Leontief, Wassily (1986), *Input–Output Economics*, 2nd edn, New York: Oxford University Press.

Levine, David P. (1986), "A Note on Wage Determination and Capital Accumulation", *Journal of Post Keynesian Economics*, **8** (3), 463–77.

Levine, Ross (1997), "Financial Development and Economic Growth: Views and Agenda", *The Journal of Economic Literature*, **35** (2), 688–726.

Lewis, H. Gregg (1986), *Union Relative Wage Effects: A Survey*, Chicago and London: University of Chicago Press.

Liang, Neng (1992), "Beyond Import Substitution and Export Promotion: A New Typology of Trade Strategies", *The Journal of Development Studies*, **28** (3), 447–72.

Linnemann, Hans (1966), *An Econometric Study of International Trade Flows*, Amsterdam: North-Holland.

Lipsey, Robert E. and Birgitta Swedenborg (1993), "The High Cost of Eating: Agricultural Protection and International Differences in Consumer Food Prices", *NBER Working Paper*, no. 4555, Cambridge, MA: National Bureau of Economic Research.

Lipsey, Robert E. and Birgitta Swedenborg (1996), "Wage Dispersion and Country Price Levels", paper presented at the Conference on Research in Income and Wealth, Washington, DC; a later version was published as *NBER Working Paper*, no. 6039, Cambridge, MA: National Bureau of Economic Research.

Lubell, Harold (1991), *The Informal Sector in the 1980s and 1990s*, Paris: OECD.

Lucas, Jr., Robert E. (1988), "On the Mechanics of Economic Development", *Journal of Monetary Economics*, **22** (1), 3–42.

Maciejewski, Edouard B. (1983), "'Real' Effective Exchange Rate Indices, A Re-Examination of the Major Conceptual and Methodological Issues", *IMF Staff Papers*, **30** (3), 491–54.

Maddison, Angus (1967), "Comparative Productivity Levels in the Developed Countries", *Banca Nazionale del Lavoro Quarterly Review*, **20** (83), 3–23.

Maddison, Angus (1980), "Economic Growth and Structural Change in the Advanced Countries", in Irving Leveson and Jimmy W. Wheeler (eds), *Western Economies in Transition: Structural Change and Adjustment Policies in Industrial Countries*, Boulder, CO: Westview Press, pp. 41–60.

Maddison, Angus (1983), "A Comparison of Levels of GDP Per Capita in Developed and Developing Countries, 1700–1980", *Journal of Economic History*, **43** (1), 27–41.

Maddison, Angus (1987), "Growth and Slowdown in Advanced Capitalist Economies: Techniques of Quantitative Assessment", *The Journal of Economic Literature*, **25** (2), 649–98.

Maddison, Angus (1990), "The ICOP Project: A Progress Report", mimeo, University of Groningen.

Maddison, Angus (1991), *Dynamic Forces in Capitalist Development: A Long-Run Comparative View*, Oxford: Oxford University Press.

Maddison, Angus (1993), "Standardised Estimates of Fixed Capital Stock: A Six Country Comparison", *Essays on Innovation, Natural Resources and the International Economy* (from *Innovazione e Materie Prime*), Milan: Ferruzi Montedison Group.

Maddison, Angus and Bart van Ark (1987), "The International Comparison of Real Output, Purchasing Power and Labor Productivity in Manufacturing Industries: A Pilot Study for Brazil, Mexico and the USA for 1975", *Research Memorandum*, no. 231, Groningen: Faculty of Economics, University of Groningen.

Maddison, Angus and Bart van Ark (1989), "International Comparison of Purchasing Power, Real Output and Labor Productivity: A Case Study of Brazilian, Mexican and U.S. Manufacturing, 1975", *The Review of Income and Wealth*, **35** (1), 31–55.

Malinvaud, Edmond (1980), *Profitability and Unemployment*, Cambridge: Cambridge University Press.

Malinvaud, Edmond (1985), *The Theory of Unemployment Reconsidered*, 2nd edn, Oxford: Basil Blackwell.

Malueg, David A. and Marius Schwartz (1994), "Parallel Imports, Demand Dispersion and International Price Discrimination", *Journal of International Economics*, **37** (3/4), 167–95.

Marris, Robin (1979), "A Survey and Critique of World Bank Supported Research on International Comparisons of Real Product", *World Bank Staff Working Paper*, no. 365, Washington, DC: The World Bank.

Marris, Robin (1984), "Comparing the Incomes of Nations: A Critique of the International Comparison Project", *The Journal of Economic Literature*, **22** (2), 40–57.

Marshall, Alfred (1920), *Principles of Economics: An Introductory Volume*, 8th edn, London: Macmillan.

Matsushita, Mitsuo (1997), "The Antimonopoly Law of Japan", in Edward M. Graham and J. David Richardson (eds), *Global Competition Policy*, Washington, DC: Institute for International Economics.

McCallum, John (1995), "National Borders Matter: Canada–U.S. Regional Trade Patterns", *The American Economic Review*, **85** (3), 615–23.

McKinnon, Ronald I. (1979), *Money in International Exchange: The Convertible Currency System*, New York: Oxford University Press.

Menon, Jayant (1996), "The Degree and Determinants of Exchange Rate Pass-Through: Market Structure, Non-tariff Barriers and Multinational Corporations", *The Economic Journal*, **106** (425), 434–44.

Messerlin, Patrick A. and Karl P. Sauvant (1990), *The Uruguay Round: Services in the World Economy*, Washington, DC and New York: The World Bank and United Nations Centre on Transnational Corporations.

Miller, Jack L. and John M. Gowdy (1992), "Vertically Integrated Productivity Measures: Tests of Standard Assumptions", *The Review of Income and Wealth*, **38** (4), 445–53.

Miyagiwa, Kaz (1991), "Scale Economies in Education and the Brain Drain Problem", *International Economic Review*, **32** (3), 743–59.

Miyagiwa, Kaz and Yuka Ohno (1995), "Closing the Technology Gap Under Protection", *The American Economic Review*, **85** (4), 755–70.

Morawetz, David (1974), "Employment Implications of Industrialisation in Developing Countries: A Survey", *The Economic Journal*, **84** (335), 491–542.

Morisset, Jacques (1998), "Unfair Trade? The Increasing Gap between World and Domestic Prices in Commodity Markets during the Past 25 Years", *The World Bank Economic Review*, **12** (3), 503–26.

Morrison, Andrew R. (1994), "Are Institutions or Economic Rents Responsible for Interindustry Wage Differentials?", *World Development*, **22** (3), 355–68.

Morrison, Christian, Henri-Bernard Solignac Lecomte and Xavier Oudin (1994), *Micro-Enterprises and the Institutional Framework*, Paris: OECD Development Centre.

Mueller, Willard F. and Larry G. Hamm (1974), "Trends in Industrial Market Concentration, 1947 to 1970", *The Review of Economics and Statistics*, **56** (4), 511–20.

Munnell, Alicia H. (1992), "Infrastructure Investment and Economic Growth", *The Journal of Economic Perspectives*, **6** (4), 189–98.

Murphy, Kevin M. and Andrei Schleifer (1997), "Quality and Trade", *Journal of Development Economics*, **53** (1), 1–15.

Murphy, Kevin M., Andrei Schleifer and Robert W. Vishny (1989), "Industrialization and the Big Push", *Journal of Political Economy*, **97** (5), 1003–26.

Nadiri, M. Ishaq (1993), "Innovations and Technological Spillovers", *NBER Working Paper*, no. 4423, Cambridge, MA: National Bureau of Economic Research.

Nakane, Chie (1973), *Japanese Society*, Harmondsworth: Penguin Books.

Naug, Bjorn and Ragnar Nymoen (1996), "Pricing to Market in a Small Open Economy", *Scandinavian Journal of Economics*, **98** (3), 329–50.

Needham, Douglas (1978), *The Economics of Industrial Structure, Conduct and Performance*, London: Holt, Rinehart & Winston.

Nixson, F.I. (1984), "Business Behaviour in the Private Sector", in C.H. Kirkpatrick, N. Lee and F.I. Nixson, *Industrial Structure and Policy in Less Developed Countries*, London: George Allen & Unwin, pp. 86–149.

Nolan, Peter (1996), "Large Firms and Industrial Reform in Former Planned Economies: The Case of China", *Cambridge Journal of Economics*, **20** (1), 1–29.

Norman, Neville R. (1996), "A General Post Keynesian Theory of Protection", *Journal of Post Keynesian Economics*, **18** (4), 509–31.

Nugent, Jeffrey B. and Mustapha K. Nabli (1989), "An Institutional Analysis of the Size Distribution of Manufacturing Establishments: An International Cross-Section Study", *KDI Working Paper*, no. 8921, Seoul: Korea Development Institute.

Nuxoll, Daniel A. (1994), "Differences in Relative Prices and International Differences in Growth Rates", *The American Economic Review*, **84** (5), 1423–36.

Oberai, A.S. (1981), *Changes in the Structure of Employment with Economic Development*, 2nd edn, Geneva: International Labor Office.

Ocampo, Jose Antonio and Lance Taylor (1998), "Trade Liberalisation in Developing Countries: Modest Benefits but Problems with Productivity Growth, Macro Prices and Income Distribution", *The Economic Journal*, **108** (450), 1523–46.

Ochoa, Eduardo M. (1986), "An Input–Output Study of Labor Productivity in the U.S. Economy, 1947–1972", *Journal of Post Keynesian Economics*, **9** (1), 111–37.

O'Connell, Paul G.J. (1998), "The Overvaluation of Purchasing Power Parity", *Journal of International Economics*, **44** (1), 1–19.

O'Connell, Paul G.J. and Shang-Jin Wei (1997), "'The Bigger They Are, The Harder They Fall': How Price Differences Across U.S. Cities Are Arbitraged", *NBER Working Paper*, no. 6089, Cambridge, MA: National Bureau of Economic Research.

OECD (1988), *National Accounts: Main Aggregates, 1960–86*, 1, Paris: OECD.

OECD (1991), *Basic Science and Technology Statistics*, Paris: OECD.

OECD (1992a), *Structural Change and Industrial Performance: A Seven Country Growth Decomposition Study*, Paris: OECD.

OECD (1992b), *Switzerland: Economic Survey 1991/1992*, Paris: OECD.

OECD (1995a), *The OECD Input–Output Database*, Paris: OECD.

OECD (1995b), *The OECD STAN Database for Industrial Analysis, 1975–1994*, Paris: OECD.

OECD (1996a), *Technology and Industrial Performance*, Paris: OECD.

OECD (1996b), *Indicators of Tariff and Non-Tariff Trade Barriers*, Paris: OECD.

OECD (no date), *The Analytical Business Enterprise Research and Development (ANBERD) Database*, data diskette, Paris: OECD.

Officer, Lawrence H. (1974), "Purchasing Power Parity and Factor Price Equalization", *Kyklos*, **27** (4), 868–78.

Officer, Lawrence H. (1976a), "The Purchasing–Power–Parity Theory of Exchange Rates: A Review Article", *IMF Staff Papers*, **23** (1), 1–60.

Officer, Lawrence H. (1976b), "The Productivity Bias in Purchasing Power Parity: An Econometric Investigation", *IMF Staff Papers*, **23** (3), 545–79.

Officer, Lawrence H. (1989), "The National Price Level: Theory and Estimation", *Journal of Macroeconomics*, **11** (3), 351–73.

Okun, Arthur M. (1975), "Inflation: Its Mechanics and Welfare Costs", *Brookings Papers on Economic Activity*, no. 2, pp. 351–90.

Oliveira Martins, Joaquim (1993), "Market Structure, International Trade and Relative Wages", *OECD Working Paper*, no. 134, Paris: OECD, Economics Department.

Osborne, Dale K. (1992), "Banking Structure and Competition", in Peter Newman, Murray Milgate and John Eatwell (eds), *The New Palgrave Dictionary of Money and Finance*, Vol. 1, New York: Stockton Press, pp. 152–5.

Oshima, Harry T. (1971), "Labor-Force 'Explosion' and the Labor-Intensive Sector in Asian Growth", *Economic Development and Cultural Change*, **19** (2), 161–83.

Pack, Howard (1984), "Technology and Employment: Constraints on Optimal Performance", in Samuel M. Rosenblatt (ed.), *Technology and Economic Development: A Realistic Perspective*; reprinted in and quoted from Gerald M. Meier. *Leading Issues in Economic Development*, 4th edn, New York: Oxford University Press, pp. 352–5.

Pack, Howard and Larry E. Westphal (1986), "Industrial Strategy and Technological Change", *Journal of Development Economics*, **22** (1), 87–128.

Panagariya, Arvind (1988), "A Theoretical Explanation of Some Stylized Facts of Economic Growth", *The Quarterly Journal of Economics*, **103** (3), 509–26.

Parsley, David C. and Shang-Jin Wei (1996), "Convergence to the Law of One Price Without Trade Barriers or Currency Fluctuations", *The Quarterly Journal of Economics*, **111** (4), 1211–36.

Pasinetti, Luigi L. (1973), "The Notion of Vertical Integration in Economic Analysis", *Metroeconomica*, **25** (1), 1–29.

Pasinetti, Luigi L. (1974), *Growth and Income Distribution: Essays in Economic Theory*, Cambridge: Cambridge University Press.

Pasinetti, Luigi L. (1977), *Lectures on the Theory of Production*, New York: Columbia University Press.

Pasinetti, Luigi L. (1981), *Structural Change and Economic Growth: A Theoretical Essay on the Dynamics of the Wealth of Nations*, Cambridge: Cambridge University Press.

Peterson, William (1979), "Total Factor Productivity in the UK: A Disaggregated Analysis", in K.D. Patterson and Kerry Schott (eds), *The Measurement of Capital: Theory and Practice*, New York: Holmes and Meier Publishers, pp. 212–25.

Pilat, Dirk (1991a), "Levels of Real Output and Labor Productivity by Industry of Origin, A Comparison of Japan and the United States, 1975 and 1970–1987", *Research Memorandum*, no. 408, Groningen: Faculty of Economics, University of Groningen.

Pilat, Dirk (1991b), "Productivity Levels in the Korean Economy, A Comparative Assessment", mimeo, University of Groningen.

Pilat, Dirk (1994), *The Economics of Rapid Growth: The Experience of Japan and Korea*, Aldershot, UK and Brookfield, US: Edward Elgar.

Pindyck, Robert S. and Daniel L. Rubinfeld (1981), *Econometric Models and Economic Forecasts*, 2nd edn, Tokyo: McGraw-Hill.

Pritchett, Lant (1996), "Measuring Outward Orientation in LDCs: Can it be done?", *Journal of Development Economics*, **49** (2), 307–35.

Pryor, Frederic L. (1972), "An International Comparison of Concentration Ratios", *The Review of Economics and Statistics*, **54** (2), 130–40.

Psacharopoulos, George (1994), "Returns to Education: A Global Update", *World Development*, **22** (9), 1325–43.

Pyo, Hak K. (1992), "A Synthetic Estimate of the National Wealth of Korea 1953–1990", *KDI Working Paper*, no. 9212, Korea Development Institute.

Quibria, M.G. (1990), "Note on International Differences in Service Prices and Some Related Empirical Phenomena", *Journal of Development Economics*, **33** (2), 357–70.

Quigley, John M. (1998), "Urban Diversity and Economic Growth", *The Journal of Economic Perspectives*, **12** (2), 127–38.

Rangan, Subramanian and Robert Z. Lawrence (1993), "The Responses of U.S. Firms to Exchange Rate Fluctuations: Piercing the Corporate Veil", in William C. Brainard and George L. Perry (eds), *Brookings Papers on Economic Activity*, no. 2, pp. 341–79.

Read, L.M. (1968), "The Measure of Total Factor Productivity Appropriate to Wage–Price Guidelines", *Canadian Journal of Economics*, **1** (2), 349–58.

Rebitzer, James B. (1993), "Radical Political Economy and the Economics of the Labor Markets", *The Journal of Economic Literature*, **31** (3), 1394–434.

Republic of Korea (1981), *Yearbook of Labor Statistics 1981*, Seoul: Ministry of Labor.

Republic of Korea (1986), *Korea Statistical Yearbook, 1986*, Seoul: National Statistical Office.

Republic of Korea (1989), *Korea Statistical Yearbook, 1989*, Seoul: National Statistical Office.

Republic of Korea (1991), *Korea Statistical Yearbook, 1991*, Seoul: National Statistical Office.

Republic of Korea (1995), *History of Korean Statistics* [in Korean], August, Seoul: Statistics Administration.

Ricardo, David [1821] (1948), *The Principles of Political Economy and Taxation*, London: J.M. Dent.

Robinson, Joan (1933), *The Economics of Imperfect Competition*, London: Macmillan.

Robinson, Joan (1962), "Philosophy of Prices", in *Collected Economic Papers*, Vol. 2, Cambridge, MA: MIT Press.

Robinson, Joan (1969), *The Accumulation of Capital*, 3rd edn, Philadelphia: Porcupine Press.

Rodríguez-Clare, Andrés (1996), "Multinationals, Linkages and Economic Development", *The American Economic Review*, **86** (4), 852–73.

Rodrik, Dani (1992a), "Conceptual Issues in the Design of Trade Policy for Industrialization", *World Development*, **20** (3), 309–20.

Rodrik, Dani (1992b), "The Limits of Trade Policy in Developing Countries", *The Journal of Economic Perspectives*, **6** (1), 87–105.

Rodrik, Dani (1994), "King Kong Meets Godzilla: The World Bank and *The East Asian Miracle*", in "Miracle or Design? Lessons from the East Asian Experience", *Policy Essay*, no. 11, Washington, DC: Overseas Development Council, pp. 13–53.

Rodrik, Dani (1995), "Trade and Industrial Policy Reform", in Jere Behrman and T.N. Srinivasan (eds), *Handbook of Development Economics*, Vol. 3B, Amsterdam: Elsevier, pp. 2925–82.

Rogoff, Kenneth (1996), "The Purchasing Power Parity Puzzle", *The Journal of Economic Literature*, **34** (2), 647–68.

Romer, David (1993), "The New Keynesian Synthesis", *The Journal of Economic Perspectives*, **7** (1), 5–22.

Romer, Paul M. (1986), "Increasing Returns and Long-Run Growth", *Journal of Political Economy*, **94** (5), 1002–37.

Romer, Paul M. (1989), "Increasing Returns and New Development in the Theory of Growth", *NBER Working Paper*, no. 3098, Cambridge, MA: National Bureau of Economic Research.

Ros, Jaime (1980), "Pricing in the Mexican Manufacturing Sector", *Cambridge Journal of Economics*, **4** (4), 729–40.

Rosen, Sherwin (1996), "Public Employment and the Welfare State in Sweden", *The Journal of Economic Literature*, **34** (2), 211–31.

Rosenberg, Sam and Thomas E. Weisskopf (1981), "A Conflict Theory Approach to Inflation in the Postwar U.S. Economy", *The American Economic Review*, **71** (2), 42–7.

Rosenstein-Rodan, P.N. (1943), "Problems of Industrialisation of Eastern and South-Eastern Europe", *The Economic Journal*, **53** (210), 202–11.

Rothschild, Kurt W. (1947), "Price Theory and Oligopoly", *The Economic Journal*, **47**, 299–320; reprinted in and quoted from *Readings in Price Theory*, American Economic Association, London: George Allen & Unwin, 1952, pp. 440–64.

Rothschild, Kurt W. (1987), "Degree of Monopoly", in John Eatwell, Murray Milgate and Peter Newman (eds), *The New Palgrave: A Dictionary of Economics*, Vol. 1, New York: Stockton Press, pp. 766–8.

Rousslang, Donald J. and Theodore To (1993), "Domestic Trade and Transportation Costs", *Canadian Journal of Economics*, **26** (1), 208–21.

Rowthorn, R.E. (1977), "Conflict, Inflation and Money", *Cambridge Journal of Economics*, **1** (3), 215–39.

Rymes, T.K. (1972), "The Measurement of Capital and Total Factor Productivity in the Context of the Cambridge Theory of Capital", *The Review of Income and Wealth*, **18** (1), 79–108.

Rymes, T.K. (1983), "More on the Measurement of Total Factor Productivity", *The Review of Income and Wealth*, **29** (3), 297–316.

Sabolo, Yves (1975), *The Service Industries*, Geneva: ILO.

Salter, W.E.G. (1959), "Internal and External Balance: The Role of Price and Expenditure Effects", *The Economic Record*, **35** (71), 226–38.

Samuelson, Paul A. (1954), "The Pure Theory of Public Expenditure", *The Review of Economics and Statistics*, **36** (4), 387–9.

Samuelson, Paul A. (1964), "Theoretical Notes on Trade Problems", *The Review of Economics and Statistics*, **46** (2), 145–54.

Samuelson, Paul A. (1974), "Analytical Notes on International Real-Income Measures", *The Economic Journal*, **84** (335), 595–608.

Sanyal, Bishwapriya (1991), "Organizing the Self-Employed: The Politics of the Urban Informal Sector", *International Labor Review*, **130** (1), 39–56.

Satterthwaite, Mark A. (1985), "Competition and Equilibrium as a Driving Force in the Health Services Sector", in Robert P. Inman (ed.), *Managing the Service Economy: Prospects and Problems*, Cambridge: Cambridge University Press, pp. 239–67.

Savage, Donald T. (1992), "Concentration in Banking and other Financial Services", in Peter Newman, Murray Milgate and John Eatwell (eds), *The New Palgrave Dictionary of Money and Finance*, Vol. 1, New York: Stockton Press, pp. 420–22.

Sawyer, M. (1992), "Kinked Demand Curve", in Peter Newman, Murray Milgate and John Eatwell (eds), *The New Palgrave Dictionary of Money and Finance*, Vol. 3, New York: Stockton Press, pp. 52–4.

Scherer, F.M. (1982), "Inter-Industry Technology Flows and Productivity Growth", *The Review of Economics and Statistics*, **64** (4), 627–34.

Scherer, F.M. (1987), "Market Structure", in John Eatwell, Murray Milgate and Peter Newman (eds), *The New Palgrave: A Dictionary of Economics*, Vol. 3, New York: Stockton Press, pp. 342–5.

Scherer, F.M. and David Ross (1990), *Industrial Market Structure and Economic Performance*, 3rd edn, Boston: Houghton Mifflin.

Schmalensee, Richard (1987), "Advertising", in John Eatwell, Murray Milgate and Peter Newman (eds), *The New Palgrave: A Dictionary of Economics*, Vol. 1, New York: Stockton Press, pp. 34–6.

Schmalensee, Richard (1989), "Inter-Industry Studies of Structure and Performance", in Richard Schmalensee and Robert Willig (eds), *Handbook of Industrial Organization*, Amsterdam: North-Holland.

Schultz, Theodore W. (1961), "Investment in Human Capital", *The American Economic Review*, **51** (1), 1–17.

Scitovsky, Tibor (1954), "Two Concepts of External Economies", *Journal of Political Economy*, **62** (2), 143–51.

Semmler, Willi (1982), "Competition, Monopoly and Differentials of Profit Rates: Theoretical Considerations and Empirical Evidence", *Review of Radical Political Economy*, **13** (4), 39–52.

Semmler, Willi (1984), *Competition, Monopoly and Differential Profit Rates: On the Relevance of the Classical and Marxian Theories of Production Prices for Modern Industrial and Corporate Pricing*, New York: Columbia University Press.

Sethuraman, S. (ed.) (1981), *The Urban Informal Sector in Developing Countries: Employment, Poverty and Environment*, Geneva: ILO.

Shaffer, Sherrill (1992), "Competitiveness in Banking", in Peter Newman, Murray Milgate and John Eatwell (eds), *The New Palgrave Dictionary of Money and Finance*, Vol. 1, New York: Stockton Press, pp. 415–16.

Shafik, Nemat (1992), "Modeling Private Investment in Egypt", *Journal of Development Economics*, **39** (2), 263–77.

Shepherd, William G. (1987), "Concentration Ratios", in John Eatwell, Murray Milgate and Peter Newman (eds), *The New Palgrave: A Dictionary of Economics*, Vol. 1, New York: Stockton Press, pp. 563–4.

Silberston, Aubrey (1970), "Surveys of Applied Economics: Price Behaviour of Firms", *The Economic Journal*, **80** (319), 511–82.

Silvestre, Joaquim (1987), "Economies and Diseconomies of Scale", in John Eatwell, Murray Milgate and Peter Newman (eds), *The New Palgrave: A Dictionary of Economics*, Vol. 2, New York: Stockton Press, pp. 80–84.

Simon, Julian L. (1990), "Great and Almost-Great Magnitudes in Economics", *The Journal of Economic Perspectives*, **4** (1), 149–56.

Singh, Ajit (1994), "Openness and the Market Friendly Approach to Development: Learning the Right Lessons from Development Experience", *World Development*, **22** (12), 1811–23.

Singh, Ajit (1995a), "Corporate Financing Patterns in Industrializing Economies", *Technical Paper*, no. 2, Washington, DC: International Finance Corporation.

Singh, Ajit (1995b), "The Causes of Fast Economic Growth in East Asia", *UNCTAD Review*, New York: United Nations, pp. 91–127.

Singh, Ajit (1995c), "Pension Reform, the Stock Market, Capital Formation and Economic Growth: A Critical Commentary on the World Bank's Proposals", *Working Paper Series*, no. 2, New York: Center for Economic Policy Analysis, New School for Social Research.

Singh, Ajit (1997), "Financial Liberalisation, Stockmarkets and Economic Development", *The Economic Journal*, **107** (442), 771–82.

Singh, Ajit (1998), "Savings, Investment and the Corporation in the East Asian Miracle", *The Journal of Development Studies*, **34** (6), 112–37.

Singh, Ajit and Bruce A. Weisse (1998), "Emerging Stock Markets, Portfolio Capital Flows and Long-Term Economic Growth: Micro and Macroeconomic Prespectives", *World Development*, **26** (4), 607–22.

Smith, Adam [1776] (1986), *An Inquiry into the Nature and Causes of the Wealth of Nations*, London: Penguin.

Sraffa, Piero (1926), "The Laws of Returns under Competitive Conditions", *The Economic Journal*, **36** (144), 535–50.

Sraffa, Piero (1960), *Production of Commodities by Means of Commodities: Prelude to a Critique of Economic Theory*, Cambridge: Cambridge University Press.

Steindl, Josef [1952] (1976), *Maturity and Stagnation in American Capitalism*, New York and London: Monthly Review Press.

Stewart, Frances and Ejaz Ghani (1991), "How Significant are Externalities for Development?", *World Development*, **19** (6), 569–94.

Stigler, George J. (1956), *Trends in Employment in the Service Industries*, Princeton: Princeton University Press.

Stiglitz, Joseph (1987), "The Causes and Consequences of the Dependence of Quality on Price", *The Journal of Economic Literature*, **25** (1), 1–48.

Stiglitz, Joseph (1993), "The Role of the State in Financial Markets", *Proceedings of the World Bank Annual Conference on Development Economics 1993*, Washington, DC: The World Bank, pp. 19–52.

Stiglitz, J.E. and A. Weiss (1981), "Credit Rationing in Markets with Imperfect Information", *The American Economic Review*, **71** (3), 393–410.

Summers, Robert (1985), "Services in the International Economy", in Robert P. Inman (ed.), *Managing the Service Economy: Prospects and Problems*, Cambridge: Cambridge University Press, pp. 27–48.

Summers, Robert and Alan Heston (1984), "Improved International Comparisons of Real Product and Its Composition: 1950–1980", *The Review of Income and Wealth*, **30** (2), 207–62.

Summers, Robert and Alan Heston (1988), "A New Set of International Comparisons of Real Product and Price Levels: Estimates for 130 Countries, 1950–1985", *The Review of Income and Wealth*, **34** (1), 1–25.

Summers, Robert and Alan Heston (1991), "The Penn World Table (Mark 5): An Expanded Set of International Comparisons, 1950–1988", *The Quarterly Journal of Economics*, **106** (2), 327–68.

Summers, Robert, Irving B. Kravis and Alan Heston (1980), "International Comparisons of Real Product and Its Components: 1950–77", *The Review of Income and Wealth*, **26** (1), 19–66.

Sutton, John (1996), "Technology and Market Structure", *European Economic Review*, **40** (3–5), 511–30.

Sutton, John (1997), "Gibrat's Legacy", *The Journal of Economic Literature*, **35** (1), 40–59.

Sweezy, Paul M. (1939), "Demand Under Conditions of Oligopoly", *Journal of Political Economy*, **47**, 568–73.

Sylos-Labini, Paolo (1979), "Prices and Income Distribution in Manufacturing Industry", *Journal of Post Keynesian Economics*, **2** (1), 3–25.

Sylos-Labini, Paolo (1984), *The Forces of Economic Growth and Decline*, Cambridge, MA: MIT Press.

Sylos-Labini, Paolo [1969] (1993), *Oligopoly and Technical Progress*, Fairfield, NJ: Augustus M. Kelley.

Szirmai, Adam and Dirk Pilat (1990), "The International Comparison of Real Output and Labor Productivity in Manufacturing: A Study for Japan, South Korea and the USA for 1975", *Research Memorandum*, no. 354, Groningen: Faculty of Economics, University of Groningen.

Taussig, F.W. (1927), *International Trade*, New York: The Macmillan Company.

Taylor, Lance (1988), *Varieties of Stabilization Experience: Towards Sensible Macroeconomics in the Third World*, New York: Clarendon Press.

Taylor, Lance (1991), *Income Distribution, Inflation and Growth: Lectures on Structuralist Macroeconomic Theory*, Cambridge, MA and London: MIT Press.

Taylor, Lance (1995), "Pasinetti's Processes", *Cambridge Journal of Economics*, **19** (5), 697–713.

Teitel, Simón (1978), "The Strong Factor-Intensity Assumption: Some Empirical Evidence", *Economic Development and Cultural Change*, **26** (2), 327–39.

Thirlwall, A.P. (1983), *Growth and Development, With Special Reference to Developing Economies*, 3rd edn, London: Macmillan.

Thompson, Alexander M. (1992), "Unproductive Expenditure in Manufacturing", *Cambridge Journal of Economics*, **16** (2), 147–68.

Thompson, G. Rodney and Andrew J. Stollar (1983), "An Empirical Test of an International Model of Relative Tertiary Employment", *Economic Development and Cultural Change*, **31** (4), 775–85.

Udall, Alan T. (1976), "The Effects of Rapid Increases in Labor Supply on Service Employment in Developing Countries", *Economic Development and Cultural Change*, **24** (4), 765–85.

UNESCO (1995), *Statistical Yearbook, 1995*, Paris: UNESCO Publishing and Bernan Press.

United Nations (1961), "Standard International Trade Classification, Revised", *Statistical Papers*, Series M, no. 34, New York: United Nations.

United Nations (1968), *A System of National Accounts*, Studies in Methods, Series F, no. 2, rev. 3. New York: United Nations.

United Nations (1987a), *World Economic Survey 1987*, New York: United Nations.

United Nations (1987b), *National Accounts Statistics: Study of Input–Output Tables, 1970–80*, New York: United Nations.

United Nations (1988), *World Economic Survey 1988*, New York: United Nations.

United Nations (1990a), *Agricultural Trade Liberalization in The Uruguay Round: Implications for Developing Countries*, New York: United Nations.

United Nations (1990b), *World Economic Survey 1990*, New York: United Nations.

United Nations (1990c), "International Standard Industrial Classification of All Economic Activities", *Statistical Papers*, Series M, no. 4, rev. 3, New York: United Nations.

United Nations (1991), *World Economic Survey 1991*, New York: United Nations.

United Nations (1992a), "Handbook of the International Comparison Programme", *Studies in Methods*, Series F, no. 62, New York: United Nations.

United Nations (1992b), *National Accounts Statistics: Main Aggregates and Detailed Tables, 1990*, New York: United Nations.

United Nations (1993), *World Economic Survey 1993*, New York: United Nations.

United Nations (1994), *National Accounts Statistics: Main Aggregates and Detailed Tables, 1992*, New York: United Nations.

United Nations (1996), *World Economic and Social Survey 1996*, New York: United Nations.

United Nations (1998), *World Economic and Social Survey 1998*, New York: United Nations.

United Nations Centre for Transnational Corporations (1989), "Transnational Service Corporations and Developing Countries: Impact and Policy Issues", *UNCTC Current Studies*, Series A, no. 10, New York: United Nations.

United Nations Centre for Transnational Corporations (1990), *Transnational Corporations, Services and the Uruguay Round*, New York: United Nations.

United Nations Centre for Transnational Corporations (1991), *World Investment Report 1991: The Triad in Foreign Direct Investment*, New York: United Nations.

United Nations Centre for Transnational Corporations and the United Nations Conference on Trade and Development (1991), *The Impact of Trade-Related Investment Measures on Trade and Development*, New York: United Nations.

United Nations Conference on Trade and Development (1993), *World Investment Report 1993: Transnational Corporations and Integrated Production*, New York and Geneva: United Nations.

United Nations Conference on Trade and Development (1994), *Directory of Import Regimes, Part I: Monitoring Import Regimes*, New York: United Nations.

United Nations Conference on Trade and Development (1997), *World Investment Report 1997: Transnational Corporations, Market Structure and Competition Policy*, New York and Geneva: United Nations.

United Nations Economic Commission for Europe (1988), "International Comparison of Gross Domestic Product in Europe, 1985", *Conference of European Statisticians, Statistical Standards and Studies*, no. 411, New York: United Nations.

United Nations and EUROSTAT (1986), *World Comparisons of Purchasing Power and Real Product for 1980, Phase IV of the International Comparison Project*, Part I, ST/ESA/STAT/SER.F/42, New York: United Nations.

United Nations and EUROSTAT (1987), *World Comparisons of Purchasing Power and Real Product for 1980, Phase IV of the International Comparison Project*, Part II, ST/ESA/STAT/SER.F/42, New York: United Nations.

United Nations and EUROSTAT (1994), *World Comparisons of Real Gross Domestic Product and Purchasing Power, 1985, Phase V of the International Comparison Programme*, ST/ESA/STAT/SER.F/64, New York: United Nations.

United Nations Industrial Development Organization (1985a), *Input–Output Tables for Developing Countries*, Vols. I and II, New York: United Nations.

United Nations Industrial Development Organization (1985b)," Industrialization and Development Generation in the Service Sector of Developing Countries: An Appraisal", *Industry and Development*, no. 15, pp. 55–108.

United Nations Statistical Commission and Economic Commission for Europe (1994), "International Comparison of Gross Domestic Product in Europe, 1990", *Conference of European Statisticians, Statistical Standards and Studies*, no. 45, New York and Geneva: United Nations.

US Bureau of Labor Statistics (1986), *Employment and Earnings*, **33** (1).

US Department of Commerce (1987), *County Business Patterns, 1985*, Washington, DC: US Department of Commerce.

US Department of Commerce (1990), *Survey of Current Business*, **70** (1).

US Department of Commerce (1992), *National Income and Product Accounts of the United States*, Vol. 2, 1959–88, Washington, DC: US Department of Commerce.

US Department of Commerce (1993a), *Fixed Reproducible Tangible Wealth in the United States, 1925–89*, Washington, DC: US Department of Commerce.

US Department of Commerce (1993b), *Survey of Current Business*, **73** (5).

US Department of Commerce (1994a), *Survey of Current Business*, **74** (4).

US Department of Commerce (1994b), *Statistical Abstracts of the United States 1994*, Lanham: Bernan Press.

Van Ark, Bart (1992), "The ICOP Approach: Its Implications and Applicability", paper presented at the conference "Explaining Economic Growth", 8–10 April, University of Groningen, The Netherlands.

Van der Hoeven, Rolph (1988), *Planning for Basic Needs: A Soft Option or a Solid Policy? A Basic Needs Simulation Model Applied to Kenya*, Aldershot: Gower.

Van Ees, Hans, Gerard H. Kuper and Elmer Sterken (1997), "Investment, Finance and the Business Cycle: Evidence from the Dutch Manufacturing Sector", *Cambridge Journal of Economics*, **21** (3), 395–407.

Van Wegberg, Marc, Arjen van Witteloostuijn and Michiel Roscam Abbing (1994), "Multimarket and Multiproject Collusion: Why European Integration May Reduce Intra-Community Competition", *De Economist*, **142** (3), 253–85.

Varian, Hal R. (1978), *Microeconomic Analysis*, New York: W.W. Norton.

Vassilakis, Spyros (1987), "Increasing Returns to Scale", in John Eatwell, Murray Milgate and Peter Newman (eds), *The New Palgrave: A Dictionary of Economics*, Vol. 2, New York: Stockton Press, pp. 761–5.

Velenchik, Ann D. (1997), "Market Power, Firm Performance and Real Wage Growth in Zimbabwean Manufacturing", *World Development*, **25** (5), 749–62.

Viner, Jacob (1937), *Studies in the Theory of International Trade*, New York: Harper & Brothers Publishers.

Wei, Shang-Jin (1996), "Intra-National Versus International Trade: How Stubborn are Nations in Global Integration?", *NBER Working Paper*, no. 5531, Cambridge, MA: National Bureau of Economic Research.

Wei, Shang-Jin and David C. Parsley (1995), "Purchasing Power Disparity During the Floating Rate Period: Exchange Rate Volatility, Trade Barriers and other Culprits", *NBER Working Paper*, no. 5032, Cambridge, MA: National Bureau of Economic Research.

Weintraub, Roy (1979), *Microfoundations: The Compatibility of Microeconomics and Macroeconomics*, Cambridge: Cambridge University Press.

Weiss, John (1984), "Manufacturing as an Engine of Growth – Revisited", *Industry and Development*, no. 13, 39–62.

Williamson, John (ed.) (1994), *Estimating Equilibrium Exchange Rates*, Washington, DC: Institute for International Economics.

Willmore, Larry (1989), "Determinants of Industrial Structure: A Brazilian Case Study", *World Development*, **17** (10), 1601–17.

Wolf, Holger C. (1997), "Patterns of Intra- and Inter-State Trade", *NBER Working Paper*, no. 5939, Cambridge, MA: National Bureau of Economic Research.

Wolff, Edward N. (1985), "Industrial Composition, Interindustry Effects and the U.S. Productivity Slowdown", *The Review of Economics and Statistics*, **67** (2), 268–77.

Wood, Adrian (1978), *A Theory of Pay*, Cambridge: Cambridge University Press.

World Bank (1983), *World Development Report 1983*, New York: Oxford University Press.

World Bank (1992), *Global Economic Prospects and the Developing Countries 1992*, Washington, DC: The World Bank.

World Bank (1993a), *Purchasing Power of Currencies: Comparing National Incomes Using ICP Data*, Washington, DC: The World Bank.

World Bank (1993b), *The East Asian Miracle: Economic Growth and Public Policy*, New York: Oxford University Press.

World Bank (1994a), *Global Economic Prospects and the Developing Countries 1994*, Washington, DC: The World Bank.

World Bank (1994b), *World Development Report 1994*, New York: Oxford University Press.

Yang, Jiawen (1997), "Exchange Rate Pass-Through in U.S. Manufacturing Industries", *The Review of Economics and Statistics*, **79** (1), 95–104.

Yang, Y. Yung and Min Hwang (1994), "Price Behavior in Korean Manufacturing", *The Review of Economics and Statistics*, **76** (3), 461–70.

Yeats, Alexander J. (1978), "Monopoly Power, Barriers to Competition and the Pattern of Price Differentials in International Trade", *Journal of Development Economics*, **5** (2), 167–80.

Yeats, Alexander J. (1990a), "Do African Countries Pay More for Imports? Yes", *The World Bank Economic Review*, **4** (1), 1–20.

Yeats, Alexander J. (1990b), "On the Accuracy of Economic Observations: Do Sub-Saharan Trade Statistics Mean Anything?", *The World Bank Economic Review*, **4** (2), 135–56.

Yotopoulos, Pan A. (1996), *Exchange Rate Parity for Trade and Development: Theory, Tests and Case Studies*, Cambridge: Cambridge University Press.

Yotopoulos, Pan A. and Sagrario L. Floro (1992), "Income Distribution, Transaction Costs and Market Fragmentation in Informal Credit Markets", *Cambridge Journal of Economics*, **16** (3), 303–26.

You, Jong-Il (1995), "Small Firms in Economic Theory", *Cambridge Journal of Economics*, **19** (3), 441–62.

Young, Allyn A. (1928), "Increasing Returns and Economic Progress", *The Economic Journal*, **38** (152), 527–42.

Zietz, Joachim (1996), "The Relative Price of Tradables and Nontradables and the U.S. Trade Balance", *Open Economies Review*, **7** (2), 147–60.

Index

NEW DIRECTIONS IN MODERN ECONOMICS